THE CHARTERED INSTITUTE OF MARKETING

Professional Diploma in Marketing

STUDY TEXT

Project Management in Marketing

Valid for assessments up to September 2013

 The Chartered Institute of Marketing

BPP
LEARNING MEDIA

First edition July 2012

ISBN 9781 4453 9148 9
e-ISBN 9781 4453 7621 9

British Library Cataloguing-in-Publication Data
A catalogue record for this book
is available from the British Library

Published by

BPP Learning Media Ltd
Aldine House, Aldine Place
142-144 Uxbridge Road
London W12 8AA

www.bpp.com/learningmedia

Printed in the United Kingdom by Polestar Wheatons

Hennock Road
Marsh Barton Industrial Estate
Exeter, Devon
EX2 8RP

Your learning materials, published by BPP Learning
Media Ltd, are printed on paper obtained from
traceable sustainable sources.

We are grateful to The Chartered Institute of Marketing for
permission to reproduce in this text the unit syllabus.

Lead Author: Frank McKee

Contents

Review form

1 Studying for The Chartered Institute of Marketing (CIM) qualifications

There are a few key points to remember as you study for your CIM qualification:

(a) You are studying for a **professional** qualification. This means that you are required to use professional language and adopt a business approach in your work.

(b) You are expected to show that you have 'read widely'. Make sure that you read the quality press (and don't skip the business pages), *Marketing*, *The Marketer*, *Research* and *Marketing Week* avidly.

(c) Become aware of the marketing initiatives you come across on a daily basis, for example, when you go shopping look around and think about why the store layout is as it is; consider the messages, channel choice and timings of ads when you are watching TV. It is surprising how much you will learn just by taking an interest in the marketing world around you.

(d) Get to know the way CIM writes its exam papers and assignments. It uses a specific approach (the Magic Formula) which is to ensure a consistent approach when designing assessment materials. Make sure you are fully aware of this as it will help you interpret what the examiner is looking for (a full description of the Magic Formula appears later).

(e) Learn how to use Harvard referencing. This is explained in detail in our CIM Professional Diploma Assessment Workbook.

(f) Ensure that you read very carefully all assessment details sent to you from CIM. There are strict deadlines to meet, as well as paperwork to complete for any assignment or project you do. You also need to make sure you have your CIM membership card with you at the exam. Failing to meet any assessment entry deadlines or completing written work on time will mean that you will have to wait for the next round of assessment dates and will need to pay the relevant assessment fees again.

2 The Professional Diploma Syllabus

The Professional Diploma in Marketing is aimed at anyone who is employed in a marketing management role such as Brand Manager, Account Manager or Marketing Executive. If you are a graduate, you will be expected to have covered a minimum of a third of your credits in marketing subjects. You are therefore expected at this level of the qualification to be aware of the key marketing theories and be able to apply them to different organisational contexts.

The aim of the qualification is to provide the knowledge and skills for you to develop an 'ability to do' in relation to marketing planning. CIM qualifications concentrate on applied marketing within real workplaces.

The complete qualification is made from four units:

- Unit 1 Marketing Planning Process
- Unit 2 Delivering Customer Value through Marketing
- Unit 3 Managing Marketing
- Unit 4 Project Management in Marketing

CIM stipulates that each module should take 50 guided learning hours to complete. Guided learning hours refer to time in class, using distance learning materials and completing any work set by your tutor. Guided learning hours do not include the time it will take you to complete the necessary reading for your studies.

The syllabus as provided by CIM can be found below with reference to our coverage within this Study Text.

Unit characteristics – Project Management in Marketing

This unit will focus on the proactive development and delivery of a justified management process to support the initiation, implementation and control of marketing projects, including the use of research and information and preparing proposals and briefs to identify needs comprehensively.

The unit will also focus upon evaluating marketing project proposals and prioritising them on the basis of fit with market conditions, organisational capacity, competitor activity and strategic management, while concurrently managing the associated risk of implementing particular plans.

Ultimately, the unit will also cover the implementation of marketing proposals including an in-depth view of project management, but also integrating knowledge from the other units at this level.

By the end of this unit, you should be able to develop an effective business case within different organisational contexts and justify their project proposals in terms of fit with the marketing strategy, evaluation of risk and the effective use of organisational capacity and capability.

Overarching learning outcomes

By the end of this unit you should be able to:

- Identify the organisation's information needs, scope of research projects and resource capability to underpin the development of a business case to support marketing projects

- Develop an effective business case, complete with justifications, financial assessments and consideration of the organisation's resource capacity and capability to deliver

- Undertake a risk assessment programme with suggestions on how to mitigate for risks facing the organisation and the achievement of its business and marketing objectives

- Design, develop and plan significant marketing programmes, using project management tools and techniques, designed to deliver marketing projects effectively, in terms of quality, resource and delivery

- Integrate a range of marketing tools and techniques to support the development and implementation of a range of marketing projects

- Monitor and measure the effectiveness and outcomes of marketing projects through the end-to-end project process.

 The Chartered Institute of Marketing

SECTION 1 – Using marketing information to develop a justified case for marketing projects (weighting 15%)

		Covered in chapter(s)
1.1	Critically assess the scope and type of marketing information required to develop effective business cases using both primary and secondary data: ■ Applied contextual research ■ Situational specific evidence ■ Gap analysis ■ Empirical prerogatives	1
1.2	Critically assess how organisations determine their marketing information requirements and the key elements of user specifications for the purposes of building a case: ■ Business intelligence ■ Product/process innovation ■ Culture ■ Source management ■ Output dissemination ■ Specialist sources ■ Consultancy/advice	1
1.3	Critically assess the scope, structure and characteristics of MIS and MkIS as marketing management support systems and evaluate their importance to business cases for marketing projects: ■ Corporate data ■ Operational data ■ Functional data ■ The data fuelled organisation ■ Data manipulation and utilisation ■ Confidentiality and integrity ■ Business databases	2
1.4	Develop a research brief to meet the requirements of an individually specific case for marketing: ■ Problem definition ■ Objectives ■ Information requirements ■ Data collection ■ Report parameters ■ Timescales ■ Resource allocation ■ Control and contingency	3

1.5	Critically evaluate a full research proposal to fulfil the brief supporting the information needs of the case and make recommendations for improvement:	3
	▪ Proposal scoring	
	▪ Brief reviewing	
	▪ The brief/proposal mechanic	
	▪ Effort required for proposal versus available budget	
	▪ Decision to use in-house or external agency resources	
	▪ Utilisation of existing data	
1.6	Identify and evaluate the most effective methods for presenting marketing information and making specific marketing recommendations relating to product/service development and implementation as part of the case:	4
	▪ The marketing dashboard	
	▪ Graphs, charts and tables	
	▪ Pie charts	
	▪ Flow diagrams	
	▪ Spreadsheets	
	▪ Correlation and regression	
	▪ Strategic impact statements	
	▪ Effect and outcome metrics	
	▪ Investment and income budgets	
	▪ Measurement and control	
	▪ Project reports	

SECTION 2 – Building a case for marketing projects (weighting 20%)

		Covered in chapter(s)
2.1	Define business case objectives for marketing plans and specific high expenditure marketing activities:	5
	▪ Customer objectives	
	▪ Management objectives	
	▪ Profit objectives	
2.2	Critically evaluate and assess the marketing potential for business case activities, including consideration of the assessments required to achieve the potential proposition:	6
	▪ Projections	
	▪ Forecasting	
	▪ Pre/post trend extrapolation	
	▪ Historical data review	
	▪ Econometrics	

2.3	Critically assess and evaluate customer groups relevant to the business case, matching their buying characteristics to the marketing proposition through the use of market research information:	7
	■ Customer specific profiling	
	■ Cross criteria scoring	
	■ Contextualised positioning	
2.4	Determine the extent to which an organisation's marketing mix may need to be amended or adjusted to meet the requirements of the customer and broader stakeholders, and consider the impact of the change on the organisation:	7
	■ Management of the marketing mix	
	■ Investment/divestment	
2.5	Critically assess the resource capability and capacity to deliver the business case proposals and consider the competency and skill requirements of both internal and external resources to deliver the business case proposition:	7
	■ Skills and competence	
	■ Role definition	
	■ Cross functionality	
	■ Agency management	
	■ Investment and income budgets	
	■ Recruitment	
2.6	Present the business case and associated marketing plans for consultation and consideration, with full justifications for the proposed product/service initiatives and how they will support the delivery of marketing strategies and plans:	8
	■ The marketing report	
	■ A structured presentation	
	■ Knowing the audience	
	■ Key impact indicators	
	■ Findings, prioritisation and conclusion	

SECTION 3 – Assessing, managing and mitigating risk associated with marketing projects (weighting 25%)

		Covered in chapter(s)
3.1	Critically evaluate the importance of developing an understanding of risk assessments in organisations in order to protect long-term stability of a range of marketing projects:	9
	■ Definition of risk	
	■ Risk perspective	
	■ Probability management	
	■ Risk culture	
	■ Strategic management	

3.2	Critically evaluate the differences between the following types of organisational risk:	9
	▪ Strategic	
	▪ Operational	
	▪ Financial	
	▪ Knowledge	
	▪ Compliance	
	▪ Project-based areas of risk	
3.3	Analyse and assess the potential sources of risk, of both internal and external origins, directly related to a specific case and consider the impact of these risks on the organisation:	10
	▪ Internal strategic, operational, financial and hazard	
	▪ External social, legal, economic, political and technological	
3.4	Design a risk management programme appropriate to measuring the impact of risk in the context of marketing projects:	11
	▪ Risk audit	
	▪ Risk evaluation	
	▪ Risk report	
	▪ Risk treatment	
	▪ Risk monitoring	
3.5	Undertake risk assessments on marketing projects and assess the impact of short/long-term tactical changes to the marketing plan:	11
	▪ Customer assessment	
	▪ Management assessment	
	▪ Profit assessment	
3.6	Critically evaluate the different approaches organisations can take to mitigate risk in order to reduce its potential to harm the organisation or its reputation:	11
	▪ Organise for risk	
	▪ Incorporate risk management	
	▪ Risk avoidance	
	▪ Risk transfer	
	▪ Risk financing	
3.7	Critically assess the strategic impact of implementing proposed risk control measures versus the strategic impact of taking no action:	11
	▪ Business impact analysis	
	▪ Event tree analysis	
	▪ Threat analysis	
	▪ Scenario analysis and planning	
	▪ Assumption analysis	
	▪ Probability analysis	

 The Chartered Institute of Marketing

3.8	Develop a range of methods for monitoring, reporting and controlling risk on an ongoing basis for project implementation:	11
	■ Risk audits	
	■ Risk management objectives	
	■ Risk reporting	
	■ Risk awareness	
	■ Risk response	
	■ Industry benchmarking	

SECTION 4 – Project management for analysis, planning, implementation and control (weighting 40%)

		Covered in chapter(s)
4.1	Critically evaluate different approaches to developing a culture of project planning within the marketing function and the organisation:	12
	■ Managing dynamics	
	■ The marketing/project interface	
	■ The project structured organisation	
	■ Planning, implementation and control	
	■ Policies, strategies and methodologies	
	■ Managing the project life cycle	
4.2	Critically evaluate soft and hard projects in the context of marketing and consider the differences in terms of project implementation:	12
	■ Types of project	
	■ Strategic context	
	■ Operational context	
	■ Tactical context	
	■ Short/medium/long term objectives	
	■ Quality, investment and delivery	

4.3	Develop the main stages of a marketing project plan, identifying the activities, estimating time and cost, sequencing of activities, and assess the competency and skills required of the people needed to deliver the project:	13

- Project initiation
- Scope and objectives
- Beginning/end dates
- Key/core deliverables
- Methodology adaptation
- Project limitations
- Risk management
- Outline budgeting
- Project implementation
- Schedules/schemes of work
- Resource reviews
- Personnel requirements
- Project termination
- Project evaluation

4.4	Critically assess the importance of and techniques for establishing the marketing project's scope, definition and goals relative to the organisational marketing plan:	13

- The project scoping document
- Goals, objectives and critical success factors
- In/out of scope
- Risk highlights
- Assumptions
- Roles and responsibilities
- Stakeholder management

4.5	Utilise a range of tools and techniques to support project planning, scheduling, resourcing and controlling of activities within the project to enable effective and efficient implementation:	14

- Work breakdown structure
- Cost analysis
- Estimate forecasting
- Gantt charts
- Critical path analysis
- Histograms
- Phase management
- Feedback control systems

The Chartered
Institute of Marketing

4.6	Utilise a variety of methods, measurements and control techniques to enable effective monitoring and measuring of progress throughout the project to ensure that it is completed to specification, on time and within budget: ■ The project scorecard ■ Objective review ■ Budget review ■ Update reporting ■ Productivity ■ Corrective action plans	15
4.7	Critically assess the main techniques for evaluating effectiveness, success or failure of a marketing project on its completion: ■ Variance analysis ■ Outcome matrices ■ Profit/loss analysis ■ Liquidity analysis ■ Investment performance analysis ■ Productivity analysis ■ Value analysis ■ Marketing mix analysis ■ Lessons learned	15

3 Assessment

The unit covered by this Study Text (Unit 4 *Project Management in Marketing*) is assessed by a work-based project requiring an in-depth study of a specific and focussed area of business activity. Tasks will require application to real settings and will be directly relevant to a work context.

In order to help you revise and prepare for your project we have also written a Professional Diploma in Marketing Assessment Workbook which is available either through your usual book retailer or our website www.bpp.com/learningmedia.

4 The Magic Formula

The Magic Formula is a tool used by CIM to help both examiners write exam and assignment questions, and you, to more easily interpret what you are being asked to write about. It is useful for helping you to check that you are using an appropriate balance between theory and practice for your particular level of qualification.

Contrary to the title, there is nothing mystical about the Magic Formula and simply by knowing it (or even mentioning it in an assessment) will not automatically secure a pass. What it does do, however, is to help you to check that you are presenting your answers in an appropriate format, including enough marketing theory and applying it to a real marketing context or issue.

The Magic Formula for the Professional Diploma in Marketing is shown below:

Figure A   The Magic Formula for the Professional Diploma in Marketing

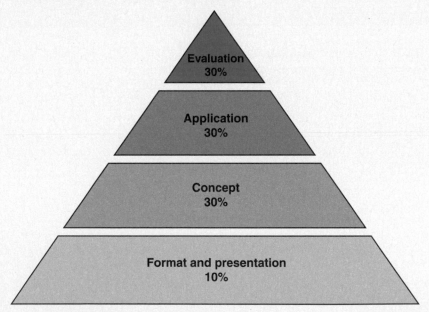

You can see from the pyramid that for the Professional Diploma marks are awarded in the following proportions:

- **Presentation and format – 10%**

  You are expected to present your work professionally which means that assignments and projects should **always** be typed. Even in an exam situation attention should be paid to making your work look as visually appealing as possible. CIM will also stipulate the format that you should present your work in. The assessment formats you will be given will be varied and can include things like reports to write,

slides to prepare, e-mails, memos, formal letters, press releases, discussion documents, briefing papers, agendas and newsletters.

- **Concept – 30%**

  Concept refers to your ability to state, recall and describe marketing theory.

- **Application – 30%**

  Application-based marks are given for your ability to apply marketing theories to real life marketing situations. For example, a question may ask you to discuss the definition of marketing and how it is applied within your own organisation. Here you are not only using the definition but are applying it in order to consider the market orientation of the company.

- **Evaluation – 30%**

  Evaluation is the ability to asses the value or worth of something, sometimes through careful consideration of related advantages and disadvantages, or weighing up of alternatives. Results from your evaluation should enable you to discuss the importance of an issue using evidence to support your opinions.

  For example, if you were asked to evaluate whether or not your organisation adopts a marketing approach you should provide reasons and specific examples of why you think it might take this approach, as well as considering why it may not take this approach, before coming to a final conclusion.

  You should have noticed that for the Professional Diploma, you are expected to consider the equal weightings of concept, application and evaluation in order to gain maximum marks in assessments.

5 A guide to the features of the Study Text

Each of the chapter features (see below) will help you to break down the content into manageable chunks and ensure that you are developing the skills required for a professional qualification.

Chapter feature	Relevance and how you should use it
Introduction	Shows why topics need to be studied and is a route guide through the chapter
Syllabus reference	Outlines the syllabus learning outcomes covered in the chapter
Chapter topic list	Study the list, each numbered topic denotes a numbered section in the chapter
Key Term	Highlights the core vocabulary you need to learn
Activity	An application-based activity for you to complete
The Real World	A short case study to illustrate marketing practice
Exam tip/Assessment tip	Key advice based on the assessment
Chapter roundups	Use this to review what you have learnt
Quick quiz	Use this to check your learning
Further reading	Further reading will give you a wider perspective on the subjects you're covering

6 Additional resources

To help you pass the Professional Diploma in Marketing we have created a complete study package. The **Professional Diploma Assessment Workbook** covers all four units of the Professional Diploma level. Practice questions and answers, tips on tackling assignments and work-based projects are included to help you succeed in your assessments.

Our A6 set of spiral bound **Passcards** are handy revision cards and are ideal to reinforce key topics for the Delivering Customer Value through Marketing exam.

7 Your personal study plan

Preparing a study plan (and sticking to it) is one of the key elements to learning success.

CIM has stipulated that there should be a minimum of 50 guided learning hours spent on each unit. Guided learning hours will include time spent in lessons, working on distance learning materials, formal workshops and work set by your tutor. We also know that to be successful, you should spend approximately an additional 100 hours conducting self-study. This means that for the entire qualification with four units you should spend 200 hours working in a tutor-guided manner and at least an additional 400 hours completing recommended reading, working on assignments, and revising for exams. This Study Text will help you to organise this 100-hour portion of self-study time.

Now think about the exact amount of time you have (don't forget you will still need some leisure time!) and complete the following tables to help you keep to a schedule.

	Date	Duration in weeks
Course start		
Course finish		Total weeks of course:

Project received	Submission date	Total weeks to complete

Content chapter coverage plan

Chapter	To be completed by	Considered in relation to the project?
1 Marketing information for business cases		
2 Marketing information systems		
3 Research briefs and proposals		
4 Presentation of findings		
5 Setting aims, goals and objectives		
6 Forecasts and projections		
7 Operational management		
8 The case report		
9 Identifying risk		

 The Chartered Institute of Marketing

Chapter	To be completed by	Considered in relation to the project?
10 Risk assessment and evaluation		
11 Risk management and mitigation		
12 Foundations of project management		
13 Project process		
14 Project tools and techniques		
15 Project control, termination, review and evaluation		

Section 1:

Using marketing information to develop a justified case for marketing projects (weighting 15%)

LEARNING OBJECTIVES

By the end of this section, you will be able to:

- Assess the scope and type of marketing information requirements
- Assess the structure and characteristics of marketing information systems
- Understand the relationship between brief and proposal
- Understand how to select from, and use, a range of primary research tools
- Select and adapt different report and presentation techniques

SYLLABUS REFERENCES

1.1 Critically assess the scope and type of marketing information required to develop effective business cases using both primary and secondary data

1.2 Critically assess how organisations determine their marketing information requirements and the key elements of user specifications for the purposes of building a case

1.3 Critically assess the scope, structure and characteristics of MIS and MkIS as marketing management support systems and evaluate their importance to business cases for marketing projects

1.4 Develop a research brief to meet the requirements of an individually specific case for marketing

1.5 Critically evaluate a full research proposal to fulfil the brief supporting the information needs of the case and make recommendations for improvement

1.6 Identify and evaluate the most effective methods for presenting marketing information and making specific marketing recommendations relating to product/service development and implementation as part of the case

CHAPTER 1

Marketing information for business cases

Introduction

Peter Chisnall in his 2004 book *Marketing Research* calls information the raw material of management. Without information we cannot make informed decisions. There will always be risk attached to business decisions, but good information will help us measure, manage and assess the degree of risk involved in making business and marketing decisions.

This section of the syllabus allows the student to contextualise research around a specific undertaking. The emphasis here is on the ability to disseminate varying amounts of information from disparate sources, identify gaps and consequently rationale for primary research. As a result, candidates should be able to manipulate their findings and present a justified case for the development and management of a specific marketing project.

Topic list

The business case	1
Defining the issues or problem	2
Carry out exploratory research	3
Data input, coding and editing	4
Results, findings and recommendations	5
User specifications for information	6

1.1	Critically assess the scope and type of marketing information required to develop effective business cases using both primary and secondary data
	■ Applied contextual research
	■ Situational specific evidence
	■ Gap analysis
	■ Empirical prerogatives
1.2	Critically assess how organisations determine their marketing information requirements and the key elements of user specifications for the purposes of building a case:
	■ Business intelligence
	■ Product/process innovation
	■ Culture
	■ Source management
	■ Output dissemination
	■ Specialist sources
	■ Consultancy/advice

1 The business case

▶ **Key terms**

A **business case** is required to justify any non-routine expenditure. In particular, any project requiring the allocation of scarce resources for its achievement will only be approved if a convincing business case can be created.

Marketing research: 'The collection, analysis and communication of information undertaken to assist decision-making in marketing.' (Wilson, 2006) Marketing research includes market research, price research and so on.

Qualitative research is 'exploratory research that aims to understand consumers' attitudes, values, behaviour and beliefs'. (Jobber, 2010, p251)

Quantitative research is structured to collect specific data regarding a specific set of circumstances.

User specifications will define information requirement and utilisation output.

The essence of a business case is that it relates directly to the achievement of the **organisation's mission**. It should explain why the proposed work will improve the value added by the organisation in a cost-effective way. Thus, a plan to air condition an office cannot be justified in business terms by saying that it will improve working conditions, or even that it will improve the accuracy and diligence with which staff do their work.

A business case may vary in nature from an informal verbal summary to a fully-researched and detailed position paper. Matters dealt with are likely to include (at least) a consideration of the present position or problem; the desired future state; the possible solutions or courses of action; reasoning as to why the selected solution has been chosen (including financial analysis); and discussion of the risks involved.

2 Defining the issues or problem

Defining the problem, despite appearances, is not easy. Problems can generally be solved in many ways. The problem definition needs to reflect the organisation's resources, or be expressed in a way that clearly identifies the opportunity that is being looked at.

Sometimes, a view of the problem for a pressured executive may not actually be the real issue. The research company that is asked to review marketing communications activity may find that there are particular political issues with the current agency or that the brand is poorly managed or that the pricing strategy is wrong. Very often we have to carry out informal or exploratory research to identify and define the research question we are trying to answer.

Poorly researched questions or problem definitions can lead to expensive and unnecessary work being carried out.

Clearly then, being able to define a problem and set objectives in an appropriate way is very important.

Often managers appear to want the answer to the meaning of life by 5.00 p.m. Understanding the business so as to be able to isolate and define a problem is a skill that comes with experience. For example, the ill-informed manager may say set an objective to determine 'why are our sales falling?', while the experienced manager might say 'what are the perceptions of our service standards against our key competitors?' He has already limited the research to a narrow problem area and researchers have a much clearer idea of the purpose to which the research will be put. It may be that the researcher has to carry out this refining and defining process, but it can be helped by good communication and understanding at this stage.

THE REAL WORLD

1   A possible approach to an effective business case might emphasise that a certain proportion of customer service failures are directly traceable to staff fatigue, short temper and poor motivation, which the improvement will tend to reduce. However, it would then be necessary to quantify the financial benefit of the improvement and show that it exceeded the cost involved.

2   Here is a list of questions that managers of marketing projects might need answered in any given real world scenario.

(a)   **Markets**. Who are our customers? What are they like? How are buying decisions made?

(b)   **Share of the market**. What are total sales of our product? How do our sales compare with competitors' sales?

(c)   **Products**. What do customers think of our product? What do they do with it? Are our products in a 'growth' or 'decline' stage of their life cycle? Should we extend our range?

(d)   **Price**. How do our prices compare with others: higher, average, lower? Is the market sensitive to price?

(e)   **Distribution**. Should we distribute directly, indirectly or both? What discounts are required?

(f)   **Sales force**. Do we have enough/too many salespeople? Are their territories equal to their potential? Are they contacting the right people? Should we pay commission?

(g)   **Advertising**. Do we use the right media? Do we communicate the right message? Is it effective?

(h)   **Customer attitudes**. What do they think of our product/firm/service/delivery?

(i)   **Competitors' activities**. Who are our competitors? Are they more or less successful businesses? Why are they more or less successful?

(j)   **Environmental factors**. What factors impact on marketing planning?

Yet another useful approach is taken by Wilson (2006) who distinguishes four roles for marketing information.

Descriptive information answers questions such as which products are customers buying, where are they buying them?

Comparative information looks at how one thing compares with another, for instance how good is an organisation's after-sales support compared with its competitors?

Diagnostic information is intended to explain customer behaviour: why are they buying less of product A?

Predictive information attempts to determine the outcome of marketing actions. How would customers respond if this were made available in larger sized packs? And so on.

3 Carry out exploratory research

This stage, as outlined above, is designed to clarify the research problem. It is largely informal and may involve a range of techniques. It should involve discussions with those who are involved with the problem and its solution. It may involve a review of the trade press and simple scanning of internal documents and resources. The aim is to inform the process and to become 'immersed' in the problem and its potential solutions.

Even at this stage, the researcher may be thinking ahead about methods that could be used to deliver the information required. The key thing is to uncover the real purpose of the research and, possibly, the constraints in terms of time and budget that may affect the process.

We also need, at this stage, to think about the value of the research. There is little point in spending more on research than will be gained by making the right decision as a result of it – it has to be cost-effective. Research cannot eliminate risk entirely, but tries to reduce it to acceptable levels within identifiable margins of error. An understanding of the commercial constraints of carrying out research may be gained through intuition or experience, but it can also be worked out more scientifically.

If research is required to justify packaging redesign, then we can estimate the improved sales of such a move and offset the cost of research against this. This objective-and-task approach to setting research budgets is the best way of managing research budgets. However, it is not always possible to carry out this process accurately.

If the cost of a research project to decide between two product flavours was £25,000, and the research-based launch generated incremental profits of £40,000, then clearly the research is worthwhile. It should always be possible to estimate the likely impact on a project, if it is done with or without research and this can help in determining whether the research should be done (in the first place) and the extent of what research is needed.

ACTIVITY 1.1

You should spend about ten minutes, before you carry on reading, thinking about information you use at work and then try and classify it into the major marketing and selling activities described under ACTIVITY in the table below. (Use a separate sheet of paper if necessary.) The second column headed INFORMATION should describe the type of information, for example: control chart, written report, oral report, telephone call, database and so on. The third column is for you to describe what you USE the information for. You may find that you use certain types of information to do more than one marketing or sales management activity, in which case feel free to list it more than once.

Table 1.1   Summary data sheet

ACTIVITY	INFORMATION	USE
Analysing		
Planning		
Implementing		
Controlling		

3.1 Previous research

As part of this process, previously carried out research should be reviewed to see if the problem has been dealt with elsewhere. It may be that the solution lies in work that has been done in other departments. For example, work to improve the navigation of the website may have been done in the IT department. Access to previously commissioned work may be through the intranet or the company library. Or it may be that individual managers have commissioned research which has not been distributed widely through the organisations.

The Chartered
Institute of Marketing

3.2 Internal research

Internal research will involve the use of the MkIS (Marketing Information System – a subset of Management Information System) and the database. It may be that the problem, as we said, can be solved at this stage. Normally it is worth spending time now on internal records to either solve the problem or at least help to define it.

For example, a problem that involves finding out the average age of a company's existing customers may be solved through a simple interrogation of the customer database.

3.2.1 Redefine the problem

The output of this stage is a clear statement of the research problem that is agreed by all parties. After this, a brief can be written based on the work to date.

3.3 Desk research

Desk or secondary research is information that has already been gathered for some other purpose. It may be held within the organisation or by other organisations. It is called desk research because it is usually accessible from a desk via the intranet or online or in hard copy. This is dealt with in detail in the next section. In the research plan, desk research is carried out before primary research. This is because it is generally cheaper. It may solve the problem without any need for expensive primary work.

ACTIVITY 1.2

Use the grid below as an exercise to identify the relevant and likely sources of data for this or any specifically defined information gathering set.

Table 1.2   Summary data source grid

Question	Examples of information needed	Sources of information: forms of marketing research
Where are we now? Situation analysis	Current sales by product/market Market share by product/market Competitors' market shares Customer attitudes and behaviour Corporate image versus competitors' image Company strengths and weaknesses	
Where do we want to be? Setting project objectives	Market forecasts by segment Environmental changes Growth capabilities Opportunities and threats Competitor response New product/market potentials	

Question	Examples of information needed	Sources of information: forms of marketing research
How might we get there? Shaping the project	Marketing mix evaluation Buying behaviour New product development Risk evaluation Alternative strategic options	
How can we ensure arrival? Controlling the project	Budgets Performance evaluation	

3.4 Field research

Field or primary research is research carried out to meet a specific objective. It is something new that adds to the body of world research. Primary research is the common currency of marketing research. It is what most of us have come across either through telephone research, or face-to-face interviews or increasingly through online research.

Primary research may be based on observation and may be qualitative or quantitative.

Observation research is data gathered by observing behaviour. No questions are asked of participants, whereas much research is based upon structured questionnaires designed to give a consistent quality of response to a range of predetermined questions as expanded upon below.

The Marketing Research Society (MRS) defines observational research as: 'A non-verbal means of obtaining primary data as an alternative or complement to questioning.'

3.5 Qualitative research

Qualitative research describes research that cannot be quantified or subjected to quantitative analysis. It typically uses small sample sizes and is designed to produce a depth of understanding, context and insight. It helps to uncover the motivation behind the behaviour rather than to identify the behaviour itself. It seeks to get under the skin of respondents, uncovering their deeper feelings. It is essentially subjective but it is a highly developed and important research methodology.

MRS defines qualitative research as: 'A body of research techniques that seeks insights through loosely structured, mainly verbal data rather than measurements. Analysis is interpretative, subjective, impressionistic and diagnostic.'

3.6 Quantitative research

This questions 'who' and 'how many' rather than the depth of insight as to why. It uses a structured approach to problem-solving using a sample of the population to make statistically based assumptions about the behaviour of the population as a whole.

MRS defines quantitative research as: 'Research that seeks to make measurements as distinct from qualitative research.'

Note that the distinction between qualitative and quantitative can sometimes become blurred – a scaled response to a question can be measured depending on number of occurrences within the points along the scale. However, the response to the questions may indicate a depth of feeling. Often a more open-ended supplementary question is specifically created to get a deeper level of quantitative analysis.

 The Chartered Institute of Marketing

3.6.1 Fieldwork

Fieldwork is the generic term given to the collection of primary data. It may cover the collection of observational, quantitative and qualitative data. The administration of a major quantitative study may involve serious logistical considerations while qualitative work may involve highly qualified and skilled researchers. The management of fieldwork is often given to specialist field managers or fieldwork agencies. The process is very important as the failure to adhere to methodology at this stage may compromise the entire project.

THE REAL WORLD

The Nielson Company was a pioneer in market research fieldwork. It was founded in 1923 by Arthur C Nielson Snr and was at the forefront of consumer behaviour analytics from its inception. Originally the main emphasis of research was on test marketing and sales data and consumer behaviour and feedback analysis. However, throughout the evolution of increasingly sophisticated technology, the firm is today truly positioned at the forefront of the digitised fieldwork on consumer data manipulation.

(Nielsen, 2012)

4 Data input, coding and editing

Data that is gathered from respondents must be recorded and edited to produce a data set that is capable of being analysed. In qualitative work, this may mean producing a transcript of the interview. In quantitative work, it means creating a data set that the computer can work with.

All potential responses must be given a different code to enable analysis. Data is checked for completeness and consistency, and if there are significant problems the respondent may be called back to check details. Often today, data is input straight into the computer via systems known as CATI (computer-assisted telephone interviewing), CAPI (computer-assisted personal interviewing) and CAWI (computer-assisted web interviewing) http://www.marketresearchworld.net.

Note that some sources may use the phrase computer-aided rather than computer-assisted.

4.1 Data analysis

Data is analysed using computers to produce a range of results, but while computers may do the calculations it is people that have to interpret the potential impact of those results and make decisions accordingly. Data is a series of facts, but it is finding a use for appropriate data that changes it to information. The right questions need to be asked.

For example, 'half past three this afternoon' makes no sense until it is framed as a response to the question 'what time is the next bus to the city centre'?

5 Results, findings and recommendations

A marketing decision should result from the results of the research. Results should be presented clearly in a way that focuses on the problem to be solved. It is easy with today's statistical packages to produce hundreds of tables to a high degree of statistical sophistication. Results must be presented in a way that is accessible to the audience and that presents clearly the solution to the problem posed.

We live in the knowledge age where so much can be found at the click of a mouse button. There is a danger of information overload that hides the reason why a question was posed in the first place.

5.1 Report or presentation

Presentation of the results will usually be in the form of a written report and often this is supported by an oral presentation. The data will need to be presented, but this should be in the appendices. The body of the report remains solutions-focused.

5.2 Decision

The output should be marketing decisions that are made at reduced risk and a feedback loop should exist to the business situation. Feedback should continue to monitor the situation post-implementation, so that fine-tuning can be made.

We will examine this again in greater depth when we explore the process of research to include briefs and proposals in Chapter 3.

6 User specifications for information

It is worth stressing from the outset how important it is that managers specify in advance what their information needs are. It can be very wasteful of time and money to collect answers to questions that did not need to be asked, or which were the **wrong questions** in the first place!

Key elements of user specifications will include the following.

- **Rationale**. How the need for information arises and what the users intend to do with the information when they have it, in other words what decisions will be taken.

- **Budget**. In general the benefits of collecting information should be greater than the costs of collecting it, but benefits in particular are not always easy to quantify. In any case, the budget may be limited by other organisational factors such as availability of cash or a head office allocation of, say, £5,000 per annum for marketing research purposes. Clearly, this will affect the scale and type of information search that can be carried out.

- **Timescale**. Quite obviously, if the decisions have to be made by May, for example, then the information needs to be collected and analysed before then. Once again this will have an impact on the sale and type of information search that can be carried out.

- **Objectives**. The precise information needed, set out as clearly as possible. For instance 'To determine customer response to a price reduction of £250 in terms of repeat purchasing, word-of-mouth recommendations and willingness to purchase our other products and services'. The objectives should relate **only** to the rationale: it might be 'nice to know' what type of car customers drive, but if this will make no difference to the decisions that will be taken once the information has been collected, there is no need to know about customers' cars in the first place.

- **Methods**. This need only be an outline, setting out, for instance, the scale of the search, the mix of quantitative and qualitative information needed, the segments of the market to be included.

- **Reports**. How the final information should be presented. Considerations here might include style of reports, degree of summarisation, use of charts and other graphics, format for quantitative information (eg in Excel spreadsheets, for ease of further analysis).

Your company manufactures cruelty-free beauty products for a number of supermarket chains. You have been given responsibility for researching the market for a new line of cruelty-free cosmetics. List the likely information you would need to collect to lay the foundations for a business case.

THE REAL WORLD

The Department for Business, Innovation and Skills (BIS) has previously published estimates of the total number of enterprises in the publication *Small and Medium Enterprise Statistics for the UK and Regions (SME Statistics)*. This National Statistics series ran from 1994 to 2009, containing data on the number of enterprises at the start of the year with their associated employment and turnover2.

In December 2008 BIS launched a public consultation on *SME Statistics*, a key component of which was a set of questions on proposals to change the methodology (see BIS 2008).

Respondents on the whole welcomed the ideas BIS put forward for improving the methodology. In June 2009 BIS published the *Government Response to the Consultation on Small and Medium Enterprise Statistics for the UK and Regions* (see BIS 2009). In this response BIS committed to further investigate the options for improving the methodology and implementing changes where appropriate.

BIS identified a number of areas where improvements could be made to the estimate of the number of enterprises. One key area is the over-count in the self-employment estimate used to produce *SME Statistics*. It is only recently that a change to the Labour Force Survey questionnaire has allowed a robust methodology to be developed for estimating the 'true' level of self-employment. Other improvements were identified, such as more closely following ONS practice when selecting enterprises from the Inter-Departmental Business Register (IDBR) and using HMRC self-assessment data for the first time. Recent improvements to the timing of employment estimates on the IDBR have presented BIS with the opportunity to use an earlier IDBR data extract and produce estimates sooner than before. For the first time all the constituent data sources used in producing *SME Statistics* are available in the Standard Industrial Classification 2007 (SIC2007), allowing the publication to be based on this format.

In order to minimise the number of discontinuities in the series, all of the improvements to the methodology will be applied at the same time. *SME Statistics for the UK and Regions* has been renamed *Business Population Estimates for the UK and Regions* to ensure users are aware of the significant change in methodology between the 2009 and 2010 estimates.

(Office for National Statistics, 2012. Contains public sector information licensed under the Open Government Licence v1.0)

▶ **Assessment tip**

The ability to recognise and highlight that gaps exist within the information available from secondary sources is always rewarded. Better still is the use and presentation of supporting primary data collection undertaken to fill the gaps.

CHAPTER ROUNDUP

- We established what a business case entails.

- We looked at the fact that problems need to be defined.

- We established that the research should start with the most cost effective sources of information, ie secondary or desk research. If this does not produce the required information, then we move to primary work.

- We outlined the different types of marketing research and looked at qualitative and quantitative work.

- We saw that qualitative work should precede and inform the development of quantitative methodology.

- We looked at the difference between qualitative and quantitative work.

- We examined how data is collected and collated.

- We established how data needs to be manipulated, reported and used for decision-making.

- We identified the main elements of user specifications.

FURTHER READING

McDaniel, C. and Gates, R. (2010) *Marketing Research Essentials*. 7th edition. Minneapolis/St. Paul, John Wiley & Sons Inc.

REFERENCES

Chisnall, P. (2004) *Marketing Research*. 7th edition. Maidenhead, McGraw-Hill.

Jobber, D. (2010) *Principles and Practice of Marketing*. 6th edition. Maidenhead, McGraw Hill.

Nielsen (2012) http://www.nielsen.com/uk/en [Accessed 23 June 2012].

Shaw, J. (2011) Economic and Labour Market Review April 2011. ONS. http://data.gov.uk/dataset/economic_and_labour_market_review [Accessed 30 May 2012].

Wilson, A. (2006) *Marketing Research: an Integrated Approach*. 2nd edition. London, Financial Times/Prentice Hall.

QUICK QUIZ

1   What is the essence of a business case?

2   What are the four roles of information, according to Alan Wilson?

3   What are the two main types of research?

4   What are the two main methodologies for research?

5   What are the main elements of user specifications?

Activity 1.1

The answer will be specific to your circumstances.

Activity 1.2

Table 1.3

Sources of information: forms of marketing research
Accounting system
Customer database
Market analysis/surveys
Competitor intelligence
Customer surveys
Internal/external analyses
Industry forecasts/surveys
PESTEL
PIMS
Competitor research
Product/market research
Internal/external audits
Customer research
Concept testing/test marketing
Feasibility studies/competitor response modelling/focus groups/marketing mix research
Internal accounting, production and human resource systems
Marketing information systems
Marketing audit
Benchmarking
External (financial) auditing

Activity 1.3

We've not given you enough information to enable you to be too precise. You would have much more information in real life, of course. It might look something like this though:

To collect information about the market for a new line of cruelty-free cosmetics with a view to drawing up a business case and implementing a marketing project

(a)   The size of market, value, number of items sold, number of customers

(b)   The leading companies and their respective market share

(c) The breakdown of market by type of cosmetic (lipstick, eye shadow and so on)

(d) Current consumer trends in buying cruelty-free cosmetics (price, colour and so on)

(e) Consumer preferences in terms of packaging and presentation

(f) The importance to consumers of having a choice of colours within the range

(g) The influence on consumers of advertising and promotion that emphasises the cruelty-free nature of products

QUICK QUIZ ANSWERS

1 It relates directly to the achievement of the organisation's mission. It should explain why the proposed work will improve the value added by the organisation in a cost-effective way.

2 Descriptive, comparative, diagnostic and predictive

3 Secondary/Desk research and primary/field research

4 Qualitative and quantitative

5 Rational, budget, timescale, objectives, methods and reports

The Chartered Institute of Marketing

CHAPTER 2

Marketing information systems

Introduction

Without pertinent, reliable, accurate and timely information, decision-making would be impossible. Management decisions would be made in a vacuum. Without information and intelligent analysis of the data, the organisation is disconnected from its markets, suppliers, people, customers and future.

Some markets change quickly, others evolve, but they always change. As Hugh Davidson (1997) says, 'tomorrow's standards are always higher'. The information strategy of the organisation must be set up to ensure that these changes can be anticipated, monitored and acted upon. Risk can never be eliminated from business decision-making. The key thing is to manage and, where possible, reduce the risk to which the organisation is subject to acceptable levels relative to the required return on shareholders' investments.

Integrated information is critical to effective decision-making. Marketing information sources can be thought of as separate jigsaw pieces; only when they are connected does the whole picture become clear. Taking decisions by looking at each of the pieces individually is not only inefficient, but is also likely to result in wrong assumptions and decisions being made (Wilson, 2006).

What we see here is that advantage in the marketplace does not simply come from carrying out research; it is about identifying, collating, understanding, analysing and acting upon the many diverse sources of knowledge within an organisation. Wal-Mart is one organisation that manages this very well.

Topic list

Knowledge management	1
The marketing information system (MkIS)	2
The database	3
Customer relationship management systems	4
Data protection and freedom of information	5

1.3	Critically assess the scope, structure and characteristics of MIS and MkIS as marketing management support systems and evaluate their importance to business cases for marketing projects:
	▪ Corporate data
	▪ Operational data
	▪ Functional data
	▪ The data fuelled organisation
	▪ Data manipulation and utilisation
	▪ Confidentiality and integrity
	▪ Business databases

1 Knowledge management

▸ **Key terms**

The **marketing database** is a manual or computerised source of data relevant to marketing decision-making about an organisation's customers.

Data mining: the process of extracting hidden and actionable information from large databases.

Data warehouse: a database whose records contain information aggregated from multiple locations on a customer basis.

Data mart: cut-down version of a data warehouse, containing only that data deemed useful for analysis and reporting purposes.

Data capture: the process and system for gathering and recording data on customers.

A **marketing information system** is built up from several different systems which may not be directly related to marketing. Typical components are an internal reporting system, a marketing intelligence system, a marketing research system and a decision and analytical marketing system.

Knowledge management involves the identification and analysis of available and required knowledge, and the subsequent planning and control of actions to develop knowledge assets so as to fulfil organisational objectives.

Groupware is a term used to describe software that provides functions for the use of collaborative work groups.

An **intranet** is an internal network used to share information. Intranets utilise internet technology and protocols. The firewall surrounding an internet fends off unauthorised access.

An **extranet** is an intranet that is accessible to designated authorised users outside the company.

A **marketing intelligence system** is a set of procedures and sources used by managers to obtain everyday information about pertinent developments in the marketing environment.

The aim of knowledge management is to integrate systems and individuals to enable and encourage knowledge transfer between employees and other stakeholders. For example, knowledge management systems may work between retailers and their suppliers to ensure 'just-in-time' delivery of new stock, to plan and implement sales-promotion campaigns and to jointly manage the marketing research that underpins new product development.

Knowledge can be analysed into two categories.

(a)   **Explicit knowledge** includes facts, transactions and events that are clearly stated and stored in management information systems. Explicit knowledge is created, manipulated, stored and retrieved by rationally-designed **systems and procedures**.

(b)   **Tacit knowledge** is expertise held by people within the organisation that has not been formally documented. It is a difficult thing to manage because it is **invisible**. The organisation may not even appreciate the extent to which it exists and the possessors may be reluctant to share it

We do not know what knowledge exists within a person's brain, and whether he or she chooses to share knowledge is a matter of choice. The **motivation to share** hard-won experience is sometimes low; the individual is 'giving away' their value and may be very reluctant to lose a position of influence and respect by making it available to everyone. Knowledge management is an attempt to address the two problems associated with tacit knowledge: invisibility and reluctance to share. It attempts to turn all relevant knowledge, including personal knowledge, into corporate knowledge assets that can be easily and widely shared throughout an organisation and appropriately applied.

1.1 Where does knowledge reside?

There are various actions that can be taken to try to determine the prevalence of knowledge in an organisation.

One is the **identification and development of informal networks** and communities of practice within organisations. These self-organising groups share common work interests, usually cutting across a company's functions and processes. People exchange what they know and develop a shared language that allows knowledge to flow more efficiently.

Another means of establishing the prevalence of knowledge is to look at knowledge-related business **outcomes**. One example is **product development and service innovation**. While the knowledge embedded within these innovations is invisible, the products themselves are tangible.

1.2 Customer knowledge within the organisation

Many business functions deal with customers, including marketing, sales, service, logistics and financial functions. Each function will have its own reasons for being interested in customer information, and may have its own way of recording what it learns or even its own customer information system. The diverse interests of different departments make it **difficult to pull together** customer knowledge in one common format and place and the problem is magnified because all have some political reason to keep control of (in other words **not share**) what they know about customers.

While much of this book is about the processes of **market research** (which generates **explicit knowledge**, often by going outside the organisation), it is also worth remembering the necessity to **motivate employees to record, share and use** knowledge gained in a **less formal** manner. This includes experiential observations, comments made, lessons learned, interactions among people, impressions formed and so on.

Organisational means of encouraging sharing include emphasising it in the corporate **culture**, **evaluating** people on the basis of their knowledge behaviour and **rewarding** those who display good knowledge-sharing practice.

On a more practical level, **information and communications technology** can be of great assistance too, as we will see in the next section.

1.3 Systems that aid knowledge management

Any system – even a basic e-mail system – that helps and encourages people to work together and share information and knowledge will aid knowledge management. We have already covered expert systems, which may help to solve specific marketing problems, but marketing management is also likely to have the support of more general information sharing tools.

1.3.1 Groupware

Typically, groups utilising groupware are small project-oriented teams that have important tasks and tight deadlines. Perhaps the best-known general purpose groupware product is **Lotus Notes**. However, the components of **Microsoft Exchange** used on a networked system could also be considered to be a form of groupware, as could a CRM system.

Features might include the following:

(a)   A **scheduler** allowing users to keep track of their schedule and plan meetings with others.

(b)   An **address book**.

(c)   '**To do**' lists.

(d)   A **journal**, used to record interactions with important contacts, record items (such as e-mail messages) and files that are significant to the user, and record activities of all types and track   them all without having to remember where each one was saved.

(e)   A **jotter** for jotting down notes as quick reminders of questions, ideas, and so on.

(f)   File sharing and distribution utilities.

There are clearly advantages in having information such as this available from a computer at the touch of a button, rather than relying on scraps of paper, address books, and corporate telephone directories. However, it is when groupware is used to **share information** with colleagues that it comes into its own. Here are some of the features that may be found:

(a)   **Messaging**, comprising an **e-mail** in-box which is used to send and receive messages from the office, home, or the road and **routing** facilities, enabling users to send a message to a single person, send it sequentially to a number of people (who may add to it or comment on it before passing it on), or sending it to everyone at once.

(b)   Access to an **information database**, and customisable '**views**' of the information held on it, which can be used to standardise the way information is viewed in a workgroup.

(c)   **Group scheduling**, to keep track of colleagues' itineraries. Microsoft Exchange Server, for instance, offers a 'Meeting Wizard' which can consult the diaries of everyone needed to attend a meeting and automatically work out when they will be available, which venues are free, and what resources are required.

(d)   **Public folders**. These collect, organise, and share files with others on the team or across the organisation.

(e)   One person (for instance a secretary or a stand-in during holidays or sickness) can be given '**delegate access**' to another's groupware folders and send mail on their behalf, or read, modify, or create items in public and private folders on their behalf.

(f)   **Conferencing**. Participation in public, online discussions with others.

(g)   **Assigning tasks**. A task request can be sent to a colleague who can accept, decline, or reassign the task. After the task is accepted, the groupware will keeps the task status up-to-date on a task list.

(h)   **Voting** type facilities that can, say, request and tally responses to a multiple-choice question sent in a mail message (eg 'Here is a list of options for this year's Christmas party').

(i)   **Hyperlinks** in mail messages. The recipient can click the hyperlink to go directly to a web page or file server.

(j)   **Workflow management** (see below) with various degrees of sophistication.

Workflow is a term used to describe the defined series of tasks within an organisation to produce a final outcome. Sophisticated workgroup computing applications allow the user to define different **workflows** for different types of jobs. For example, when preparing a brochure, a document might be automatically routed between writers and then on to an editor, a proof reader and finally the printers.

At **each stage** in the workflow, **one individual** or group is **responsible** for a specific task. Once the task is complete, the workflow software ensures that the individuals responsible for the **next** task are notified and receive the data they need to complete their stage of the process.

1.3.2 Intranets

The idea behind an 'intranet' is that companies set up their own **mini version of the internet**. Intranets use a combination of the organisation's own networked computers and internet technology. Each employee has a browser, used to access a server computer that holds corporate information on a wide variety of topics, and in some cases also offers access to the internet.

Potential applications include company newspapers, induction material, online procedure and policy manuals, employee web pages where individuals post details of their activities and progress, and **internal databases** of the corporate information store.

Most of the **cost** of an intranet is the **staff time** required to set up the system.

The **benefits** of intranets are diverse.

(a)   Savings accrue from the **elimination of storage**, **printing** and **distribution** of documents that can be made available to employees online.

(b)   Documents online are often **more widely used** than those that are kept filed away, especially if the document is bulky (eg manuals) and needs to be searched. This means that there are **improvements in productivity** and **efficiency**.

(c)   It is much **easier to update** information in electronic form.

Wider access to corporate information should open the way to **more flexible working patterns**, eg material available online may be accessed from remote locations.

1.3.3 Extranets

Whereas an intranet is accessible only to people who are members of the same company or organisation, an extranet provides various levels of accessibility to outsiders.

Only those outsiders with a valid username and password can access an extranet, with varying levels of access rights enabling control over what people can view. Extranets are becoming a very popular means for **business partners to exchange information** for mutual benefit.

ACTIVITY 2.1

When marketing management support systems are being designed, what factors might you consider?

THE REAL WORLD

As a quick example of a marketing management support system in action, let us visualise a company that has identified **quality service** as a strategic priority. To meet this goal, the system must be capable of performing a wide range of tasks, including the following:

(a)   Provide managers with **real time** information on how customers and staff **perceive the service** being given, on the assumption that **what is not measured can't be managed**.

(b)   Measure quality of both service and customer care so as to provide evidence that they do matter, the implication being that **what is seen to be measured gets done**.

(c)   Monitor how (if at all) the **customer base is changing**.

(d)   Perhaps, provide a basis on which marketing staff bonus payments can be determined, on the grounds that **what gets paid for gets done even better**.

2 The marketing information system (MkIS)

The MkIS is a term that has largely fallen out of favour in the marketing world. It has been replaced by a whole tranche of new descriptors, the most common amongst these being CRM systems and database marketing. What we are looking at in this section is the range of tools that exists to help the marketing manager handle the vast amount of information that he or she has access to today.

The MkIS is the system that organisations use to put information at the heart of the decision-making process.

The MkIS defined by Kotler 'consists of people, equipment and procedures to gather, sort, analyse, evaluate and distribute timely and accurate information to marketing decision-makers' (Kotler *et al*, 2007).

A MkIS is built up from several different systems which **may not be directly related to marketing**. It is likely to contain the following **components**:

(a) Internal records – These include sales records, accounts records, details on past communications and the results of previously commissioned marketing research.

(b) The marketing intelligence system – This refers to the published data existing in the marketplace. It may include published research reports, government statistics or the national or trade press. We will look at this in detail when we examine secondary research.

(c) The marketing research system – This is the backbone of the marketing information system. However, the MkIS also contains other elements. These are as follows:

(d) The decision-support system – This contains the tools needed to make sense of data; it may include statistical packages and the intranet, with a range of tools and information designed to help marketers make decisions.

Figure 2.1   The marketing information system

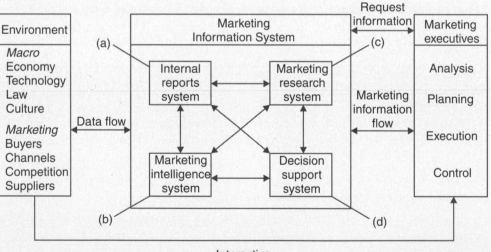

Despite being designed a long while ago, Kotler's (1996) model of a marketing information systems remains true to this day because it is simple and clear.

The internal reporting system sits on top of the transaction processing system already discussed. Although the data and records have been generated for some other purpose, they provide an invaluable insight into the current activity and performance of the company. Data such as sales records, invoices, production records and accounts can all be used in an internal reporting system. Many of these records are stored in computerised databases and therefore storage, retrieval and analysis is relatively quick and easy.

These records prove invaluable in an MkIS as the current operations of a business can be analysed and understood. It is good marketing practice to build any strategy or plan from an understanding of 'where we are now' and this system provides that understanding.

For example, these records may be used to provide an understanding of size and growth of customer segments, buying patterns, product profitability and many other areas.

The marketing intelligence system collects and stores everyday information about the external environment – information such as industry reports, competitors' marketing materials and competitors' quotes. Information collected here allows a company to build a more accurate profile of the external environment. The data may take the form of press cuttings, information derived from websites and so forth, but can also incorporate subscriptions to external sources of competitive data.

This could allow a company to calculate market sizes and growth patterns, competitor positioning and pricing strategy, and so on. This information may help in decision-making in many areas such as gap analysis, segmentation and targeting, market development and pricing strategy.

The market research system uses marketing research techniques to gather, evaluate and report findings in order to minimise guesswork in business decisions. The system is used to fill essential information gaps which are not covered by the other components of the MkIS system. In this way it provides targeted and detailed information for the decision-making problem at hand.

A company might use marketing research to provide detailed information on new product concepts, attitudes to marketing communication messages, testing advertising effectiveness and understanding customer perceptions of service delivery.

The decision support system comprises analytical techniques that enable marketing managers to make full use of the information provided by the other three sources. This analysis may range from simple financial ratios and projections of sales patterns to more complex statistical models, spreadsheets and other exercises in extrapolation.

An example would be a price sensitivity analysis tool using internal data from sales records together with market share and pricing information on competitors to calculate the price sensitivity of products.

3 The database

These elements of the MkIS are often incorporated within the marketing database. Alan Wilson (2006) defines the marketing database as: 'A manual or computerised source of data relevant to marketing decision-making about an organisation's customers'.

There are a few things about this definition that need to be explained.

A database does not have to be computer-based. It can be kept on hard copy. However, access to database technology is very easy and cost effective. Even the cheapest and simplest software is capable of storing a significant number of records. Microsoft Access is perfectly serviceable for many businesses.

While the definition limits itself to 'customers', other definitions spell out the fact that the database will collect data about past and potential customers as well as current customers. Jobber uses the following definition of database marketing:

Database marketing has been defined as: 'An interactive approach to marketing, that uses individually addressable marketing media and channels to: provide information to a company's target audience; stimulate demand; and stay close to them by recording and storing an electronic database memory of customer, prospects, and all communication and transactional data' (Jobber, 2010, p549).

The Institute of Direct Marketing (IDM) defines the marketing database as: 'A comprehensive collection of inter-related customer and/or prospect data that allows the timely accurate retrieval, use or manipulation of that data to support the marketing objectives of the enterprise'

Wilson says that the database differs from an accounting system in that the data must be relevant to marketing decision-making. This is a subtle but important difference. Clearly, the accounting system may reveal very interesting information to the marketer. It may contain details of what the customer has bought and when, and the frequency of purchase. We will see later that this information is important to successful database marketing. However, it is important that the data fed into the marketing database is relevant to marketing decisions now and in the future. It costs money to store and process data, and in this information age it is easy to have too much data.

Customer databases can contain a wide variety of information about the customer such as **contact details**, **transaction history**, **personal details** and **preferences** and so on. Information may come from a variety of sources besides transaction processing systems, including specialist geodemographic data and lifestyle information. Retailers are encouraging the collection of such data by introducing loyalty cards which are swiped through the till at the checkout, and contain information about the customer and their purchases.

A marketing database can provide an organisation with lots of information about its customers and target groups. **Every purchase a customer makes has two functions**:

- Provision of **sales revenue**
- Provision of **information** as to future market opportunities

A typical customer database might include the following:

Table 2.1   Summary database entry form

Element	Examples
Customer or company details	Account numbers, names, addresses and contact (telephone, fax, e-mail) details; basic 'mailing list' data, relationship to other customers. For business customers these fields might include sales contact, technical contact, parent company or subsidiaries, number of employees
Professional details	Company; job title; responsibilities – especially for business-to-business marketing; industry type
Personal details	Sex, age, number of people at the same address, spouse's name, children, interests, and any other relevant data known, such as newspapers read, journals subscribed to
Transaction history	What products/services are ordered, date, how often, how much is spent (turnover), payment methods
Call/contact history	Sales or after sales service calls made, complaints/queries received, meetings at shows/exhibitions, mailings sent, etc
Credit/payment history	Credit rating, amounts outstanding, aged debts
Credit transaction details	Items currently on order, dates, prices, delivery arrangements
Special account details	Membership number, loyalty or incentive points earned, discount awarded (where customer loyalty or incentive schemes are used)

The **sources** of information in a customer database, and the **uses** to which it can be put, are outlined in the diagram below.

The Chartered Institute of Marketing

Figure 2.2   Database inputs/outputs

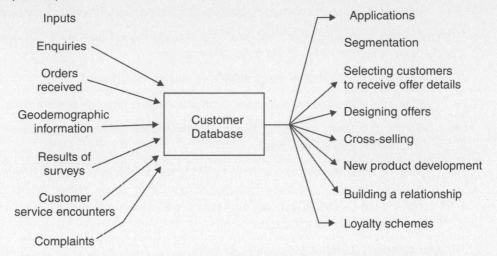

- The **majority** of customer information will be gleaned from the orders they place and the enquiries that they make. A relatively recent development in this area is the combination of cookies or user log-ins and server logging software, which enables **tracking and recording** of a customer's progress through a **website**, perhaps revealing interests that would otherwise have gone unnoticed.

- **Geodemographic** information relates to the characteristics of people living in different areas. Even simple post-code information can contain a lot of data about the customer.

- **Customer service** can be used to indicate particular concerns of customers. For example, in a DIY store, if customers have to ask service staff where items are stored, the volume of complaints might indicate poor signage and labelling.

- **Complaints** also indicate deficiencies in the product or the fact that customer expectations have been poorly communicated.

- The specific information held may **vary by type of market**. For example, an industrial database will hold data on key purchasers, influencers and decision-makers, organisational structure, industry classification (SIC codes), and business size.

Customer data can be categorised into four groups:

(a) **Behavioural data** which is collected by the organisation as a result of its interactions with the customer (eg contact records, letters, complaints, competition entries, orders, payments, online enquiries, tracked web pages visited, discussion forums used, loyalty or membership cards swiped etc).

(b) **Volunteered data** is generated when customers complete forms, register with websites, request more information and provide their own details, respond to calls for more information, agree to be contacted by relevant third parties and update their online profiles.

(c) **Attributed data** is data generated as a result of a specific research project. This information is confidential and therefore individual respondents cannot be added to a database using their personal identity. The results of a research study, however, can be used to add more detail to your database. For example, a charity may have conducted some research into the type of communications message that is most likely to elicit a response from different groups of potential donors. If, for example, it found that a plea for help worked well with mothers aged between 20 and 40 years old then it could place a code next to individuals within that group on its database to show that they are best communicated using that type of message. Professional men aged 40 – 50 may have been found to respond more to altruistic appeals, and therefore males fitting this profile could be tagged accordingly. The next time the charity sent a piece of direct mail, it could then adapt its tone and send more targeted messages to the individuals on its database.

(d)   **Profile data** is collected when it is linked with data from another source (eg lifestyle databases purchased, corporate databases, geodemographic profiles). Profiling is explored in more detail later.

Databases may be populated by information that the organisation collects for themselves or through information that is hired or purchased from third-party data providers.

Databases can provide **valuable information** to marketing management.

- Computer databases make it easier to collect and store more **data/information**.

- Computer software allows the data to be **extracted** from the file and **processed** to provide whatever information management needs.

- In some cases businesses may have access to the databases of **external organisations**. Reuters, for example, provides an online information system about money market interest rates and foreign exchange rates to firms involved in money market and foreign exchange dealings, and to the treasury departments of a large number of companies.

Other benefits of database systems might include:

(a)   Increased **sales and/or market share** (due to enhanced lead follow-up, cross-selling, customer contact)
(b)   Increased **customer retention** (through better targeting)
(c)   Better use of **resources** (targeting, less duplication of information handling)

Databases enable marketing managers to improve their **decision-making**.

- Understanding customers and their preferences
- Managing customer service (helplines, complaints)
- Understanding the market (new products, channels etc)
- Understanding competitors (market share, prices)
- Managing sales operations
- Managing marketing campaigns
- Communicating with customers

A database built for marketing purposes will, like the marketing function itself, be **future orientated**. It will be possible to **exploit** the database to **drive future marketing programmes**, not just to reflect on what has happened in the past.

3.1 Using the database to profile your customers

Profiling is something that the database allows us to do quite easily. Because of the range of information that we capture on our customers, we can create quite sophisticated profiles of our customers. By linking our database to services like Mosaic and Acxiom's products, we can extend this profile significantly. For example, a Mosaic code based on a customer's postcode will also unlock information collected by British Market Research Bureau (BMRB) through a service called the Target Group Index (TGI). This means that we can effectively link our base with TGI data on the basis of over 25,000 customer interviews.

Simple profiling might be used to identify the best-value customers according to certain demographic or lifestyle indicators. This would be based on the value of past purchases, how often they purchased and when they last purchased. This is known as recency, frequency and value analysis or RFV analysis. You may also see it written as FRAC (frequency, recency, amount and category) analysis. By matching this to other data, for example, income, family status and postcode, we can identify similar people in the market who do not transact with us and target them for acquisition.

Of course, the process of identifying these top customers allows us to begin the process of retaining them. It is believed that it costs between 3 and 30 times more to acquire a customer than it does to retain a customer.

Reichheld's book *The Loyalty Effect* goes into this in far more detail (Reichheld, 2001).

The Chartered Institute of Marketing

Academic research shows that the use of modelling and profiling via the database is a far more reliable and profitable approach to decision-making in marketing.

ACTIVITY 2.2

Think about a marketing project process. How does marketing information help this process? Write as many things as you can. Use your textbooks when you run out of ideas.

4 Customer relationship management systems

Unfortunately, the label 'CRM' (customer relationship management) now tends to be applied (especially by software vendors) to any and all systems designed to support marketing and sales.

Traditional functional organisation structures tended to create stand-alone systems oriented to the separate requirements of the distinct departments responsible for the four main types of interaction with the customer: marketing, sales, fulfilment and after-sales. The modern philosophy is that a single system should store and allow access to all customer information wherever it is created or required for use. A CRM system is above all an **integrated system**, covering the entire sales and marketing process. It brings together a number of marketing and customer-facing systems within one system or homogeneous software application. The following features are usually associated with CRM:

- Data warehouses
- Customer service systems
- Call centres
- E-commerce
- Web marketing
- Operational systems (eg invoicing and payment)
- Sales systems (eg mobile communications)

With an effective CRM system, whenever there is contact with customers, whether by letter or telephone or online, the customer should be recognised and dealt with appropriately: this will require that their contact histories are accessed, and that information and attention suitable to their individual requirements are provided. CRM software provides advanced suitable personalisation and customised solutions to customer demands, and gives marketing management a range of key information about each customer which can be applied to the current and future transactions.

However, some commentators would argue that it is now **customers** who **manage** the relationship with **companies**, and not the other way around.

ACTIVITY 2.3

Find out how an IT system based on a data warehouse works.

5 Data protection and freedom of information

The United Kingdom has had data protection legislation since 1984. The current Data Protection Act that was passed in 1998 and came into force in 2000 was introduced in response to the 1995 European Union Directive on Data Protection. The Act regulates 'processing' of data; this covers data on any living person, and there are separate rules for sensitive data, for example, health, sexuality, religion, disabilities and so on. If you collect data on Halal meals, then your data falls in this separate, more sensitive category. The Freedom of Information Act (2000) came into force on 1 January 2005. The Act regulates access to information held by public authorities.

The guiding principles of transparency and consent in the Data Protection Act are most relevant for marketing research professionals. Individuals must have a clear understanding of why their data is being captured and what it will be used for, and they must consent to its use and be given the opportunity to opt-out of any later use of this data.

Opt-out is the standard at the moment. However, this is changing, and the latest rules seem to be asking people to actively 'opt-in' to future use of their data (an extension of the principle of permission marketing). This is very likely to become the standard, and it is good practice now to ask individuals to actively opt-in to the future use of their data.

We will examine the aspects of legal compliance in greater depth when we look at the research process and data manipulation in Chapter 3.

Proctor & Gamble

Proctor & Gamble senior management meet every Monday morning in their Ohio headquarters to review the data. The room resembles a surround view and sound mini studio with massive curved screens. This room is the centre of the business's data review and manipulation analysis and provides instant sight of the metrics involved with their entire portfolio, trading in 80 different countries and generating approximately four billion transactions every day. Each tap or click of a key on an iPad will present those present with any specific set or combination of data variables under any given input. For example, comparative metrics could suggest that in the next four weeks in Australia, 600,000 more cases of a particular brand of shampoo will need to be sold for sales of that brand just to remain flat in the period in the territory.

The Business Sphere, as this room and its inhabitants are referred to internally, was totally ramped up in the first quarter of 2011. The technology is cutting edge and is drawn from 14 different vendors allowing the data not only to be displayed and reviewed in this room, but to be shared and used by senior management teams in over 40 different locations worldwide. The simultaneous and instantaneous use of this data allows the organisation to manage the outputs in such a fashion that agreement and decision making is enhanced and ultimately flexible. Tracking progress against objectives can be viewed in real time and if called for, the data can pinpoint a particular retailer in any part of the world. Such data sophistication is priceless.

As the biggest consumer products company on the planet, Proctor & Gamble is at the forefront of data capture and manipulation and fully recognises how such a rich resource adds significant competitive advantage. The harnessing and leveraging of this data will continue unabated. The firm began profit forecasting on a monthly basis nearly 40 years ago by analysing masses of data on such elements as volume sales, commodity prices and exchange rates. Today however, given the massive dynamic within technology and the data capture opportunities presented by high speed networking, data visualisation and multiple analysis streams, decisions can be made in minutes.

(Forbes, 2011)

▶ **Assessment tip**

When dealing with projects that require customer profiling, it is imperative to fully investigate and interrogate all available customer data from all available sources and outline this in a synthesised and cohesive manner

CHAPTER ROUNDUP

- We looked at the categories of knowledge management, where knowledge resides, how knowledge can systematically be managed and what benefits knowledge management brings to the organisation.

- We looked at the component parts of a marketing information system.

- We looked at databases, how these are constituted and what they are used for.

- We established that a dedicated approach should be created and formulated into a customer relationship management system.

- We looked at marketing and the law when it comes to data protection.

FURTHER READING

Davenport, T. and Prusak, L. (2000) *Working Knowledge: How Organisations Manage What They Know*. 2nd edition. Boston, Harvard Business School Press.

REFERENCES

Davidson, H. (1997) *Even More Offensive Marketing*. Harmondsworth Penguin.

Jobber, D. (2010) *Principles and Practice of Marketing*. 6th edition. Maidenhead, McGraw Hill.

Kotler, P. *et al*, (2007) *Marketing Management*. 12th edition. Harlow Pearson.

Hardy, Q. (2011) At Proctor & Gamble, Toothpaste Is Data. Forbes, http://www.forbes.com/sites/quentinhardy/2011/08/03/at-procter-gamble-toothpaste-is-data/ [Accessed 23 May 2012].

Reichheld, F.F. (2001) *The Loyalty Effect: The Hidden Force Behind Growth, Profits and Lasting Value*. Revised edition. Watertown, Harvard Business School Press.

Wilson, A. (2006) *Marketing Research: an Integrated Approach*. 2nd edition. London Financial Times/Prentice Hall.

QUICK QUIZ

1   What is knowledge management?

2   What type of information can a customer database contain?

3   A marketing information system has four typical components. Fill in the gaps.

I	R	System
M	I	System
M	R	System
A	M	System

 The Chartered Institute of Marketing

4   List six ways in which groupware helps organisations to share information.

5   What is the most important thing that is achieved by CRM systems as opposed to earlier types of system?

ACTIVITY DEBRIEFS

Activity 2.1

When marketing management support systems are being designed, the following factors should be considered:

(a)   Users should **understand** the systems and be in a position to evaluate and control them. Management's **access** to the information must be **easy and direct** and the true meaning of the information provided must be clear.

(b)   The **cost** of data/information **gathering** should be **minimal**.

(c)   **Data gathering** should not cause excessive inconvenience to information sources. Preferably the data will be gathered without customers having to make any extra effort (for example, through analysis of supermarket checkout receipts which show consumer purchase patterns).

(d)   **Data gathering should be regular and continuous** since a small amount of data gathered regularly can build a considerable database. Regular data gathering produces more reliable results because it reduces the likelihood of bias of one kind or another.

(e)   The system must be **flexible**. It should be regularly **reviewed** and **improved** where possible.

Activity 2.2

Information is key and will always be used to inform such elements as problem definition, project scope and objectives, resource requirements and knowledge gaps.

Activity 2.3

A **data warehouse** receives data from transaction processing systems, such as a sales order processing system, and stores them in their most fundamental form, without any summarisation of transactions. Analytical and query software is provided so that reports can be produced at any level of summarisation and incorporating any comparisons or relationships desired. The value of a data warehouse is enhanced when **data-mining** software is used. True data-mining software discovers previously unknown relationships and provides insights that cannot be obtained through ordinary summary reports. These hidden patterns and relationships constitute knowledge that can be used to guide decision-making and to predict future behaviour.

1   Knowledge **management** involves the identification and analysis of available and required knowledge, and the subsequent planning and control of actions to develop knowledge assets so as to fulfil organisational objectives.

2   **Customer databases** can contain a wide variety of information about the customer such as **contact details**, **transaction history**, **personal details** and **preferences** and so on.

3   Internal Reporting System
     Marketing Intelligence System
     Marketing Research System
     Analytical Marketing System

4   The features mentioned in the text of the chapter are: messaging, access to databases, scheduling, shared public folders, delegate access, conferencing, task assignment, voting, hyperlinks and workflow management.

5   Integration of information from all the systems that impact upon marketing.

CHAPTER 3

Research briefs and proposals

Introduction

We now move on to the discipline of marketing research. In this chapter, we explore the process of planning research and briefing researchers to carry out the process. This will be an important part of your course. The senior examiner in a recent briefing to tutors told them to focus on the process of developing research briefs, responding to those briefs through the presentation of the proposal and then presenting the final report.

This activity represents the day-to-day management of the research function in business and you may expect it to form a relative part of your assessment in this unit.

The brief is very important. Even if the research is to be carried out in-house, a briefing document is required. It provides a fixed reference that all parties involved should sign off.

For the commissioner of the research, it provides 'bulletproof' evidence that certain dates or budgets were agreed on. In complex research studies, it keeps all parties on track and can help the process of project management.

Topic list

The marketing research brief	(1)
The marketing research industry	(2)
Selecting a supplier	(3)
Choosing and using consultants	(4)
A research brief	(5)
The marketing research proposal	(6)
Ethical and social responsibilities	(7)

1.4	Develop a research brief to meet the requirements of an individually specific case for marketing:
	▪ Problem definition
	▪ Objectives
	▪ Information requirements
	▪ Data collection
	▪ Report parameters
	▪ Timescales
	▪ Resource allocation
	▪ Control and contingency
1.5	Critically evaluate a full research proposal to fulfil the brief supporting the information needs of the case and make recommendations for improvement
	▪ Proposal scoring
	▪ Brief reviewing
	▪ The brief/proposal mechanic
	▪ Effort required for proposal versus available budget
	▪ Decision to use in-house or external agency resources
	▪ Utilisation of existing data

1 The marketing research brief

> ▶ **Key terms**
>
> A **research brief** is a detailed commissioning document that fully sets out why the research is needed, what questions need to be addressed, how the research should be carried out and presented and what the research budget is.
>
> A **research proposal** is a detailed response document to a research brief.

We will now look more in detail at the marketing research brief. The briefing document is perhaps the most important stage of the research process. As the old aphorism states, 'be careful what you ask for, you may get it'. A tight brief is vital to the management of the marketing research process. It provides a focus for discussion and a guiding hand through the project.

Many companies see the briefing process as part of an almost gladiatorial trial of strength where a brief is issued, limited information is given, and the resulting proposals are torn to bits in the arena of the pitch. The justification is that ideas are tested in the heat of the moment and that if an agency cannot justify an approach under fire, they are unlikely to be effective. The lack of detail is seen as allowing the agency to interpret and explore ideas. Some research briefs are given on one side of a page of A4. This may be sufficient, but is almost certainly inadequate for complex multifaceted research tasks.

Equally, some companies go the other way, even specifying the colour and weight of paper for the final presentation. This may be overkill.

On the other side, some agencies receive a brief as Drayton Bird (2007) says, 'rather like a baby bird waiting to be fed by its mother, passively, humbly and gratefully'. Both approaches are wrong. The best marketing solutions come through co-operation and active involvement.

The Chartered Institute of Marketing

You are the marketing manager for a major soft drinks producer. Sales have stagnated in the over 50s segment and you have been asked to look at the development of a new drink to target the older market. What core information would you need to be establishing to enable you to undertake such a project?

Agencies need the right information in order to be able to produce a suitable proposal. If there are issues over confidentiality, then confidentiality agreements can be signed before the brief is issued. Members of the MRS are obliged to comply with the code of conduct that ensures client confidentiality. However, the agency needs the tools to do the job – in this case, information. The development of the brief should be a team activity.

If you read other books on marketing research you will find many slight variations on the suggested 'stages' of the market research process, partly depending on whether the book is written from the point of view of a client or a market research agency. There is fairly general agreement, however, that the process will entail the following stages, in this order. (The process spells **DODCAR**, if you like mnemonics!)

Stage 1   **Definition**: identify and define the **opportunity or threat**

Stage 2   **Objectives**: determine precisely what you need to know to deal with the opportunity or threat

Stage 3   **Design** the research and the methods to be used

Stage 4   **Collect** the **data**

Stage 5   **Analyse** the data

Stage 6   **Report** on the findings

Where an organisation is using an agency or agencies to do the research it will send out a **research brief** at the end of Stage 2, and the various agencies that are asked to tender for the work will then submit **research proposals** (in outline, at least) covering Stage 3, explaining how they would do the work and why they should be chosen. Research proposals are discussed at more length later in this chapter.

1.1 Stage 1: Identify and define the opportunity or threat

We have phrased the heading above so that it reminds you of SWOT analysis, since the identification of a need for market research will usually arise from strategic and marketing planning processes and reviews.

(a)   An **opportunity** is something that occurs in the organisation's environment that could be advantageous – a **change in the law**, say, or a **new technology** that could be exploited.

(b)   A **threat** is an environmental development that could create problems and stop the organisation achieving its objectives – a **new competitor**, perhaps, or an adverse change in **buying behaviour**.

In either case the organisation will **want to know more**. How can it best take advantage? What action is most likely to stave off or reverse the problem? The answers will depend on **how the market reacts** to different possible solutions, and the organisation can be much surer about this if it conducts **research**.

Bear in mind that marketing research, however well organised, is not a substitute for decision-making. It can help to reduce the risks, but it will not make the decision. Professional marketing depends partially on sound judgement and reliable information, but it also needs flair and creativity.

1.2 Stage 2: Determine the objectives of the research

The objectives should set out the precise information needed, as clearly as possible. It is very wasteful of time and money to collect answers to questions that did not need to be asked or which were the wrong questions. The objectives should relate only to the problem or opportunity. They should be stated carefully, completely and precisely. The **SMART** mnemonic gives some clues, though there are several versions of just what this acronym stands for. Here is one reasonable possibility

(a)   They should be as **specific** as possible: vague objectives will lead to inconclusive, vague research.

(b)   They should relate to **measurable** matters: quantified information should be the target, but even when a topic can only be dealt with in qualitative terms, the objectives should require as much quantification as possible.

(c)   They should be **attainable** with reasonable resources: objectives that are impossible to achieve are nonsensical.

(d)   They should focus on **results** rather than methods.

(e)   They should be **time-bound**: an overall time frame for the research should be agreed, with suitable progress gates incorporated.

Marketing research can sometimes be a waste of effort and resources.

(a)   The research undertaken may be designed without reference to the decisions that will depend on, or be strongly influenced by, the results of the research.

(b)   The research results may be ignored, misused, misunderstood, or misinterpreted. Sometimes this happens accidentally; more often it is deliberate because the results do not agree with some senior person's prejudices or established beliefs.

(c)   The research is poorly designed or carried out.

(d)   The results of the research are themselves inconclusive, giving rise to different opinions about what the research signifies.

With issues like this in mind, Wilson (2006) suggests **early consultation and involvement** of all the parties that will be involved in actioning the decisions taken as a result of the proposed research, for example by setting up a project team. This has the advantage that those closest to the project will probably have the best idea of what **knowledge** the organisation **already possesses**, and does not need to be researched. Also it means that the questions that **need** to be answered are more likely to get asked.

ACTIVITY 3.2

Using the example again of a company that manufactures cruelty-free beauty products for a number of supermarket chains, you have been given responsibility for outlining the likely research objectives.

Other matters that would be considered at this stage would be the available budget and the timescale for the work, and perhaps there would be outline thoughts about the methods to be used (for instance the scale of the research and the segments of the market to be included). All of this information, together with the requirements for the final report, would be included in the research brief if the work was now to be put out to tender.

1.3 Stage 3: Design the research and the methods to be used

The **category** of research must first be decided upon: the methods used will depend on that. Research may be **exploratory**, **descriptive** or **causal**.

1.3.1 Exploratory research

As the name suggests, **exploratory** research tends to **break new ground**. For instance, if your organisation has a **completely new idea** for a product or service which consumers have never been offered before, then exploratory research will be most appropriate in the first instance.

(a)   Potential consumers may be totally uninterested, in which case exploratory research will quickly show that it is best to **abandon the idea** before any more money is spent on developing it.

(b)   Consumers **may not understand** how the offer could benefit them, in which case exploratory research would show that it may be worth simplifying the product and introducing it to them in a different way, with different promotional techniques and messages.

(c)   On the other hand, consumers may not have responded because the **research methods used** were not appropriate, or because the wrong consumer group was chosen: exploratory research can help to define how more detailed research should be carried out.

Exploratory research may therefore be a **preliminary** to more detailed development of marketing ideas or a more detailed research project. It may even lead to abandonment of a product idea.

Research **methods** should involve as **little cost** and take as **little time** as possible. If use can be made of **existing research** by others then that is certainly desirable, as are methods that are not too labour and cost intensive such as **telephone** research or limited **internet surveys**.

1.3.2 Descriptive research

Descriptive research aims to describe what is happening now (a single snapshot) or what has happened over a limited period of time (several snapshots).

(a)   Now (a '**cross-sectional study**'): 'At present 45% of the target market are aware of our product whereas 95% are aware of Competitor A's product'.

(b)   Over time (a '**longitudinal study**'): 'During the period of the in-store promotion (February to April) awareness of our product rose from 45% to 73%'.

In other words, descriptive research is useful for answering 'where are we now?' questions, and it can also be used to summarise how things have changed over a period in time. Published market research reports are examples of descriptive research: if you subscribe today you will find out 'where you were' when the report was last published, and if you wait a while for the next edition you will find out how you have progressed.

The main problem (for researchers) with longitudinal descriptive research is to ensure that their respondents are either the same people each time or, if that is not possible, that answers from very similar respondents are aggregated. Research **methods** are likely to include **telephone** research, with the consumer's agreement, and specially invited **panels** of respondents.

1.3.3 Causal research

Although descriptive research is very common and is much used it may not really tell us the **cause** of the event or behaviour it describes. To paraphrase Wilson (2006), virtually all marketing research projects fall somewhere along a continuum between purely descriptive and purely **causal**.

For example, the descriptive result 'During the period of the in-store promotion (February to April) awareness of our product rose from 45% to 73%' appears to suggest a reason for the change, but the only thing we know for certain is that two to three months have gone by. The change may be little or nothing to do with the in-store promotion. It may be due to a completely random factor such as temporary unavailability of a competitor's product, or uncontrolled and unmeasured actions taken by in-store staff, or to other promotional efforts such as TV ads.

The relationship between variables like this is not formally taken into account in descriptive research. **Causal** research attempts to identify and establish the relationship between all the variables, and determine whether one variable influences the value of others. **Experimental** research can be carried out, where one variable is deliberately changed to see the effect, if any, on other variables. The most obvious example is to see if lowering the price causes sales to rise.

Research **methods** might be similar to those for longitudinal descriptive research (panels of consumers for instance), but the information they are asked to provide will be more extensive and the time span may be longer. The researcher will need to consider the **sampling** method and parameters (how many people and of what type), where the people can be found, and the means of obtaining information (**interviews**, **questionnaires** and so on).

1.4 Stage 4: Collect the data

Data can be collected from either primary or secondary data sources.

(a) **Primary data** is information **collected specifically for the study** under consideration. Primary data may be **quantitative** (statistics), **qualitative** (attitudes etc) or **observational** videos of people browsing in a store, for instance).

(b) **Secondary data** is data collected for another purpose not specifically related to the proposed research, for instance, all the **internal** information in the company's marketing information systems and databases, or information such as **published research** reports, **government** information, **newspapers** and trade journals and so on.

1.5 Stage 5: Analyse the data

This stage will involve getting the data into analysable form by entering it into a computer and using statistics (for quantitative data) and other means of analysis and summary (qualitative data) to find out what it reveals.

1.6 Stage 6: Report on the findings

The final report is likely to take the form of a **presentation** given to an audience of interested parties and a detailed **written report** explaining and summarising the findings, with appendices of figures and tables and so on.

In putting together the research plan, decisions need to be made under the following headings.

Table 3.1   Summary research plan

Data sources	Primary data (data the organisation collects itself for the purpose)
	Secondary data (collected by someone else for another purpose which may provide useful information)
Type of data required	Continuous/*ad hoc*
	Quantitative (numbers)
	Qualitative (important insights)
Research methods	Observation
	Focus groups
	Survey
	Experiment

Research tools	Interviews (semi-structured, structured, unstructured; open vs closed questions)
	Questionnaires
	Mechanical tools (video, audio)
Sampling technique (if required)	Sampling unit
	Sample size
	Sample procedure
Contact methods	Telephone
	Mail
	Face-to-face

2 The marketing research industry

2.1 Internal marketing research departments

Most organisations will have somebody who is responsible for marketing research, even if that simply means liaising with external agencies who actually carry out the work.

Larger organisations that have a regular need for marketing research information (particularly FMCG organisations) are likely to set up their own **marketing research department**.

2.2 Specialist agencies

As the name implies a specialist agency specialises in a particular type of work.

(a) Some agencies specialise in particular **markets** or market **sectors** or **regions**.

(b) Others specialise in a particular **research service** such as questionnaire design, or collection and analysis of qualitative information.

(c) **Field agencies** have specialised skills in **conducting** personal or telephone interviews and **administering** postal or e-mail surveys.

(d) **Data analysis agencies** can be employed to code up, read in or input data collected (in questionnaires, say, or perhaps recorded in personal interviews) and analyse it using state-of-the-art hardware (such as highly accurate scanners) and software (for instance highly specialised statistical packages).

(e) There are numerous **independent consultants** who will undertake a variety of tasks, usually on a **smaller scale**. Such people are typically ex-employees of larger research organisations or have gained their expertise in related disciplines such as IT or librarianship.

2.3 Syndicated research agencies

A syndicated service is one that is **not conducted for any specific client**. Regular research is conducted into areas that the agency knows for certain that many organisations will be interested in (for instance newspaper and magazine readership) and is then sold to anyone willing to pay the price.

Well-known examples of syndicated research agencies include **Datamonitor** (with products like MarketWatch: Drinks and MarketWatch: Food), and **Mintel** (http://www.mintel.co.uk) which has a huge number of regularly updated reports available on a subscription basis (eg *Agricultural Machinery, Nail Color and Care, Disposable Nappies and Baby Wipes*, and hundreds of others).

2.4 List brokers

A list broker **creates or acquires lists** of potential consumers **for the purpose of selling them on** to companies who are interested. Lists may be created from publicly available sources such as the telephone book or yellow pages or the electoral rolls but they will usually be **organised** for convenience, presented in **formats** that can be easily incorporated into clients systems, and **checked** for accuracy and currency. The client could possibly do this in-house, but it would be very **time-consuming**. Lists that have arisen as a result of some other exercise such as responses to mailshots or entry into a 'free' draw may also be **acquired** by list brokers.

2.5 Profilers

A profiler is able to take an organisation's database and **superimpose profiling information** (demographics, lifestyle and life stage information) on the basis of post codes. This allows the organisation's database to be segmented according to the criteria that are most appropriate to that organisation.

A profiler may also have access to other lists and be able to offer these to its clients, much like a list broker, except that the profiler has closer knowledge of the characteristics of the clients' existing customers and so the list may have more appropriate prospects.

2.6 Full service agencies

As the name implies a full service agency **offers all of the above services** and so will be able to conduct a research project from start to finish. Well-known international examples are **BMRB** (http://www.bmrb.co.uk), **Taylor Nelson Sofres** (http://www.tns-global.com) and **Ipsos** (http://www.ipsos.com).

In addition, many full service **advertising agencies** offer marketing research services as do firms of **management consultants** like McKinsey (http://www.mckinsey.com).

3 Selecting a supplier

Very few organisations can shoulder the cost of a large full-time staff of marketing research workers, so market research is often outsourced.

3.1 External agencies versus in-house programmes

There are a number of advantages and disadvantages to each alternative.

(a) **Using an external agency**

    (i) **Advantages**

        1   External agencies **specialising** in research will have the necessary expertise in marketing research techniques. This should allow them to develop a cost-effective research programme to a **tighter timescale**.

2   Skills in **monitoring and interpreting data** will allow the programme to be reviewed and modified as required.

3   Nationwide or global agencies will be able to offer much **broader geographical coverage**.

4   An external agency can provide an **objective input** without the bias which often results from a dependence on internal resources.

5   **Costs** can be determined from the outset, allowing better **budgetary control**.

6   When conducting **confidential research** into sensitive areas, there is less risk of information being 'leaked' to competitors.

(ii)   **Disadvantage**

Agency knowledge of the industry will be limited: a serious drawback if the agency needs a disproportionate amount of time to familiarise itself with the sector.

(b)   **In-house programme**

(i)   **Advantages**

1   **Costs can be absorbed** into existing departmental overheads.
2   It can **broaden the experience** and skills of existing staff.
3   It might promote a **team spirit** and encourage a 'results-oriented' approach.

(ii)   **Disadvantages**

1   There is a danger of **overstretching current resources** and adversely affecting other projects.

2   There is a risk of developing an **inappropriate programme**, yielding insufficient or poor quality data with inadequate analysis and control.

3   If additional **training or recruitment** is required this could prove expensive and time consuming.

4   **Bias** could result from using staff with preconceived views.

5   **Company politics** may influence the results.

6   Considerable **computing resources** with appropriate software packages would be required to analyse the data.

7   There may be a lack of **appropriate facilities**. For example, focus group research is often conducted off premises during evenings or weekends.

In view of the shortcomings of a purely in-house or external agency approach, a **combination** of the two might be more appropriate. For example, it might be deemed preferable to design the programme in-house but contract out certain aspects.

4 Choosing and using consultants

Choosing the right agency or consultant to work with is a key element in a successful working relationship. The external expert must become a trusted part of the team. It is important that the market researcher has the specialist knowledge and research service capabilities needed by the organisation. It helps if the agency has some knowledge of the market or business in which the company operates. Therefore, it may be worthwhile to develop a long-standing relationship with the research organisation, because its understanding of the company's business and the marketplace will develop over time.

The selection process will generally involve the organisation sending out its **research brief** to a number of agencies and inviting each to submit a **research proposal**.

5 A research brief

The key to good research is the quality of the research brief prepared by the organisation commissioning the research.

A research brief will normally cover the following matters.

(a)   **Background** – relevant information about the company, its products and services, its marketplace and so on.

(b)   **Rationale** – how the need for information arose and what the users intend to do with it? What decisions will be taken?

(c)   **Budget** – the benefits of collecting information should be greater than the costs of collecting it, but benefits are not always easy to quantify. The budget is always likely to be limited and this will affect the scale and type of information search that can be carried out. This item will probably not be revealed to possible external suppliers, since their response is likely to be based on how much research they are prepared to undertake for the price, rather than how they propose to meet the requirements of the brief.

(d)   **Timescale** – commercial constraints may impose severe time limits. This will also have an impact on the scale and type of information search that can be carried out.

(e)   **Objectives** – the precise information needed should be set out as clearly as possible.

(f)   **Methods** – this need only be an outline, setting out, for instance, the scale of the search, the mix of quantitative and qualitative information needed, the segments of the market to be included, for example.

(g)   **Reports** – how the final information should be presented. Considerations here might include style of reports, degree of summarisation, use of charts and other graphics, format for quantitative information (eg in Excel spreadsheets, for ease of further analysis).

THE REAL WORLD

(Note: Following is an illustrative cut-down brief presented to ensure client confidentiality.)

Purpose of the research – to establish usage and attitudes to the consumption of ambient ready meals in the five EU markets (specified elsewhere).

Background to the company

Description of the company: ownership, turnover, brands, ambient ready meal (ARM) brands.

Market size and market share data, trends, volume and values, competition.

 The Chartered Institute of Marketing

Background to the problem

Falling retail share, seek to stabilise market share through refined mix.

Research objectives

- Why are ARMs bought?
- When are they used?
- Who prepares them?
- On what occasions are they used?
- Perception of quality relative to other RM (ready meal) categories
- Perception of quality relative to competitors
- Attitudes to price
- Attitudes to advertising

Methods

1   Qualitative analysis
    Focus groups in key target audiences
2   Quantitative analysis
    Around 1500 housewives in each market, representative of households, quota sample
    Question areas built out of the qualitative study
    Brands bought, brands recognised, consumption occasion, attitudes to ARMs and other RM categories
    Client input requested on this aspect of research, design and implementation

Timing

Proposal: 2 April; Presentation: week commencing 12 April; Commission: 4 May; Report: early July.

Budget

In the region of £25,000.

Report to

Brand manager, Marketing research manager, Marketing director.

6 The marketing research proposal

The proposal should be presented in a written format and on time. A formal presentation may accompany the proposal. The proposal itself should be seen before any formal face-to-face presentation in order for it to be assessed and questions framed. These questions may be sent to the agency before the formal meeting.

Proposals may form the final contract for a project and as such can include contract details and terms and conditions as an appendix. It is also a marketing tool for the research agency, so the use of client testimonials and relevant past contracts is normal. It is fundamental that presentation, spelling and grammar should be faultless.

Research proposals are prepared by research agencies in response to the research brief. In structure, a research proposal is similar to the research brief, but it will be much more detailed in certain parts.

(a)   **Background.** This sets out the agency's understanding of the client company, its products and services, its marketplace and so on, and its understanding of why the research is required. If the agency has misunderstood the brief, this will be clear to the client.

(b)   **Objectives.** These will probably be much the same as those in the brief, although the agency's understanding of research techniques may have helped to define them more precisely still.

(c)   **Approach and method.** How the agency proposes to carry out the research, what methods will be used, where the sample will be taken from and so on.

(d)   **Reports.** How the final information will be presented, whether interim reports will be made, and so on.

(e)   **Timing**. How long the research will take and how it will be broken down into separate stages if appropriate.

(f)   **Fees and expenses**. This is self-explanatory.

(g)   **Personal CVs** of the main agency personnel who will be involved in the project.

(h)   **Relevant experience/references**. The agency will wish to assure the client that it is capable of carrying out the research, so it will include information about similar projects undertaken in the past, and possibly details of previous clients who are willing to testify to the competence of the agency.

Contractual details will set out the agency's terms of trade, and clarify matters such as ownership of the data collected.

6.1 Reviewing the research proposal

The research proposal should be reviewed very carefully, since it will form the basis of the contractual relationship with an external supplier and, even if internal resources are used, it must demonstrate that the proposed activity will meet the objectives set for the project.

Generally, a full assessment of a research proposal will inevitably spill over into an assessment of the agency making it, since it is necessary to be convinced not only that the details of the proposal are appropriate but also that the agency is capable of doing the work concerned, subject to the usual constraints of time, cost and quality. A proposal might thus be assessed against a number of criteria. Here are some examples:

(a)   The **methodology** proposed must be judged capable of achieving the overall objectives.

(b)   The agency must be considered **capable of carrying out its proposal**, both in its technical resources and in its ability to deploy and control their use.

(c)   The agency must be considered to be appropriately **stable** commercially and legally.

(d)   Proper attention must be paid to both **ethics and legal compliance**.

(e)   There must be proper and appropriate arrangements for **liaison and problem-solving** between the agency and the client.

(f)   **Time**, **quality** and **cost** constraints must be satisfied.

Assessment may be carried out on an entirely qualitative basis, especially when the bidding agencies are well-known to the client. However, some form of scoring may be useful where some of the bidders are unknown or the project requirements and selection criteria are particularly complex. When scoring is used, it is usual to weight each criterion and then score against the weight given. Thus, using the criteria outlined above, percentage weights might be allocated as shown below.

Table 3.2   Research proposal assessment criteria

Criterion	Percentage weight
Methodology	30
Capability	25
Supplier stability	15
Compliance	10
Liaison	20

Any or all of the time, cost and quality constraints may be regarded as **imperatives**; that is they are absolute, non-negotiable factors and will be built into the contract on that basis, rather than being criteria for scoring.

The Chartered Institute of Marketing

7 Ethical and social responsibilities

Marketing research aims to collect data about people. It could not take place at all if people were not willing to provide data, and that means that it is as much in the interests of the marketing research industry as it is of respondents for researchers to behave responsibly with the information collected.

7.1 Data protection

Most developed countries have specific legislation to protect the **privacy of individuals**. Many people feel unhappy about their personal details being retained by commercial organisations.

7.1.1 The Data Protection Act 1998

Data protection legislation was introduced in the UK in the early 1980s to try to prevent abuses. The latest provision is the **Data Protection Act 1998**.

The Act is concerned with '**personal data**', which is information about **living, identifiable individuals**. This can be as little as a name and address: it need not be particularly sensitive information. If it is sensitive (discussed later) then extra care is needed. The Act gives individuals (**data subjects**) certain rights and it requires those who record and use personal information (**data controllers**) to be open about their use of that information and to follow 'sound and proper practices' (the Data Protection Principles).

7.1.2 The eight data protection principles

Data must be:

- Fairly and lawfully processed
- Processed for limited purposes
- Adequate, relevant and not excessive
- Accurate
- Not kept longer than necessary
- Processed in accordance with an individual's rights
- Secure
- Not transferred to countries that do not have adequate data protection laws

7.1.3 Fair processing for limited purposes

When an organisation collects information from individuals it should be **honest and open** about why it wants the information and it should have a **legitimate reason** for processing the data.

7.1.4 Adequate, relevant and not excessive; accurate and no longer than necessary

Organisations should hold **neither too much nor too little** data about the individuals in their list. For instance, many companies collect date of birth or age range information from their customers, but in many cases all they actually need to know is that they are over eighteen.

Personal data should be **accurate and up-to-date** as far as possible. Data should be **removed when it is no longer required** for audit purposes or when a customer ceases to do business with the organisation.

7.1.5 The rights of data subjects

Individuals have various rights including the following.

- The right to **be informed** of all the information held about them by an organisation.

- The right to **prevent** the processing of their data for the purposes of direct marketing.

- The right to **compensation** if they can show that they have been caused damage by any contravention of the Act.

- The right to have any inaccurate data about them **removed** or corrected.

7.1.6 Security

Organisations should make sure that they provide **adequate security** for the data, taking into account the nature of the data, and the possible harm to the individual that could arise if the data is disclosed or lost.

- Measures to ensure that **access** to computer records **by staff** is authorised (for instance a system of passwords).

- Measures to control **access** to records by **people other than staff**. For instance, care should be taken over the siting of computers to prevent casual callers to the organisation's premises being able to read personal data on screen.

- Measures to prevent the **accidental loss or theft** of personal data, for example backups and fire precautions.

7.1.7 Overseas transfers

If an organisation wishes to transfer personal data to a country outside the European Economic Area (EEA) it will either need to ensure there is adequate protection (eg a Data Protection Act) for the data in the receiving country, or obtain the consent of the individual.

7.1.8 Sensitive data

The Act defines eight categories of sensitive personal data. If an organisation holds personal data falling into these categories it is likely that it will **need the explicit consent** of the individual concerned. It will also need to ensure that its security is adequate for the protection of sensitive data.

The eight categories are:

- The racial or ethnic origin of data subjects
- Their political opinions
- Their religious beliefs or other beliefs of a similar nature
- Whether they are a member of a trade union
- Their physical or mental health or condition
- Their sexual life
- The commission or alleged commission by them of any offence
- Any details of court proceedings or sentences against them

7.1.9 Enforcement

If an organisation is breaching the principles of the Act, the Information Commissioner has various powers to force the organisation to comply, including issuing an enforcement notice, and the power to enter and search its premises, and examine equipment and documents. It is an offence to obstruct the Commissioner, and there are also fines and criminal penalties for holding data without being registered; for failing to comply with an enforcement notice; and for unauthorised disclosure of personal data.

7.2 Professional codes of practice

In addition to adhering to legislation, marketing researchers should act in the interests of the marketing research profession, and to help them do so a number of codes of practice have been developed by the various professional bodies. These do **not have legal status**, but breaches may result in **disciplinary action** by the professional body, including barring the transgressor from membership of the body.

The best known code is the ESOMAR code: the full document can be downloaded from the organisation's website: http://www.esomar.org.

With marketing and the law in mind, list those areas of marketing activity with which you are familiar that have legal implications.

THE REAL WORLD

Marketing and the law in the digital era

Cookies and personal data

Although devices which process personal data give rise to greater privacy and security implications than those which process data from which the individual cannot be identified, new regulations apply to all uses of such devices, not just those involving the processing of personal data.

Where the use of a cookie-type device does involve the processing of personal data, service providers will need to make sure they comply with the additional requirements of the Data Protection Act 1998 (the Act). This includes the requirements which state that data controllers must not process personal data that is excessive. Where personal data is collected, the data controller should consider the extent to which that data can be effectively processed anonymously. This is likely to be particularly relevant where the data is to be processed for a purpose other than the provision of the service directly requested by the user, for example, counting visitors to a website.

Information to be provided

Cookies or similar devices must not be used unless the subscriber or user of the relevant terminal equipment:

(a)   is provided with clear and comprehensive information about the purposes of the storage of, or access to, that information; and

(b)   has given his or her consent.

The regulations are not prescriptive about the sort of information that should be provided, but the text should be sufficiently full and intelligible to allow individuals to clearly understand the potential consequences of allowing storage and access to the information collected by the device should they wish to do so.

The regulations also state that once a person has used such a device to store or access data in the terminal equipment of a user or subscriber, that person will not be required to provide the information described and obtain consent (and discussed above) on subsequent occasions, as long as they met these requirements initially. Although the regulations do not require the relevant information to be provided on each occasion, they do not prevent this.

Responsibility for providing the information and obtaining consent

The regulations do not define who should be responsible for providing the information and obtaining consent. Where a person operates an online service and any use of a cookie type device will be for their purposes only, it is clear that that person will be responsible for complying with this regulation.

Exemptions from the right to refuse a cookie

The regulations specify that service providers should not have to provide the information and obtain consent where that device is to be used:

- for the sole purpose of carrying out or facilitating the transmission of a communication over an electronic communications network; or

- where such storage or access is strictly necessary to provide an information society service requested by the subscriber or user.

In defining an 'information society service' the Electronic Commerce (EC Directive) Regulations 2002 refer to 'any service normally provided for remuneration, at a distance, by means of electronic equipment for the processing (including digital compression) and storage of data, and at the individual request of a recipient of a service'.

Wishes of subscribers and users

Regulation 6 states that consent for the cookie-type device should be obtained from the subscriber or user but it does not specify whose wishes should take precedence if they are different. There may well be cases where a subscriber, for example, an employer, provides an employee with a terminal at work along with access to certain services to carry out a particular task, where to effectively complete the task depends on using a cookie-type device. In these cases, it would not seem unreasonable for the employer's wishes to take precedence. However, it also seems likely that there will be circumstances where a user's wish should take precedence. To continue the above example, an employer's wish to accept such a device should not take precedence where this will involve the unwarranted collection of personal data of that employee.

(Information Commissioners Office, 2011. Contains public sector information licensed under the Open Government Licence v1.0)

▶ **Assessment tip**

An appreciation of, and reference to, the legal implications within your proposed cases and ultimate projects, will always demonstrate a sound ability to analyse and evaluate in context.

The Chartered Institute of Marketing

CHAPTER ROUNDUP

- We looked at the briefing process and looked at each stage in turn. We saw that the brief was an important document and that the proposal that answers or accompanies it, ultimately, will become the template for the research programme.

- We looked at the process of producing a proposal and the pros and cons of in-house versus out-of-house resources and expertise.

- We looked at the marketing research industry and identified the alternative agencies and consultancies available to any research commissioning organisation.

- We identified the key regulatory and legal compliance issues when it comes to data collecting, analysis and protection.

FURTHER READING

Creswell, J.W. (2008) *Research Design: Qualitative, Quantitative and Mixed Method Approaches*. 3rd edition. Thousand, Oaks Sage.

REFERENCES

Anon. (2011) Privacy and Electronic Communications Regulations. ICO. http://www.ico.gov.uk/for_organisations/privacy_and_electronic_communications/the_guide/cookies.aspx. [Accessed 23 May 2012].

Bird, D. (2007) *Commonsense direct and digital marketing*. 5th edition. London, Kogan Page.

Wilson, A. (2006) *Marketing research: an integrated approach*. 2nd edition. London, Financial Times/Prentice Hall.

QUICK QUIZ

1   What does DODCAR stand for?

2   List the eight data protection principles.

3   What are five disadvantages of in-house market research departments?

4   What is meant by 'rationale' in the context of a research brief?

5   Why should an agency include a discussion of the background to the project in a research proposal?

Activity 3.1

You would need as a minimum a full geo and socio demographic and economic breakdown for the segment in question and then you could go to decide how you could collect or require more qualitative data in the areas of behaviour and psychographics.

Activity 3.2

Your objectives might look something like this:

Table 3.3

Research objectives	Example
Specific	Size of market for *cruelty-free* cosmetics, not cosmetics in general
Measurable	Respective market share in percentage terms of leading players
Attainable	Good guidance on attitudes to cruelty-free products rather than absolute confidence
Results focussed	Interviewing technique is left to the experts
Time-bound	Information within three months so product can be marketed for Christmas

Activity 3.3

All aspects of marketing activity have legal implications but some of those that you should familiarise yourself with are in areas such as sale of goods, contract, packaging, marketing to minors, marketing communications, digital marketing and, of course, data protection.

QUICK QUIZ ANSWERS

1   Definition, Objectives, Design, Collect, Analyse, Report. In other words the marketing research process.

2   Data must be:

- Fairly and lawfully processed
- Processed for limited purposes
- Adequate, relevant and not excessive
- Accurate
- Not kept longer than necessary
- Processed in accordance with individual's rights
- Secure
- Not transferred to countries that do not have adequate data protection laws

The Chartered
Institute of Marketing

1   There is a danger of **overstretching current resources** and adversely affecting other projects.

2   There is a risk of developing an **inappropriate programme**, yielding insufficient or poor quality data with inadequate analysis and control.

3   If additional **training or recruitment** is required this could prove expensive and time consuming.

4   **Bias** could result from using staff with preconceived views.

5   **Company politics** may influence the results.

6   Considerable **computing resources** with appropriate software packages would be required to analyse the data.

4   How the need for information arose and what the users intend to do with it.

5   To set out the agency's understanding of the client's problem and needs in order to avoid costly mistakes.

CHAPTER 4

Presentation of findings

Introduction

The final report is perhaps the most important part of the research process. In practice, this is a very stressful time. Not only are decisions to be made as to where the work will be allocated, but for individuals, it is the chance to impress senior colleagues and enhance their reputation.

The ability to present data in the most appropriate and accessible way, while ensuring that the research problem is effectively dealt with, is a highly developed skill.

The results are generally presented in written format and this may or may not be supported by an oral presentation supported by slides.

Topic list

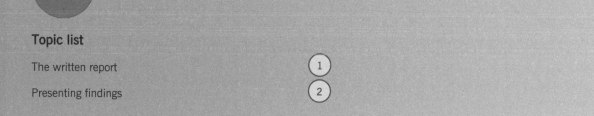

The written report   1

Presenting findings   2

1.6	Identify and evaluate the most effective methods for presenting marketing information and making specific marketing recommendations relating to product/service development and implementation as part of the case:
	■ The marketing dashboard
	■ Graphs, charts and tables
	■ Pie charts
	■ Flow diagrams
	■ Spreadsheets
	■ Correlation and regression
	■ Strategic impact statements
	■ Effect and outcome metrics
	■ Investment and income budgets
	■ Measurement and control
	■ Project reports

1 The written report

▶ **Key terms**

Report: A report is a textual work made with the specific intention of relaying information or recounting certain events. Written reports are documents which present focused, salient content to a specific audience. Reports are often used to display the result of an experiment, investigation or inquiry.

Presentation: A presentation is the practice of showing and explaining the content of a topic to an audience.

Executive summary: An executive summary is a short section of a document, produced for report purposes, that summarises a longer proposal or presentation.

Diagrammatic illustration: A diagram is a two-dimensional symbolic representation of information.

Appendices: A section of additional matter included at the end of a report or document in support of the main content.

The structure of a written report is standard and this helps considerably with the process of producing the document. Before producing the report, it helps to consider the objectives of the study again and the nature of the audience who will read and use the report.

What are the key points that the audience is interested in? What are the key constraints on marketing decisions recommended in the report? What is the business position and are the resource implications of decisions adequately considered?

1.1 The audience thinking sequence

Wilson (2006) suggests that the researcher should take account of the typical 'thinking sequence' that people go through when others are communicating with them.

(a) **Respect the client's importance**: in other words don't waste their time with irrelevant, badly structured or presented, over-long information.

(b) **Consider the client's needs**: the client needs to make a marketing decision.

(c) **Demonstrate how your information helps the client**: relate the research findings to the original objectives.

(d) **Explain the detail that underpins your information**: why should your findings be believed? Because you have evidence that 'Nine out of ten dogs prefer …' or whatever. This is the place for tables and charts, apt quotes from respondents and so on.

(e) **Remind the client of the key points**.

The Chartered Institute of Marketing

(f)   **Suggest what the client should do now**: there will usually be a variety of options. It is the client's decision, but it is usual to give recommendations.

The researcher knows more about the subject matter of the report or presentation than the report user. It is important that this information should be communicated impartially, so that the report user can make his own judgements.

- Any assumptions, evaluations and recommendations should be clearly signalled as such.

- Points should not be over-weighted (or omitted as irrelevant) without honestly evaluating how objective the selection is.

- Facts and findings should be balanced against each other.

- A firm conclusion should, if possible, be reached. It should be clear how and why it was reached.

The researcher must also **recognise the needs and abilities of the audience**.

- Beware of jargon, overly technical terms and specialist knowledge the user may not share.

- Keep your vocabulary, sentence and paragraph structures as simple as possible, for clarity (without patronising an intelligent user).

- Bear in mind the type and level of detail that will interest the user and be relevant to his/her purpose.

- The audience may range from senior manager to junior operational staff to complete layman (a non-executive director, say). Your vocabulary, syntax and presentation, the amount of detail you can go into, the technical matter you can include and the formality of your report structure should all be influenced by such concerns.

1.2 Report layout and structure

Various techniques can be used to make the content of a research report easy to identify and digest.

- The material in the report should be in a logical order.

- The relative importance of points should be signalled by headings.

- Each point may be numbered in some way to help with cross-reference.

- The document should be easy on the eye, helped by different font sizes, bold, italics, capitals, spacing and so on.

A typical report structure will use some or all of the conventions described below:

(a)   **Headings**. There should be a hierarchy of headings: there is an overall title and the report as a whole is divided into sections. Within each section main points have a heading in bold capitals, sub-points have a heading in bold lower-case and sub-sub-points have a heading in italics. (Three levels of headings within a main section is usually considered the maximum number that readers can cope with.) It is not necessary to underline headings.

(b)   **References**. Sections are lettered, A, B and so on. Main points are numbered 1, 2 etc, and within each division paragraphs are numbered 1.1, 1.2, 2.1, 2.2. Sub-paragraphs inherit their references from the paragraph above. For instance the first sub-paragraph under paragraph 1.2 is numbered 1.2.1.

(c)   **Fonts**. Word processors offer you a wealth of fonts these days, but it is best to avoid the temptation. It is often a good idea to put headings in a different font to the main text, but stop there.

A detailed report on an extensive research study may run to many pages, and may, therefore, require these elements:

(a) **Title page.** This should contain the title of the report, the author, the organisation and the date of presentation.

(b) A **list of contents**. This should contain full details of sections, subsections and page numbers, and include lists of tables and figures. It should make the report navigable. If presenting on the web, the use of hyperlinks that take the browser to the relevant section can be considered.

Most word processing software can produce these automatically.

(c) A **summary** of findings (to give the reader an initial idea of what the report is about). This is usually called the **executive summary**, the implication being that senior managers don't have time to read it all. Production of the executive summary is a tough job. As Churchill said, 'Sorry, for such a long letter. I didn't have time to write a short one'. It is hard to condense the report into a one- or two-page summary. It is also the section of the report that will be read by senior managers and so it is worth putting time and effort into its production.

The executive summary should be written after the rest of the report has been completed, but should be positioned at the start of the report. Some people feel that it should follow the contents page and some feel that it should precede it. Some companies produce a separate summary of the work and this can be useful for a wider and more efficient distribution of the key findings of the report. In business, different organisations will have their preferred structure and layout – a house style.

Generally, companies that are producing a large number of reports will include the format of the report in their identity guidelines or will have formal guidelines elsewhere that should be followed. The font size and appearance must do justice to the work and the sequencing of the report with its headers and subheaders should make the report more accessible. A style guide might also be used to help with language, grammar and even brand messages through the report.

If you are unsure of your use of English, then it is always best to get somebody professional to proofread your work for spelling, grammar and punctuation. Remember that proofreading is different from reading the report through. Each word and sentence needs to be considered individually as well as in connection with the rest of the report.

(d) **Introduction/problem definition**. This is likely to be very similar to the rationale and objectives set out in the research brief and proposal. This section outlines the background to the problem and reviews business and marketing objectives. It drills down into the problem's definition and the detailed objectives for the research programme, and reprises the sections of the brief and proposal.

(e) **Research method (and limitations)**. Again this is likely to be similar to the equivalent section in the proposal, although it must be updated if anything had to be changed during the implementation of the research or if the research did not go to plan (lower than expected response rates and so on). This section outlines the detailed methodology for the study. It should cover the research method; the data-capture mechanism, the topic, discussion guide or questionnaire, the definition of the population of interest, the sampling approach and the method of data analysis.

This section should not be too long. Details should be put into the appendices. It should cover potential sources of error, including sample size.

(f) **Research findings**. This is the main body of the report. The main body of the report looks at the findings relevant to the objectives. It should be constructed to present a solution to the problem, not on a question-by-question basis. The research data should present data to support a line of argument and the focus should be on analysis and insight. Tables or quotes from respondents can support key ideas. It may include tables and graphics, and should be linked by a narrative.

Remember that your audience is in solutions to the problem far more than a restating of the background – get the balance the right way around.

(g) **Conclusions**. This section should point out the implications of the findings for the client with reference to the initial problem. This section brings the report to a close. It should present a summary of key findings and recommendations for marketing decisions and future research.

(h) Supporting **appendices**. These might include the questionnaire used or the original discussion document, more detailed tables of figures, lists of secondary sources used and so on. Appendices contain subsidiary detailed material, that may well be of interest to some readers, but which might lessen the impact of the findings if presented in full detail in the body of the report.

(i) Possibly, an **index**.

THE REAL WORLD

Here is the format and structure of a recent report by Keynote on the UK market for **Premium Lagers, Beers and Spirits 2012**.

Table of Contents

Foreword

Executive Summary

Market Definition

(A)   Market Sectors
(B)   Market Trends
(C)   Economic Trends

Market Size

(A)   Total
(B)   Sector

Current Issues

(A)   UK Taxation
(B)   Consumer Equity
(C)   Pub Closures

Forecasts

(A)   Market Growth
(B)   Future Trends

Company Profiles

References

This report analyses and evaluates the current market in the UK for premium lagers, beers and spirits. The total market volume is calculated at c£10bn and represents over 80% of total consumption within the categories. However the economic crisis in the UK over the last five years has pushed the market into decline. This is forecasted to remain stagnant in 2012 and not to recover in real term growth until 2016.

(Keynote, 2012)

2 Presenting findings

The key thing in preparing a presentation is that it is not simply a regurgitation of the written report. The presentation, of course, draws on the same data and makes the same conclusions but the findings can be presented in a much livelier and, maybe, accessible and memorable way.

Tables and graphs will enliven reports and presentations, but with the range of technology available, overkill is possible.

THE REAL WORLD

This is an example of how CIM present a breakdown of assessment grades and attainment.

Figure 4.1   Breakdown of assessment grades

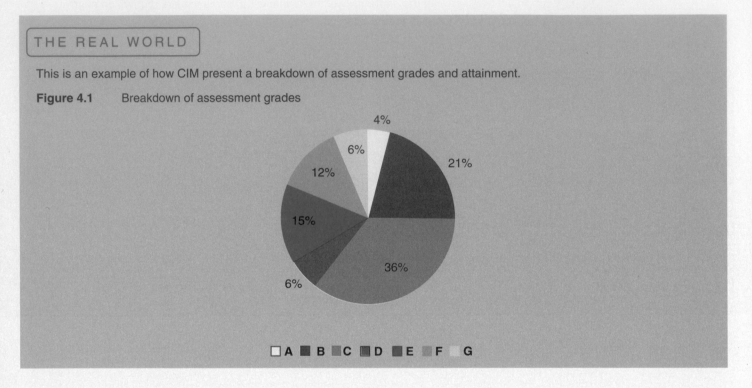

□ A ■ B ■ C ■ D ■ E ■ F ■ G

2.1 Tables

Tables should be presented with the title and a number. The tables should be labelled with base numbers; that is, the figures for the sample and subsamples should be shown, especially when percentages are being used. Seventy-five per cent is an impressive statistical value, but if the full picture is that the sample was only ten people, it is less so. Where quantities are indicated in the table, you must specify if they are in volumes or value. If numbers are used, specify the units. If currency is used, make sure that it is included in the table description.

Tables should be structured so that data is ordered from large to small items. The layout should enable data to be read easily. If data is imported, it should always be referenced or sourced. Tables should, if appropriate, contain totals and subtotals. Numbers should be right justified. You should normally work to two decimal places.

Other illustrative approaches should be examined and applied and can include pictograms, histograms, flow charts, graphs, bar charts and pie charts

You are likely to present data in tabular form very often. Here are the key points to remember:

(a)   The table should have a clear **title**.

(b)   All columns and rows should be clearly **labelled**.

(c)   Where appropriate, there should be **sub-totals** and a **right-hand total column** for comparison.

(d)   A total figure is often advisable at the **bottom of each column** of figures also, for comparison. It is usual to double-underline totals at the foot of columns.

(e)   **Numbers** should be **right-aligned** and they are easier to read if you use the **comma separator** for thousands.

(f)   **Decimal points should line up**, either by using a decimal tab or by adding extra noughts (the latter is preferable, in our opinion).

(g)   A grid or border is optional: see what looks best and is easiest to read.

(h)   Tables should not be packed with too much data. If you try to get too much in, the information presented will be difficult to read.

2.2 Line graphs

In business, line graphs are usually used to illustrate **trends over time** of figures such as sales or customer complaints. It is conventional to show **time** on the **horizontal** axis. By using different symbols for the plotted points, or preferably by using different colours, several lines can be drawn on a line graph before it gets too overcrowded, and that means that **several trends** (for example, the sales performance of different products) can be compared.

Figure 4.2   Sales of products A and B in 2010

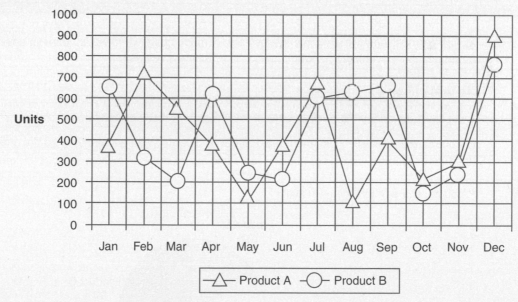

The scale of the vertical axis should be just large enough for you to tell with reasonable accuracy the sales figure at any given point during the period. In the example above we have used a scale of 100 and you can tell, for instance that sales of product A in April were a little less than 400.

2.3 Charts

2.3.1 Bar charts

The bar chart is one of the most common methods of visual presentation. Data is shown in the form of bars which are the same in width but variable in height. Each bar represents a different item, for example, the annual production cost of different products or the number of hours required to produce a product by different work teams.

Figure 4.3 Sales in Quarter 1, 2012

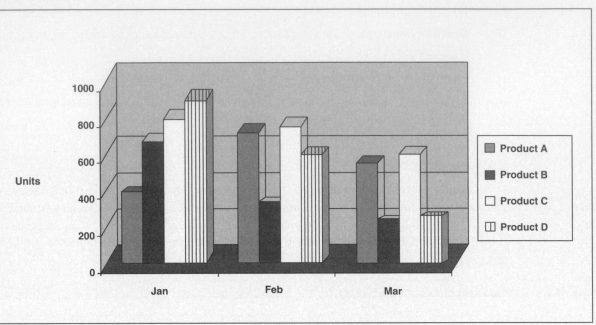

As you can see, here we are more interested in comparing a few individual items in a few individual months (although you can still get a visual impression of trends over time).

2.3.2 Pie charts

A pie chart illustrates the **relative** sizes of the things that make up a total.

Pie charts are most effective where the number of slices is small enough to keep the chart simple, and where the difference in the size of the slices is large enough for the eye to judge without too much extra information.

Figure 4.4 Products, share of total sales in 2012

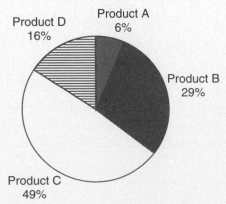

2.3.3 Flow charts, organisation charts and other labelled diagrams

Flow charts and organisation charts are useful ways of presenting and summarising information that involves a series of **steps** and **choices** and/or **relationships** between the different items.

On the following pages there are some examples of this type of presentation. If you choose any of these forms of presentation here are some points to bear in mind.

(a)   Be consistent in your use of layout and symbols (and colours, if used). For instance, in our flow chart example below a decision symbol is consistently a diamond with italic text; a YES decision consistently flows downwards; a NO decision consistently flows to the right.

(b)   Keep the number of connecting lines to a minimum and avoid lines that 'jump over' each other at all costs.

(c)   Keep the labels or other text brief and simple.

(d)   Hand-drawn diagrams should be as neat and legible as possible. If they are likely to be seen by a lot of people (not just your team) it is better to use a business graphics programme like Microsoft Visio.

(e)   Everyone can draw ... but only so well. If you are not expert you can waste an enormous amount of time playing with computer graphics. If it needs to be really beautifully presented and you are not an expert, sketch it quickly by hand, and then give it to a professional!

Figure 4.5   A flow chart

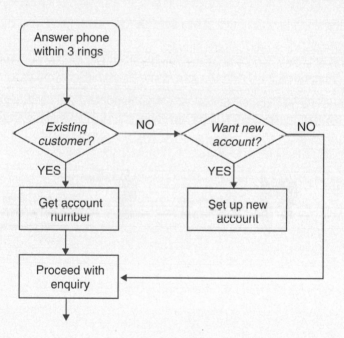

Figure 4.6   An organisation chart

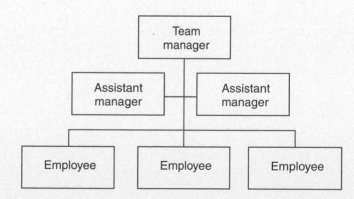

2.4 Pictograms

A pictogram is a simple graphic image in which the **data is represented by a picture or symbol**, with a clear key to the items and quantities intended. Different pictures can be used on the same pictogram to represent different elements of the data. For example, a pictogram showing the number of people employed by an organisation might use pictures of … people!

Figure 4.7   Pictogram 1

You can see quite easily that the workforce has grown and that the organisation employs far more female workers than before.

Pictograms present data in a simple and appealing way.

- The symbols must be clear and simple.
- There should be a key showing the number that each symbol represents.
- Larger quantities are shown by more symbols, not bigger symbols.

Bear in mind, however, that pictograms are **not appropriate** if you need to give **precise** figures. You can use portions of a symbol to represent smaller quantities, but there are limits to what you can do.

Figure 4.8   Pictogram 2

150 female employees

Over 100 employees, mostly male. But how many others and what sex are they?

2.5 Spreadsheets

Figure 4.9   A spreadsheet

	A	B	C	D	E	F	G	H
1	Name	Yearly Sale	Bonus	Total Income	Deduction	Net Salary		
2	Smith B.	45789	4578.9	50367.9	3022.074	47354.83		
3	Wilson C.	41245	4124.5					
4	Thompson D.	39876	3987.6					
5	James D.	432111	4321.1					
6								
7								

Spreadsheets were originally developed as aids to calculation. They have since been developed into extremely sophisticated computer applications that can be used for a wide range of purposes that require computation and other manipulation of data. They are frequently used for purposes that involve very little computation, such as form design and the presentation of tabulated data of all kinds. When they are used for computational purposes, great care must be taken with their design since it is very easy when designing formulae to make syntax errors that are invisible to users.

ACTIVITY 4.1

As an example, a package delivery service may be **fast** or **slow**, and it may deal with **large** or **small** packages. Interpret the diagram below.

Figure 4.10   Sample positioning map

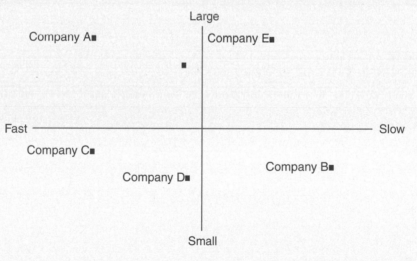

The Chartered Institute of Marketing

2010 Marketing Trends Survey – Wave 10

Summary Report

In the tenth wave of The Chartered Institute of Marketing's Marketing Trends Survey, thoughts on the economy appear to have stabilised since the surge in optimism last year. Pre-election times have shown a mixed and cautious outlook for the year to come but there are definitely signs of growth throughout the industry.

Awareness of digital and social media has risen significantly and with it come new plans to integrate Web 2.0 applications into everyday business. Job security looks to be recovering well, with marketers feeling more comfortable about retaining their professional positions. The 2012 Olympic Games are on marketers' minds and there are mixed feelings as to how these will benefit businesses.

The year ahead will be important for all industries as the UK continues on its path of financial recovery and many other topics. We look at the impacts that the downturn is having on marketers and their customers and how well company sales generally and marketing spend in particular are holding up.

The economy

Views on the predicted economic condition of the UK have dipped slightly after a marked surge in positive sentiment in October 2009. This year, just over two-thirds (43%) predict that the situation is going to improve in the next 12 months, compared with just over half (51%) in October. In line with this, there has been a slight overall increase of those who believe the condition will deteriorate, 17% this year compared to 12% last wave – see chart below.

Those in the technology and telecoms sector still look to be the most optimistic with just over half (52%) predicting that conditions will improve, although this is ten percent lower than in October last year.

Those working for the public sector and for charities are least positive about the economy, although even here most think that it will either stay the same (41%) or improve (36%) in the next year.

Technical note

A total of 846 marketers completed The Chartered Institute of Marketing's Marketing Trends Survey. It was an online questionnaire conducted for the Institute by the independent market research organisation, Ipsos MORI, from 8 April to 3 May 2010. A broad cross section of organisations by sector, turnover and geographic location was interviewed.

(The Chartered Institute of Marketing, 2010)

ACTIVITY 4.2

Examine a report you have recently written. Was it properly formatted and structured in line with the recommendations in this chapter?

ACTIVITY 4.3

Criticise your own recent presentations. Did you think about your audience? Did you get the message across with imagery as opposed to text? How could you improve it?

> **▶ Assessment tip**
>
> The more diagrammatic illustration and presentation you can get into your assignment submissions the better. The examiner is always looking to see your analytical mind and how you can translate modular data.

CHAPTER ROUNDUP

- This chapter looked at the process of delivering results from research. It looked at the structure of a written research report and covered each of these. A certain emphasis was placed on diagrammatic illustration.

- The chapter also examined the differing options for presenting data in illustrative format and promoted the use and employment of a variety methods.

FURTHER READING

Easterby-Smith, M. *et al* (2002) *Management Research: An Introduction*. 2nd edition. London, Sage.

Jankowicz, A.D. (2004) *Business Research Projects*. 4th edition. London, Thomson Learning.

REFERENCES

Anon. (2012) Premium Lagers, Beers and Cider 2012. Keynote, http://www.keynote.co.uk/market-intelligence/view/product/10541/premium-lagers-beers-%26ciders?highlight=premium+lagers+beers+and+spirits&utm_source=kn.reports.search [Accessed 24 May 2012].

The Chartered Institute of Marketing (2010) Marketing Trends Survey Spring 2010. CIM, http://www.cim.co.uk/resources/understandingmarket/mts.aspx [Accessed 24 May 2012].

Wilson, A. (2006) *Marketing Research, An Integrated Approach*. 2nd edition. London, FT/Prentice Hall.

QUICK QUIZ

1 What kind of graphic is used to show how a variable changes over time?

2 A graphic aid used to show steps and relationships between processes and events is a .... chart.

3 If 💰 represents $100m, draw a pictogram for $550m.

4 What is an appendix?

5 What is a spreadsheet primarily used for?

The Chartered Institute of Marketing

Activity 4.1

Company details

Company A specialises in delivering large packages quickly.
Company B delivers smaller packages slowly.
Company C delivers smaller packages quickly.
Company D delivers fairly small packages slightly more quickly than average.
Company E delivers very large packages very slowly.
Company F delivers medium to large packages more quickly than average.

Activity 4.2

This will be specific to the reader's situation.

Activity 4.3

This will be specific to the reader's situation.

QUICK QUIZ ANSWERS

1   A line graph

2   Flow chart

3   💰 💰 💰 💰 💰 💰

4   An additional piece of material inserted at the end of a report or document in support of the main content.

5   Spreadsheets are used mostly for mathematical calculations, basic database functions and for creating graphs and charts.

Section 1:

Senior Examiner's comments

The Project Management in Marketing Unit dictates that students must have an appreciation and understanding of all the units at Level 4, as this knowledge will be relied upon, broadened and more deeply applied. With particular reference here, Unit 3 of the Professional Certificate in Marketing, Marketing Information and Research, is very important.

This section of the syllabus allows the student to contextualise research around a specific undertaking. Therefore, a relative understanding of the core fundamentals and principles is insufficient. Now, this must be developed and added to an ability to apply in context. The emphasis here is on the ability to disseminate varying amounts of information from disparate sources, identify gaps and consequently the rationale for primary research. As a result, the candidates should be able to manipulate their findings and present a justified case for the development and management of a specific marketing project.

In addition, the section explores the interface between the research brief and the research proposal and how this inter-relationship should manifest in an organisational mechanic that limits the risk of failure. The students must understand and appreciate how this applies in practice and will need to demonstrate their rigour in delivering and presenting these fundamental analyses.

Furthermore, the structure, format and illustration of findings are key to the final translation of any given marketing problem when managing solutions is the core business function. Therefore, a range of professional presentation tools needs to be explored, adapted and applied in context.

This section should equip the students with the necessary knowledge and skills to physically collect, manipulate and utilise marketing data and information. The students should prioritise undertakings and concentrate on their efforts. What needs to be researched and investigated will be highlighted through the assessment brief and nothing will be gained by straying from this. The students need to appreciate that no matter what the project, the data and information they collect from secondary sources will never be complete. This identifies the information gaps, which in turn, formulates the rationale for primary research.

It is important that the primary research undertaking is highlighted within student submissions for assessment.

From an assessment perspective, the emphasis within this subject area concentrates around the ability to recognise problems and identify research requirements. The matching of these through various methodologies will be the key and there will be an expectation that some form of primary undertaking is conducted and evidenced. The writing-up and reporting of findings in a professional manner will be imperative, and the wide and varied use of illustrative diagrams and models within the presentation will be rewarded.

This section of the unit will directly impact the summary, critical analysis and prioritisation of findings.

What must be maintained throughout is relevance. The assignment brief will be specific and will detail the areas and issues that need to be investigated. There is absolutely nothing to be gained by researching and presenting any data or information that does not support the specific context of the brief.

Section 2:

Building a case for marketing projects (weighting 20%)

CHAPTERS

Chapter 5 – Setting aims, goals and objectives

Chapter 6 – Forecasts and projections

Chapter 7 – Operational management

Chapter 8 – The case report

LEARNING OBJECTIVES

By the end of this section, you will be able to:

- Prioritise and formalise business case objectives

- Prepare accurate and quantified forecasts and projections

- Understand customer profiling and scoring

- Appreciate resource requirements and tactical implementation

- Construct a case around core justifications

SYLLABUS REFERENCES

2.1   Define business case objectives for marketing plans and specific high-expenditure marketing activities

2.2   Critically evaluate and assess the marketing potential for business case activities, including consideration of the assessments required to achieve the potential proposition

2.3   Critically assess and evaluate customer groups relevant to the business case, matching their buying characteristics to the marketing proposition through the use of market research information

2.4   Determine the extent to which an organisation's marketing mix may need to be amended or adjusted to meet the requirements of the customer and broader stakeholders, and consider the impact of the change on the organisation

2.5   Critically assess the resource capability and capacity to deliver the business case proposals and consider the competency and skill requirements of both internal and external resources to deliver the business case proposition

2.6   Present the business case and associated marketing plans for consultation and consideration, with full justifications for the proposed product/service initiatives and how they will support the delivery of marketing strategies and plans

CHAPTER 5

Setting aims, goals and objectives

'If we could first know where we are, then whither we are tending, we could then decide what to do and how to do it'.

Abraham Lincoln, 1809–1865

Introduction

In Chapter 3, we considered the example of building a presentation and report as a response to a marketing research brief. That constituted a project with clear SMART objectives and the ability to measure outcomes against them. Project management, we must remember, is an organised process where the ideas apply to all projects, large or small.

With many large projects, almost the first step is to break them down into a series of smaller sub-projects. A large project may be complex to manage, and extended time frames can create a less focused feeling within the team as there appears to be a lot of time left; progress made seems insignificant compared to the size of the overall task, and it can be disheartening.

Consider briefly a full marketing plan. A strategic direction is chosen on the basis of information from a marketing audit. Detailed ideas are then considered to determine how to implement the strategy. These are evaluated and comparative risk/rewards ratios weighed up. From that process, a full implementation plan involving the marketing mix (and within that the promotional mix) is drawn up. Resources are committed and the plan is put into action. This is reviewed to monitor progress and ensure that it will meet the targets initially established.

However, within that broad overall picture, one team may have been given the task of researching information to found the marketing audit upon. That is the extent of their project. Another group may have been given the specific job of developing the segmentation, targeting and positioning (STP – see Chapter 7), while agencies may be invited to pitch for the business of preparing a promotional campaign to reposition the product or service as a result of the analysis. Their first project will be to prepare a successful pitch. If they do that, the next project is the actual campaign itself.

It is important to appreciate that the project management techniques are rarely a stop–start approach as so much within the modern business world is based on projects. A disciplined and logical approach is what is offered by the techniques, but this is only as a structure to achieve the individual marketing objectives as discussed above.

Topic list

Where are we now? ①

The potential weaknesses and limitations of secondary data ②

Qualitative techniques ③

Where do we want to be? ④

2.1	Define business case objectives for marketing plans and specific high expenditure marketing activities:
	■ Customer objectives
	■ Management objectives
	■ Profit objectives

1 Where are we now?

> ▶ **Key terms**
>
> A **goal** is often a longer term overall aspiration: Mintzberg (2011) defines **goals** as 'the intentions behind decisions or actions, the states of mind that drive individuals or collectives of individuals called organisations to do what they do.' Goals may be difficult to quantify and it may not be very helpful to attempt to do so. An example of a goal might be to raise productivity in a manufacturing department.
>
> **Objectives** are often quite specific and well-defined, though they can also embody comprehensive purposes.
>
> **Targets** are generally expressed in concrete numerical terms and are therefore easily used to measure progress and performance.

We are still within the conceptual phase of the project life cycle – building the preliminary evaluation to guide the decision as to what is feasible.

In the process of establishing the facts and the situation surrounding any given marketing problem, a systematic and rigorous examination of the business environments impacted by the problem as well as the specific core elements relative to the problem will have been undertaken.

The whole aspect of information collection, analysis and management was considered in the previous section. With this in mind, there should be no doubt as to the importance of that research and the subsequent manipulation of the data that results whenever we are trying to build our business cases for marketing.

However, whenever we are dealing with this specific type of research geared towards a specific problem and requiring a specific project, it is unlikely that all the required data and information will be available from secondary sources alone.

2 The potential weaknesses and limitations of secondary data

1   It is not related to the research question and the temptation may be to force the data to fit the question.

2   It may not be directly comparable. This is particularly the case in international markets where markets may be defined differently. For example, data on the low-alcohol drinks market varies from market to market as definitions of 'low' alcohol change.

3   Data may be incomplete. For example, the cross-channel trade in drinks and tobacco is significant but not included in official statistics.

4   Data may relate to certain markets – for example, data on food markets may relate to the retail trade rather than to the retail and catering markets, or *vice versa*. Pan-national studies will certainly find this. In many countries, a significant amount of the retail trade is made through street markets. This is very hard to quantify. In this case, it may be possible to weight data or use other techniques to complete the data set.

5   It may not be available. It may be that there are certain markets that are not adequately covered – for example, in Europe, data on the Belgian or Dutch market is often hard to obtain, as these are relatively small markets within the European Union.

6   The data may have been gathered for a particular purpose. Production statistics in certain markets are unreliable. Data may be presented to portray a company or government in a more favourable light. We see this in the United Kingdom, with the ongoing debate of how unemployment figures should be presented.

7   Information that is reviewed without access to the methodology should be viewed with suspicion and other data sources should be brought in to confirm the data under review.

8   Data for international markets may be more expensive and unreliable.

9   Data for international markets may be in a foreign language. Translating costs in business markets are very expensive.

10   Time series data may be interrupted by definition changes, for example, the most recent announcement by the British government about changes to the way inflation is calculated.

11   Secondary data in certain markets may not be up to date.

ACTIVITY 5.1

Reflect on the definitions of secondary research. What other problems do you think the researcher may experience in using secondary data?

In fact, experience suggests that around 80% of the core information may be available around specifics, which therefore leaves a significant gap to be filled. In order to build cases, these gaps cannot exist. We must fill them if we are to succeed in fully justifying and quantifying our proposals in relation to organisational improvement or enhancement.

It is this mindset that enables us to define our discipline as an 'artistic science' or a 'scientific art'. This also adds weight to our proposals and allows us to flex our 'marketing muscles'.

Interrelated and interdependent on the previous section of the book, we will look here at the core primary undertakings we can engage in to fill our information gaps, be in relatively full possession of the facts and build a quantifiably justified business case around our proposed project.

We looked at aspects of quantitative research in Chapter 1 so now we will examine qualitative research in a little more depth.

3 Qualitative techniques

Qualitative research accounts for between 10 and 15% of total research expenditure in the United Kingdom. It is growing in importance as marketing professionals recognise its vital role in providing depth of understanding about customers and their behaviour.

3.1 Data-collection techniques in qualitative research

3.1.1 Focus groups or group discussions

Wilson (2006) defines group discussions as 'depth interviews with a group of people; they differ in that they involve interaction between respondents'.

MRS defines group discussions or focus groups as:

'A number of respondents gathered together to generate ideas through the discussion of, and reaction to, specific stimuli. Under the steerage of a moderator, focus groups are often used in exploratory work or when the subject matter involves social activities, habits and status.'

Focus groups are generally made up of around 6–12 respondents. The most common number is eight. A lower number may be used when a particularly specialist topic is being discussed. The higher number would be used for a wide-ranging discussion. This design aspect is determined by the need to reflect the range of views held on a subject by the target market or concerned population.

They are run and managed by an interviewer, usually called a moderator. The moderator may be the same researcher who produced the research proposal, perhaps a specialist consultant or employed from a fieldwork agency. The moderator will control the group, keeping the discussion on track and probing for further information when needed. They will introduce other tasks that may occur within the group.

The main aim of the group is to ensure that the group members discuss the topic amongst themselves; the moderator's touch should be as light as possible. However, the skilled moderator will use a range of techniques to control the input of particularly vociferous members and to encourage quieter members of the group to make their contribution. Groups will normally last between 45 minutes and two hours. Discussions are generally tape-recorded or videoed.

Groups usually occur at the beginning of a research project as they can provide very useful information to explore through other methods. The groups may be observed remotely, and agencies offer clients the chance to view groups set up in special rooms, where the client can observe the group through a one-way window. A concealed or a discreet microphone to the observers can link the moderator so that a particularly interesting line of discussion can be probed further.

3.1.2 Depth interviews

Depth interviews involve structured or semi-structured conversations or interviews with individuals directly involved with, or having an impact upon, the problem in question. The topic for discussion can be singular or multifaceted and closed or open-ended. The broad aims are relatively similar to those of the group discussions outlined above, but are primarily used when either it is not feasible to organise a group discussion or the presence of other people will not necessarily elicit deep and truthful responses from an individual or if the individual in question holds significant power and/or influence on or over the problem at hand.

In both approaches, the content for the topic of discussion relative to building a case will be formed by the detail within the gaps identified via the secondary desk research.

Of course, relative care must be taken when trying to manipulate the resultant data here, as the sample sizes are usually quite small and there can be a tendency and a temptation to over report the more sensational and disproportionate results and responses.

However, it is this addition to our data collection and manipulation that adds weight, support and justification to everyday marketing cases.

Therefore, to all intents and purposes, a robust statement of the situation pertaining to a specific case can be presented with confidence. Without this, cases cannot be built let alone proposed. If we have no idea about where we are, we have no opportunity to suggest where we should be. If we cannot state where we want to get to, then no case exists. That is why, to get to a stage whereby the case can sustain itself on its own merits, the rigour involved in this first stage of the build is imperative. More than likely, this will involve several data-collection rounds, several data gap analyses, several primary undertakings and multiple manipulations.

Nothing can guarantee success, but we can try to limit our risk of failure.

4 Where do we want to be?

SMART and centred with no ambiguity while at the same time being capable of deep and severe cross-examination.

S	SPECIFIC
M	MEASURABLE
A	ACHIEVABLE
R	REALISTIC
T	TIMESCALED

Objectives must be able to fully stand up to SMART criteria. If they do not, they are not objectives and simply become only broad aims or goals. Broad aims or goals do not define business cases. Fully formalised and quantified SMART objectives do.

All business activity must support and be consistent with the organisation's overall strategy. This applies as much to marketing plans and projects as to any other form of activity. One important aspect of this requirement for strategic consistency is that departmental and functional objectives should support the corporate mission. Shareholder value analysis will show how marketing activities can be expected to support the typical corporate objective of maintaining and enhancing shareholder wealth. Within the framework provided by overall value analysis of proposed activity, it is important that subordinate objectives are assessed for their contribution to supporting and enabling the overall departmental or functional objectives.

THE REAL WORLD

A simple example is the development of a completely new product for a given market that can also be made viable in other markets at low incremental cost. Richard Branson's ability to use his brand Virgin with almost any consumer product is another example. There are network effects here too, in that as more and more dissimilar Virgin products become available, the brand's suitability for use with even more types of product grows.

ACTIVITY 5.2

Download or refer to other published material that states or highlights the objectives for your own organisations or an organisation of your choice. Alternatively or in addition refer to the objectives you have set for yourself or for others.

Constructively criticise these using SMART criteria.

How many are robust enough to stand up to the test?

4.1 Customer objectives

The majority of the marketing projects we have to build cases for are going to concentrate on the core areas of customers, management and profit. It stands to reason therefore that the cases we build for these projects must be focused and polished.

Customer objectives will be about market share, market development and market penetration. The emphasis will be on more customers, more business, retained business, new business and so on. Remember here, objectives could be about internal customers or even about divesting customers. Either way, and no matter the case or the project, customer objectives are entirely that, customer objectives, or any other physical manifestation of business transactions, that is consumers, clients, subscribers, end-users etc.

Customer objectives in this context are **organisational objectives** that relate to customers, rather than the **objectives of the customers** themselves (though, clearly, there is a conceptual link between customer behaviour and what we can set out to achieve in relation to it). There are a vast number of specific objectives that might be set in this context.

For a **commercial organisation**, objectives relating to customers might include the following:

(a)　Market share maintenance and enhancement

(b)　Retention of key customers

(c)　Changing the market profile by acquiring or shedding specific customer groups or customers from specific segments

(d)　Improving the enquiry conversion rate

(e)　Increasing the repeat purchase rate

(f)　Dealing more effectively with customer complaints

A not-for-profit organisation such as a **charity** might have some customer objectives that were essentially similar to those of the commercial organisation, especially if it has a trading arm. It would also be likely to have objectives relating to its **client** and **donor** customer groups.

(a)　Increasing client take-up of service in specific geographic areas or demographic groups

(b)　Increasing donations per donor

(c)　Retaining donors

THE REAL WORLD

An industrial organisation of bottled gases researched its customers' preferences to predict the likely performance of new products. They discovered that a significant number of customers showed a strong preference for suppliers that could guarantee delivery within a few hours. Based on this research they estimated the number of customers who would be willing to pay extra for guaranteed delivery. They found the size of this segment was large enough to justify the introduction of a premium guaranteed delivery service, which was then launched successfully.

ACTIVITY 5.3

Suggest some appropriate customer objectives for a local government education department.

4.2 Management objectives

Management objectives will be about organisation and structure, systems and processes and culture and orientation. The emphasis will be on flatness and integration, technology and application and areas such as customer focus, corporate social responsibility and ethics.

Managers at all levels in all departments and functions will have a range of objectives relating to their roles and responsibilities. A very simple description of the manager's work was provided by the nineteenth century French management thinker Henri Fayol (cited by Huczynski & Buchanan, 2007, p432).

(a)　**Planning**. Selecting the objectives and methods for achieving them, either for the organisation as a whole or for a part of it.

The Chartered Institute of Marketing

(b) **Organising**. Establishing the structure of tasks to be performed to achieve the goals of the organisation; grouping these tasks into jobs for an individual; creating groups of jobs within departments; delegating authority to carry out the jobs; providing systems of information and communication and co-ordinating activities within the organisation.

(c) **Commanding**. Giving instructions to subordinates to carry out tasks over which the manager has authority for decisions and responsibility for performance.

(d) **Co-ordinating**. Harmonising the activities of individuals and groups within the organisation. Management must reconcile differences in approach, effort, interest and timing.

(e) **Controlling**. Measuring and correcting activities to ensure that performance is in accordance with **plans**. Plans will not be achieved unless activities are monitored, and deviations identified and corrected as soon as they become apparent.

This analysis has, of course, been effectively superseded by more recent thinking about the nature of management, but it remains a useful description of the major roles and responsibilities of many managers. We could enhance the list by adding **communicating** and **motivating**.

We may reasonably anticipate that improvement objectives will flow from each of these aspects of managerial work. The need to plan, for example, might generate a need for project management software and the training to use it, possibly for the manager individually, possibly for chosen subordinates; the ever-present need for control and co-ordination might generate an objective of enhancing an under-performing MkIS; and so on.

4.3 Profit objectives

Profit objectives, depending upon how profit is defined, will concentrate on the bottom line, singular or triple, extracting cost out of the business, productivity, lifetime value, efficiency, economy of scale and shareholder value to name but a few.

It is important, when building and ultimately presenting business cases, that these objectives are clearly visible and overly explicit.

THE REAL WORLD

For most small- to medium-sized enterprises, **profitability**, in the most simple terms, is measured by net operating profit after tax (NOPAT). NOPAT can be increased in three ways.

(a) **Higher prices**. Marketing strategies such as building strong brands can enable the charging of premium prices. A particularly powerful route to higher prices is **innovation**, since desirable new products will normally justify increased prices.

(b) **Reduced costs**. Cost reduction depends on increased efficiency in all aspects of the business operation.

(c) **Volume increases**. Other things being equal, volume growth increases the absolute profit margin and may increase the profit rate as well.

▶ **Assessment tip**

It is imperative when building cases and proposing projects that you consistently work with formalised and quantified objectives. There can be no ambiguity, and a focused and driven mechanic must dominate whenever you are justifying the necessity for investment and action. With this, all cases for functional activity become more feasible and viable.

CHAPTER ROUNDUP

- In this chapter, we continued with the theme that a rigorous approach to the manipulation of marketing information is a management imperative if we are to be in a position to build business cases for our marketing projects.

- We established that secondary research creates information gaps relative to our marketing problems and that these can be filled somewhat by qualitative primary research.

- Having collected, analysed and manipulated the data to its fullest extent, we now appreciate we are in a position to formally state a position that will deliver a solution.

- This is formalised through our SMART objectives, which from a customer, management or profit perspective, must be up front and central.

FURTHER READING

Kotler, P. *et al* (2007) *Principles of Marketing*. 4th European edition. Harlow, Prentice Hall Europe.

REFERENCES

Huczynski, A. and Buchanan, D. (2007) *Organisational Behaviour, An Introductory Text*. 6th edition. London, Pearson Education.

Mintzberg, H. (2011) *Managing*. London, FT/Prentice Hall.

Wilson, A. (2006) *Marketing Research, An Integrated Approach*. 2nd edition. London, FT/Prentice Hall.

QUICK QUIZ

1 What must any objective be?

2 For marketing as a function, what should the primary objectives be concerned with?

3 What is an example of emphasis for a customer objective?

4 What is an example of emphasis for a management objective?

5 What is an example of emphasis for a profit objective?

 The Chartered Institute of Marketing

Activity 5.1

Other problems associated with using secondary data include issues such as bias of the original researcher, the amount of time required to locate and translate the research and of course the competence, skill and application of the secondary researcher.

Activity 5.2

Remember that these must be totally specific, measureable, achievable, realistic and timescaled in order to be true formal objectives.

Activity 5.3

The first problem with this activity is to establish who you think the customers of such a department might be. There are probably several groups, but note that it is important here not to confuse 'customers' with the wider category 'stakeholders'.

- Children of school age
- Their parents
- Potential adult education students

Just considering the first category, we might suggest the following broad objectives:

- Increasing the exam success rate
- Reducing the unauthorised absence rate
- Increasing the number of optional study subjects taken up
- Increasing the take up of healthy school meals

QUICK QUIZ ANSWERS

1   SMART

2   Customers, management and profit

3   Market share

4   Restructuring the department

5   Return on investment

CHAPTER 6

Forecasts and projections

'I often say that when you can measure what you are speaking about, and express it in numbers, you know something about it; but when you cannot measure it, when you cannot express it in numbers, your knowledge is of a very meagre and unsatisfactory kind'.

William Thomson, Lord Kelvin, 1824–1907

Introduction

Every manager, director, MD and owner in every business up and down the land, no matter what industry or sector, will utter these words 'OK! What's in this for us?' when faced with proposals to instigate any sort of investment in, or change to, the organisation. In fact, it is the statement that necessitates the diligence required in building business cases.

If we cannot present or articulate the answer to this question instantaneously, then no case exists.

In this chapter, we will examine some core tools and techniques that allow us to respond in a heartbeat. Depending upon the specific nature of the marketing project that is being considered, we may be either in the conceptual or the planning phase of the life cycle.

If we are using the following tools as part of the preliminary decision-making, then we would be in the conceptual phase, but it could also be that the project is approved and this is more detailed research work to support decisions in actually making the plan.

Topic list

Forecasting in marketing   (1)

Judgemental forecasting   (2)

Time series forecasting   (3)

Seasonal methods   (4)

Causal forecasting   (5)

Correlation and regression   (6)

2.2	Critically evaluate and assess the marketing potential for business case activities, including consideration of the assessments required to achieve the potential proposition:
	▪ Projections
	▪ Forecasting
	▪ Pre/post trend extrapolation
	▪ Historical data review
	▪ Econometrics

1 Forecasting in marketing

> ▶ **Key terms**
>
> A **forecast** is a prediction of future events and a quantification of that prediction for the purpose of planning.
>
> A **projection** is the expected future trend pattern, which is obtained by extrapolation. It tends to be concerned with quantitative factors, whereas a forecast includes judgements.

One of the underlying fundamentals of marketing management is the opportunity to be able to try and predict and extrapolate future trends relative to areas such as demand, sales levels, seasonal variability, resource requirements, inventory and capacity to name but a few.

Without viable projections related to our marketing problems, we would be unable to build, let alone justify, any business case for onward adoption of our proposals. Therefore, we must investigate the alternative methods available to us to make these projections and utilise and apply those most compatible with our own specific problems.

THE REAL WORLD

A variety of techniques is used in connection with forecasting. Different techniques are appropriate according to the **degree of uncertainty** perceived in the relevant forecast.

(a) An approach based on **discounting** may be used when the amount and timing of future cash flows are assumed to be known with something **approaching certainty**.

(b) Projects that are **repeated several times** lend themselves to the use of **expected values** and **decision trees**.

(c) **Modelling** and **sensitivity analysis** are appropriate when there is **less confidence** about the range and distribution of potential outcomes: such techniques are employed in conjunction with decision rules that reflect the degree of risk aversion of the decision-makers.

(d) It is important to remember that **certainty cannot be attained in any forecast**. Major, rapid changes, such as the collapse of the dot.com bubble and the global recession of 2008 are simply not knowable in advance.

1.1 Statistical projections

Statistical forecasts take past data and endeavour to direct it to the future, by **assuming** that **patterns or relationships which held in the past will continue to do so**. Many statistical techniques aim to reduce the uncertainty managers face. In **simple** or **static conditions the past is a relatively good guide** to the future.

The Chartered Institute of Marketing

1.1.1 Statistical forecasting techniques for static conditions

(a) **Time series analysis**. Data for a number of months/years is obtained and analysed. The aim of time series analysis is to identify:

   (i)   Seasonal and other cyclical fluctuations
   (ii) Long-term underlying trends

   For example, the UK's monthly unemployment statistics show a **headline figure** and the **underlying trend**.

(b) **Regression analysis** (as discussed earlier). Remember that the relationship between two variables may **only hold between certain values**. For example, you would expect ice cream consumption to rise as the temperature becomes hotter, but there is a maximum number of ice creams an individual can consume in a day, no matter how hot it is. Remember also the limited usefulness of **extrapolation** compared with **interpolation**.

(c) **Econometrics** is the study of economic variables and their inter-relationships, using computer models. In strict terms, econometrics is a branch of economics rather than a method of forecasting, but some short-term or medium-term econometric models might be used for that purpose.

   (i)   **Leading indicators** are indicators that change **before** market demand changes. For example, a sudden increase in the birth rate would be an indicator of future demand for children's clothes. Similarly, a fall in retail sales would be an indicator to manufacturers that demand from retailers for their products will soon fall. The number of new construction and house building starts in a period is often regarded as an indicator of future economic growth, as is purchasing activity in manufacturing.

   (ii) The firm needs the ability to **predict the span of time between a change in the indicator and a change in market demand**. Change in an indicator is especially useful for demand forecasting when they reach their highest or lowest points (when an increase turns into a decline or *vice versa*).

(d) **Adaptive forecasts** change in response to **recent** data.

1.2 Problems with statistical projections

(a) Past relationships do not necessarily hold for the future.

(b) Data can be misinterpreted, and **relationships assumed where none exist**. For example, sales of ice cream rise in the summer, and sales of umbrellas fall – the link is the weather, not any correlation between them.

(c) Forecasts do not account for special events (eg wars), the likely response of competitors and so on.

(d) The variation and depth of business cycles fluctuate.

(e) In practice, statistical forecasters **underestimate uncertainty**.

THE REAL WORLD

When an industrial air products organisation invented a technology for producing huge quantities of powdered ice, they explored potential usages. One candidate was artificial ski slopes to replace the dry slopes where skiers practise on nylon matting. They researched the build rate of dry ski slopes, the financial models of those businesses and canvassed the opinions of slope operators. All of the data used for forecasting and projection overwhelmingly presented a viable proposition. They went ahead and invested heavily in production, and to date they have supplied this material to dozens of slopes throughout Europe.

2 Judgemental forecasting

Judgemental forecasts are drawn from the subjective opinions of internal personnel such as key employees, managers or directors, or external individuals like experts or academics. These opinions are collated, manipulated, aggregated and averaged in order to instigate some form of consensus that in turn will aid predicting trends and events in the future.

Judgemental forecasts are used principally for the long-term, covering several decades. However, because of the limitations of short-term forecasting they are used for the short-term too. Effectively, they are based on **hunches or educated guesses**. Sometimes, these prove surprisingly accurate. At other times they are wide of the mark.

(a)   **Individual forecasting**. A company might forecast sales on the basis of the judgement of one or more executives.

   (i)   **Advantages** are that it is cheap and suitable if demand is stable or relatively simple.

   (ii)   The **disadvantage** is that it is swayed most heavily by **most recent** experience rather than trend.

(b)   **Genius forecasting**

An individual with expert judgement might be asked for advice. This might be the case with the fashion industry; although demand might be hard to quantify, an ability to understand the mind of the customer will be very useful.

In practice, forecasts might be prepared by an interested individual who has read the papers, say, and has promoted an item for management attention. Two of the more widely used, delphi (also shown as capital lettered Delphi) method and sales force composite are outlined below.

2.1 Delphi method

The Delphi method is an attempt to 'align' the sometimes conflicting positions of experts into a coherent and unified perspective.

The Delphi method is based on a structured process for collecting and synthesising knowledge from a group of experts by means of a series of questionnaires accompanied by controlled opinion feedback. The questionnaires are presented in the form of an anonymous and consultation procedure by means of surveys (postal and/or e-mail).

The technique is relatively simple. It consists of a series of questionnaires sent to a preselected group of experts. These questionnaires are designed to elicit and develop individual responses to the task specified and to enable the experts to refine their views as the group's work progresses in accordance with the assigned task. The rationale behind the Delphi method is to address and overcome the disadvantages of traditional forms of 'consultation by committee', particularly those related to group dynamics.

Delphi is primarily used to facilitate the formation of a group judgement. It was developed in response to problems associated with conventional group-opinion assessment techniques, such as Focus Groups, which can create problems of response bias owing to the dominance of powerful opinion leaders. It may be used in forward planning to establish hypotheses about how scenarios are likely to develop, and on their socio-economic implications. For example, it has been widely used to generate forecasts in technology, education, and other fields. Fundamentally, the method serves to shed light on the evolution of a situation, to identify priorities or to draw up prospective scenarios.

2.1.1 The main steps involved

The approach consists of questioning the experts by means of successive questionnaires, in order to reveal convergence and any consensus there may be.

The main stages of this process are:

Step 1 Determination and formulation of questions. Particular care should be given to the choice of questions, so as to obtain useful and applicable information.

Step 2 Selection of experts. These must have specific knowledge about the subject and be prepared to engage in this type of process.

Step 3 Formulation of a first questionnaire that is sent to the experts. The first questionnaire must contain a reminder of the nature of the study and include both semi-open and open questions.

Step 4 Analysis of the answers to the first questionnaire. The answers are analysed by someone other than the experts in order to determine the general trends and the most disproportionate answers.

Step 5 Formulation of a second questionnaire that is sent to experts. Each expert is informed of the results of the first round and is then asked to provide a new answer and to justify it if it differs from the general emerging themes and trends.

Step 6 Sending of a third questionnaire. This questionnaire can be a further manipulation based on Step 5. Sufficient convergence of opinions generally appears with this questionnaire. If that is not the case, the cycle continues.

Step 7 Summary of the process and drawing-up of the final report. It is important to note that the analysis of data elicited through Delphi surveys should be carried out using statistical analysis (eg cluster analysis or correlation analysis) in order to identify convergence and divergence in responses.

2.2 Sales force composite

In this method, sales personnel project volume of usage by customers in their area, territory or portfolio. The good thing about it is that the estimates are given by those people closest to the customer and also the method lends itself to product augmentation, territory development and penetration and customer segmentation, targeting and positioning.

The disadvantages are that sales persons are often not aware of broad economic forces, and also they may be evaluating sales performance and not necessarily forecasting *per se*, so they do not expend enough time and effort on the exercise. Also, there is a big aspect of potential bias, where there is a tendency to usually underestimate in order to make any resultant sales targets easier to achieve.

As the foremost customer-facing element of the business, sales professionals are extremely close to the market, demand, needs and requirements, emerging trends and potential macroenvironmental impacts.

3 Time series forecasting

Time series forecasting involves the deep and rigorous analysis of historical business data in order to establish and identify significant trends over time and fully explained via variance impact analysis. This technique and approach can then be utilised to extrapolate future results relative to specific scenarios or projects. The assumption is made that past patterns in the data can be used to forecast future data points (Figure 6.1).

Figure 6.1   Example time series data

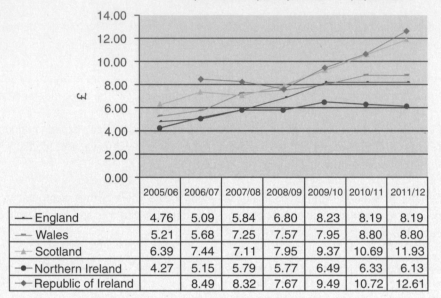

Comparison of spend per head of population

	2005/06	2006/07	2007/08	2008/09	2009/10	2010/11	2011/12
England	4.76	5.09	5.84	6.80	8.23	8.19	8.19
Wales	5.21	5.68	7.25	7.57	7.95	8.80	8.80
Scotland	6.39	7.44	7.11	7.95	9.37	10.69	11.93
Northern Ireland	4.27	5.15	5.79	5.77	6.49	6.33	6.13
Republic of Ireland		8.49	8.32	7.67	9.49	10.72	12.61

Some of the more widely used options are outlined below.

3.1 Moving averages

The forecast is based on an arithmetical average of a given number of past data points and contains the following parameters and definitions:

- An average is the mean of the observations over time.

- A trend is a gradual increase or decrease in the average over time.

- A seasonal influence is a predictable short-term cyclical pattern due to time of day, week, month, season, year etc.

- A cyclical movement is a predictable long-term cyclical pattern due to a business cycle or product/service life cycle.

- A random error is any remaining variation that cannot be explained by the other four components.

3.2 Simple moving average

Moving average techniques forecast demand by calculating an average of actual demands from a specified number of prior periods. Each new forecast drops the demand in the oldest period and replaces it with the demand in the most recent period; thus, the data in the calculation 'moves' over time.

The Chartered
Institute of Marketing

Simple moving average: For example, consider a simple two-month average forecast model:

Forecast of June sales = April sales + May sales divided by 2

Forecast of June sales = 800,000 + 600,000/2 = 700,000

The more periods over which the moving average is calculated, the less susceptible the forecast is to random variations, but the less responsive it is to changes.

3.3 Weighted moving average

A weighted moving average is a moving average where each historical demand may be weighted differently.

3.4 Exponential smoothing

Exponential smoothing gives greater weight to demand in more recent periods and less weight to demand in earlier periods, but in this method we do not have to save the values for many periods like the moving average methods. We just need the forecast and actual value for the current period and then we would be able to forecast the value for the next period.

4 Seasonal methods

What happens when the patterns you are trying to predict display seasonal effects?

What is seasonality? It can range from true variation between seasons to variation between months, weeks, days in the week and even variation during a single day or hour. To deal with seasonal effects in forecasting, two tasks must be completed:

1 A forecast for the entire period must be made using whatever forecasting technique is appropriate. This forecast will be developed using whatever the forecast must be adjusted to reflect the seasonal effects in each period.

2 The seasonal method adjusts a given forecast by multiplying the forecast by a seasonal factor.

These approaches by nature lend themselves more to the short-term aspect of forecasting.

5 Causal forecasting

Causal forecasting examines changes caused by fluctuations in one or more variables. Such variables may extend to, but not be exclusive to, such elements as competitor activities, price variations, supply shortages and so on. So with this extended analysis, time is not the only variable investigated.

Some of the more common techniques for this type of forecasting are outlined in part 6.

6 Correlation and regression

The purpose of correlation analysis is to determine whether there is a relationship between two sets of variables. We may find that:

- There is a positive correlation.
- There is a negative correlation.
- There is no correlation.

Correlation and regression are concerned with the investigation of two variables.

Correlation describes the strength of the relationship. It is not concerned with 'cause' and 'effect'.

Regression describes the relationship itself in the form of a straight-line equation that best fits the data.

Previously, we have only considered a single variable; now, we look at two associated variables.

We might want to know:

- Does a relationship exist between these variables?
- How strong that relationship is.
- What constitutes the relationship?
- Will the strength of the relationship be sufficient to aid predictions or forecasts?

THE REAL WORLD

The figures represent the sales for a particular firm of manufacturers and also the average monthly temperature.

Table 6.1

Month	Av. Temp.(°C)	Sales (£000,000)
January	3	74
February	5	58
March	6	82
April	7	95
May	13	111
June	14	125
July	17	135
August	16	140
September	13	125
October	10	104
November	6	82
December	4	81

Some initial insight into the relationship between two continuous variables can be obtained by plotting a scatter diagram and looking at the resulting graph.

Does the relationship seem to be linear or curved?

If there appears to be a linear relationship, it can be quantified and a correlation therefore exists.

If the relationship is found to be significantly strong, then its nature can be found using linear regression, which defines the equation of the straight line of best fit through the data.

For example, £x spent on Advertising would be expected to increase Sales by y%.

The best fit can be calculated to see how well the line fits the data.

Once defined by this equation, the relationship can be used for forecasting purposes (Figure 6.2).

The Chartered Institute of Marketing

Figure 6.2   Scatter diagram

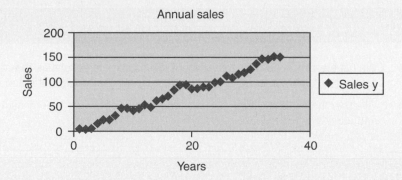

In practice, there seems to be a tendency to favour the potential accuracy of causal approaches as opposed to judgemental approaches. In relation to judgemental techniques, no one technique is more favourable or reliable, but the Delphi method is most popular. Time series analysis is more robust when more variables are examined simultaneously. Correlation and regression analysis is well used and accepted. However, no singular method is superior and the practised forecaster will use a combination of tools at their disposal.

ACTIVITY 6.1

Identify the relative advantages and disadvantages of statistical forecasting versus judgemental forecasting.

ACTIVITY 6.2

Using your own organisation as an example, create some projections and forecasts for the market potential of any of your products or services.

ACTIVITY 6.3

Using your own organisation as an example, create a six month moving average forecast for any of your products or services.

▶ **Assessment tip**

You need to able to show that projections and forecasts of future activity and results can be handled from a relatively scientific perspective. Whenever you can make grounded predictions from a qualified and quantified perspective you will always achieve marks at the higher end of what is allocated.

CHAPTER ROUNDUP

- We have established here that without significant projections as to future outcomes based on acceptable forecasting techniques, potentially our business cases could not stand up to intense scrutiny.

- Whether judgemental, time series or causal, our approach to forecasting should be relevant, applicable and varied.

FURTHER READING

Doyle, P. (2008) *Value-based Marketing.* 2nd edition. London, John Wiley and Sons Ltd.

QUICK QUIZ

1   How does the Delphi method of expert forecasting work?

2   What does time series analysis aim to identify?

3   What is econometrics?

4   What is the sales force composite method of forecasting?

5   What does regression analysis describe?

ACTIVITY DEBRIEFS

Activity 6.1

Table 6.2

Use of forecasts	Statistical	Judgement
Changes in established patterns	Past data is no guide	Can be predicted but could be ignored
Using available data	Not all past data is used	Personal biases and preferences obscure data
Objectivity	Based on specific criteria for selection	Personal propensity to optimism/pessimism
Uncertainty	Underestimated	Underestimated, with a tendency to over-optimism
Cost	Inexpensive	Expensive

Activity 6.2

Market potential can be projected by forecasts of the amount of product or service that would be purchased by specific customer groups within a specified time period at a specific intensity of industry marketing activity.

The Chartered Institute of Marketing

Activity 6.3

Your answer should be calculated using the formula:

m1 + m2 + m3 + m4 + m5 + m6/6

QUICK QUIZ ANSWERS

1   Anonymous participants respond to a questionnaire containing tightly-defined questions. The results are collated and statistically analysed, then returned by the organiser to each expert. The experts respond again, having considered each other's opinions and analyses.

2   Seasonal or other cyclical fluctuations and/or long term underlying trends.

3   The study of economic variables and their interrelationships using computer models.

4   Sales personnel project volume of customer usage in their area, territory or portfolio.

5   The relationship between two variables in the form of a straight line equation.

CHAPTER 7

Operational management

Introduction

The central core running through the business cases we construct to support our marketing projects will contain common themes and content.

Consequently, we must consider, analyse and assess major relevance to the case around customer or other stakeholder groupings, the marketing tools and techniques utilised in pursuit of better businesses and the resource capabilities and capacity required as input.

The business case explains how a proposed activity will add value. Ultimately, it is the reaction of the customer that will determine whether or not an activity was worthwhile. Careful targeting of specific customer groups is an essential feature of marketing activity and a business case must explain which customers are to be targeted, why and how. This will require the acquisition and presentation of appropriate marketing research information.

Topic list

Segmentation, targeting and positioning	(1)	Managing resources	(10)
Segmentation	(2)	Investment and income	(11)
Segmentation of the industrial market	(3)	Cost benefit analysis	(12)
Targeting	(4)		
Positioning	(5)		
Business cases and the marketing mix	(6)		
The extended marketing mix	(7)		
Managing dynamics	(8)		
Managing people	(9)		

2.3	Critically assess and evaluate customer groups relevant to the business case, matching their buying characteristics to the marketing proposition through the use of market research information: ■ Customer specific profiling ■ Cross criteria scoring ■ Contextualised positioning
2.4	Determine the extent to which an organisation's marketing mix may need to be amended or adjusted to meet the requirements of the customer and broader stakeholders, and consider the impact of the change on the organisation: ■ Management of the marketing mix ■ Investment/divestment
2.5	Critically assess the resource capability and capacity to deliver the business case proposals and consider the competency and skill requirements of both internal and external resources to deliver the business case proposition: ■ Skills and competence ■ Role definition ■ Cross functionality ■ Agency management ■ Investment and income budgets ■ Recruitment

1 Segmentation, targeting and positioning

> **▶ Key terms**
>
> **Market segmentation** may be defined as 'the subdividing of a market into distinct and increasingly homogeneous subgroups of customers, where any subgroup can conceivably be selected as a target market to be met with a distinct marketing mix'. (Kotler,1996)
>
> A **target market** is a market or segment selected for special attention by an organisation (possibly served with a distinct marketing mix).
>
> **Positioning** is the act of designing the company's offer and image so that it achieves a distinct and valued place in the target customer's mind.
>
> **Marketing mix** is a set of controllable variables that the firm can use to influence the target market. In its most basic form, the marketing mix has four elements: **product**, **price**, **place** and **promotion**.
>
> A **product** (goods or services) is anything that satisfies a need or want. It is not a 'thing' with 'features' but a package of benefits.
>
> **Cost benefit analysis** is a systematic process for calculating and comparing benefits and costs of a project.

As a general rule, no business case will be in a position to ignore the whole underlying aspect of power and influence that permeates throughout marketing projects. Whether that is a customer, internal or external, other stakeholders, internal or external, the fundamental principles of segmentation, targeting and position will be the foundations and cornerstones that a case can be built around.

The basic premise here is that we cannot be all things to all men. As a result, we need to drill down and concentrate our efforts and resources on where the best opportunity for success exists.

2 Segmentation

What needs to be established from the outset is the population in its entirety. This is the big picture whereby we can deconstruct it to its lowest common denominators. We must try and establish clusters of homogeneous entities in order to proceed with a process of exploiting opportunities.

The overall purpose of market segmentation is to be able to make sensible marketing decisions.

Jot down possible segmentation variables for adult education, magazines, and sports facilities.

Table 7.1   Segmentation benefit chart

Reason	Comment
Better satisfaction of customer needs	One solution won't satisfy all customers
Growth in profits	Some customers will pay more for certain benefits
Revenue growth	Segmentation means that more customers may be attracted by what is on offer, in preference to competing products
Customer retention	By targeting customers, a number of different products can be offered to them
Targeted communications	Segmentation enables clear communications as people in the target audience share common needs
Innovation	By identifying unmet needs, companies can innovate to satisfy them
Segment share	Segmentation enables a firm to implement a focus strategy successfully

Steps in segmentation, targeting and positioning identified by Kotler

Step 1   Identify **segmentation** variables and segment the market

Step 2   Develop segment profiles   ] Segmentation

Step 3   Evaluate the attractiveness of each segment   ] Targeting

Step 4   Select the **target** segment(s)

Step 5   Identify **positioning** concepts for each target segment   ] Positioning

Step 6   Select, develop and communicate the chosen concept

The case therefore begins by reducing a potential disaggregation.

In order to do this, several bases for segmentation must be established. If we think about the traditional use of segmentation, these are bases such as demographic, geographic and socio-economic on the quantitative side and psychographic on the qualitative side. What defines these bases, however, are the nature and scope of the project, the objectives and the deliverables.

2.1 Identifying segments

(a)   One basis will not be appropriate in every market, and sometimes two or more bases might be valid at the same time.

(b)   One basis or 'segmentation variable' might be 'superior' to another in a hierarchy of variables. There are thus primary and secondary segmentation variables.

Jobber (2009) identifies three main approaches to segmenting consumer markets:

(a) **Behavioural**. This is the fundamental form of segmentation, in that it is consumer behaviour that has direct implications for marketing decisions.

(b) **Psychographic**. Psychographic segmentation is appropriate when it is believed that consumers' purchasing behaviour correlates with their personality or lifestyle variables.

(c) **Profile**. Profile variables such as social class are required in order to define and communicate with target markets.

The implication of this is that initial segmentation is carried out in terms of behavioural or psychographic categories, with the assessment of profile variables forming a second phase, primarily for purposes of communication. However, Jobber (2009) says that, in practice, profile segmentation will be a first step, with subsequent testing for behavioural differences between the groups identified.

2.1.1 Behavioural segmentation

Behavioural segmentation segregates buyers into groups based on their attitudes to and use of the product. There are five main segmentation bases.

(a) **Benefits sought**. Benefits might be as simple as flavour in a food product or pleasure from watching a DVD or as complex as the status and image conferred by certain unusual and luxury goods. The degree of a consumer's sensitivity to price is also an important benefit segmentation variable.

(b) **Purchase occasion**. Purchase occasion covers such aspects of behaviour as whether the purchase is seasonal, daily, impulse, as a gift, part of weekly grocery shopping or for convenience.

(c) **Purchase behaviour**. Purchase behaviour includes the degree of brand loyalty and how long the consumer takes after product launch to adopt the product.

(d) **Usage**. Segmentation can be based on the extent of use of the product, whether heavy, moderate or light. It can also be based on the occasion of use: for example, whether consumed alone, in a family setting or as part of a wider social group.

(e) **Perceptions**, **beliefs and values**. Segmentation may be based on consumers' attitudes to the market and to individual products.

Table 7.2   Benefit segmentation of the toothpaste market

Segment Name	Principal benefit sought	Demographic strengths	Special behavioural characteristics	Brands dis-proportion-ately favoured	Personality character-istics	Lifestyle characteristics
The sensory segment	Flavour, product appearance	Children	Users of spearmint flavoured toothpaste	Colgate, Stripe	High self-involvement	Hedonistic
The sociables	Brightness of teeth	Teens, young people	Smokers	Macleans, Ultra-Brite	High sociability	Active
The worriers	Decay prevention	Large families	Heavy users	Crest	High hypochon-driasis	Conservative
The independent segment	Price	Men	Heavy users	Brands on sale	High autonomy	Value-oriented

A benefit of a product is that it **reduces risk**. Toothpaste reduces the risk of tooth decay, for example. This is relevant to the worriers in the table above. **Perceptions** of risk are often very subjective. **Attitudes to risk** are useful in that they **offer segmentation opportunities**.

The credit card market in the UK is becoming increasingly fragmented. Newcomers tend to offer lower interest rates than the mainstream competitors such as Barclaycard. The newcomers target or cherry-pick certain groups of customers with a good credit history, and who are motivated mainly by price.

The card operators offer different customer benefits, by linking their cards to charitable organisations, so that some of the commission on each transaction goes to charity.

2.1.2 Psychographic segmentation

Psychographic segmentation is not based on objective data so much as how people see themselves and their **subjective** feelings and attitudes towards a particular product or service, or towards life in general.

Jobber (2009) suggests that the main bases of psychographic segmentation are **lifestyle** and **personality** characteristics.

Table 7.3   Lifestyle segmentation variables

Lifestyle dimensions			
Activities	*Interests*	*Opinions*	*Demographics*
Work	Family	Themselves	Age
Hobbies	Home	Social issues	Education
Social events	Job	Politics	Income
Holiday	Community	Business	Occupation
Entertainment	Recreation	Economics	Family size
Club membership	Fashion	Education	Dwelling
Community (including online)	Food	Products	Geography
Shopping	Media	Religion	City size
Sports	Achievements	Culture	Stage in lifecycle

(Adapted from Plummer, 1974)

Three distinct types of social behaviour exist:

- **Tradition directed** behaviour is easy to predict and changes little
- **Outer directedness** is behaviour influenced by the action and views of peer groups
- **Inner directedness** is behaviour uninfluenced by views of others

The research agency Taylor Nelson also identifies three main groups with subgroups.

(a)   **Sustenance driven group**

   (i)   **Belongers**. What they seek is a quiet undisturbed family life. They are conservative, conventional, rule followers. Not all are sustenance driven.

   (ii)   **Survivors**. Strongly class-conscious, and community spirited, their motivation is to get by.

   (iii)   **Aimless**. Comprises two groups, (a) the young unemployed, who are often anti-authority, and (b) the old, whose motivation is day-to-day existence.

(b)   **Outer directed group**

   (i)   The balance of the belongers.

   (ii) **Conspicuous consumers**. They are materialistic and pushy, motivated by acquisition, competition, and getting ahead. Pro-authority, law and order.

(c)   **Inner directed group**

   (i)   **Self-explorers**. Motivated by self-expression and self-realisation. Less materialistic than other groups, and showing high tolerance levels.

   (ii) **Social resistors**. The caring group, concerned with fairness and social values, but often appearing intolerant and moralistic.

   (iii) **Experimentalists**. Highly individualistic, motivated by fast moving enjoyment. They are materialistic, pro-technology but anti-traditional authority.

Variations on the lifestyle or psychographic approach have been developed, analysing more precisely people's attitudes towards **certain goods or services**. The value of this approach is that it isolates potential consumer responses to particular product offerings.

2.1.3 Profile segmentation

Profile segmentation is of fundamental importance for marketers: the segmentation variables are clear and easily applied and the resulting segmentation is appropriate for the design of marketing communication strategy. The need to communicate means that even where target segments have been identified using behavioural or psychographic variables, there may be a need to re-analyse, in profile terms, in order to be able to communicate with them.

There are three main types of profile segmentation, though the approaches are generally combined with one another in modern practice.

- Demographic
- Socio-economic
- Geographic

Demographic segmentation

Demographic segmentation involves classifying people according to objective variables about their situation, including age, sex and life cycle stage.

The **family life cycle (FLC)** is a summary demographic variable that combines the effects of age, marital status, career status (income) and the presence or absence of children. It is able to identify the various **stages through which households progress**. The outline below shows features of the family at various stages of its life cycle. Particular products and services can be target-marketed at specific stages in the life cycle of families.

- **Bachelor:** Young working individuals who are unmarried and not living with their parents

- **Newly-married couple:** Married couple but with no children yet

- **Full nest I:** Married couple with youngest child under six years of age

- **Full nest II:** Married couple with youngest child six years or above

- **Full nest III:** Older married couple with dependent children

- **Empty nest I:** Older married couple, no children living with them and head of the family still working

- **Empty nest II:** Older married couple, no children living at home and head of the family retired

- **Solitary survivor, in labour force:** Single survivor of the family such as a widow or divorcee, who is still working

The Chartered Institute of Marketing

- **Solitary survivor, retired:** Single survivor of the family such as widow or divorcee, who is retired.

It is important to remember that the model of the family life cycle shown above displays the **classic route** from young single to older unmarried. In contemporary society, characterised by divorce and what may be the declining importance of marriage as an institution, this picture can vary. It is possible and not uncommon to be young, childless and divorced, or young and unmarried with children. Some people go through life without marrying or having children at all. Individuals may go through the life cycle belonging to more than one family group. At each stage, whether on the classic route or an **alternative path**, needs and disposable income will change. Family groupings are, however, a key feature of society.

There has been some **criticism** of the traditional FLC model as a basis for market segmentation in recent years.

(a) It is modelled on the **demographic patterns of industrialised western nations** – and particularly America. This pattern may not be universally applicable.

(b) As noted above, while the FLC model was once typical of the overwhelming majority of American families, there are now **important potential variations** from that pattern, including:

(i)	Childless couples	– Because of choice, career-oriented women and delayed marriage
(ii)	Later marriages	– Because of greater career-orientation and non-marital relationships: likely to have fewer children
(iii)	Later children	– Say in late 30s. Likely to have fewer children, but to stress quality of life
(iv)	Single parents	– (Especially mothers) because of divorce
(v)	Fluctuating labour status	– Not just in work or retired, but redundancy, career change, dual-income
(vi)	Extended parenting	– Young, single adults returning home while they establish careers/financial independence; divorced children returning to parents; elderly parents requiring care; newly-weds living with in-laws
(vii)	Non-family households	– Unmarried (homosexual or heterosexual) couples
		– Divorced persons with no children
		– Single persons (often due to delaying of first marriage and the fact that there are more women than men in the population)
		– Widowed persons (especially women, because of longer life-expectancy)

An alternative or modified FLC model is needed to take account of consumption variables such as:

(a) Spontaneous **changes** in brand preference when a household undergoes a **change of status** (divorce, redundancy, death of a spouse, change in membership of a non-family household).

(b) **Different economic circumstances** and extent of consumption planning in single-parent families, households where there is a redundancy, dual-income households.

(c) **Different buying and consumption roles** to compensate/adjust in households where the **woman works**. Women can be segmented into at least four categories – each of which may represent a distinct market for goods and services:

- Stay-at-home homemaker
- Plan-to-work homemaker
- 'Just-a-job' working woman
- Career-oriented working woman

Socio-economic segmentation

Age and sex present few problems but social class has always been one of the most dubious areas of marketing research investigation. Class is a highly personal and subjective phenomenon, to the extent that some people are class conscious or class aware and have a sense of belonging to a particular group. JICNAR's social grade definitions (A – E), which correspond closely to what are called Social Classes I – V on the Registrar General's Scale, are often used in quota setting.

Table 7.4   Social grading scale

Registrar General's social classes	JICNAR		Characteristics of occupation (of head of household)
	Social grades	Social status	
I	A	Upper middle class	Higher managerial/professional eg lawyers, directors
II	B	Middle class	Intermediate managerial/administrative/ professional eg teachers, managers, computer operators, sales managers
III (i) non-manual	C1	Lower middle class	Supervisory, clerical, junior managerial/ administrative/professional eg foremen, shop assistants
(ii) manual	C2	Skilled working class	Skilled manual labour, eg electricians, mechanics
IV	D	Working class	Semi-skilled manual labour, eg machine operators
V			Unskilled manual labour, eg cleaning, waiting tables, assembly
	E	Lowest level of subsistence	State pensioners, widows (no other earner), casual workers

The UK Office for National Statistics uses the categorisation system shown below.

Table 7.5   Social categorisation scale

New social class	Occupations	Examples
1	Higher managerial and professional occupations	CEOs, fund managers, consultant surgeons
1.1	Employers and managers in larger organisations	Bank managers, company directors
1.2	Higher professional	Doctors, lawyers
2	Lower managerial and professional occupations	Police officers
3	Intermediate occupations	Secretaries/PAs, clerical workers
4	Small employers and own-account workers	SME owner managers
5	Lower supervisory, craft and related occupations	Electricians
6	Semi-routine occupations	Drivers, hairdressers, bricklayers
7	Routine occupations	Car park attendants, cleaners

Geographic segmentation

Geographic segmentation is appropriate when there are observable differences in consumption that correlate with geographic location. Jobber (2009) gives the example of beer, which is preferred with a foamy head in the north of England, whereas southerners prefer their beer flat. In Germany, a relatively large number of local brewers produce beer that satisfies local tastes. Geographic and, especially, national cultural differences are also important in marketing communications.

The Chartered Institute of Marketing

Geographic and demographic information is combined in geodemographic segmentation. Social class information may also be included. For example, the ACORN system divides the UK into 17 groups which together comprise a total of 54 different types of areas, which share common socio-economic characteristics.

(a)   The 17 ACORN groups are as follows:

Table 7.6   Socio-economic classification scale

The ACORN targeting classification: abbreviated list		% of population
A	*Thriving (19.7%)*	
A1	Wealthy achievers, suburban areas	15.0
A2	Affluent greys, rural communities	2.3
A3	Prosperous pensioners, retirement areas	2.4
B	*Expanding (11.6%)*	
B4	Affluent executives, family areas	3.8
B5	Well-off workers, family areas	7.8
C	*Rising (7.8%)*	
C6	Affluent urbanites, town and city areas	2.3
C7	Prosperous professionals, metropolitan areas	2.1
C8	Better-off executives, inner city areas	3.4
D	*Settling (24.1%)*	
D9	Comfortable middle-agers, mature home-owning areas	13.4
D10	Skilled workers, home-owning areas	10.7
E	*Aspiring (13.7%)*	
E11	New home-owners, mature communities	9.7
E12	White collar workers, better-off multi-ethnic areas	4.0
F	*Striving (22.7%)*	
F13	Older people, less prosperous areas	3.6
F14	Council estate residents, better-off homes	11.5
F15	Council estate residents, high unemployment	2.7
F16	Council estate residents, greatest hardships	2.8
F17	People in multi-ethnic, low-income areas	2.1

(b)   As an example of a more detailed breakdown, group *E* (*'Aspiring'*) contains the following groups:

Table 7.7   Socio-economic classification scale: Group E

E	*Aspiring (13.7% of population)*	
E11	New home-owners, mature communities (9.7%)	
11.33	Council areas, some new home-owners	3.8
11.34	Mature home-owning areas, skilled workers	3.1
11.35	Low-rise estates, older workers, new home-owners	2.8
E12	White collar workers, better-off multi-ethnic areas (4.0%)	
12.36	Home-owning multi-ethnic areas, young families	1.1
12.37	Multi-occupied town centres, mixed occupations	1.8
12.38	Multi-ethnic areas, white collar workers	1.1

Unlike geographical segmentation, which is fairly crude by area, geodemographics enables similar groups of people to be targeted, even though they might exist in different areas of the country. These various classifications share certain characteristics, including:

- Car ownership
- Unemployment rates
- Purchase of financial service products
- Number of holidays
- Age profile

3 Segmentation of the industrial market

Segmentation may apply more obviously to the consumer market, but it can also be applied to industrial markets (also known as organisational markets).

Industrial markets can be segmented with many of the bases used in consumer markets such as geography, usage rate and benefits sought. Additional, more traditional bases include customer type, product/technology, customer size and purchasing procedures.

(a) **Geographic location**. Some industries and related industries are clustered in particular areas. Firms selling services to the banking sector might be interested in the City of London.

(b) **Type of business** (eg service, manufacturing)

    (i) **Nature of the customers' business**. Accountants or lawyers, for example, might choose to specialise in serving customers in a particular type of business. An accountant may choose to specialise in the accounts of retail businesses, and a firm of solicitors may specialise in conveyancing work for property development companies.

    (ii) **Components manufacturers** specialise in the industries of the firms to which they supply components.

    (iii) **Type of organisation**. Organisations in an industry as a whole may have certain needs in common. Employment agencies offering business services to publishers, say, must offer their clients personnel with experience in particular desktop publishing packages. Suitable temporary staff offered to legal firms can be more effective if they are familiar with legal jargon. Each different type of firm can be offered a tailored product or service.

The Chartered
Institute of Marketing

(iv) **Size of organisation**. Large organisations may have elaborate purchasing procedures, and may do many things in-house. Small organisations may be more likely to subcontract certain specialist services.

(c) **Use of the product**. In the UK, many new cars are sold to businesses, as benefit cars. Although this practice is changing with the viability of a 'cash alternative' to a company car, the varying levels of specification are developed with the business buyer in mind (eg junior salesperson gets an Escort, Regional Manager gets a Mondeo).

Wind and Cardozo (1974) developed a two-stage framework.

(a) **Stage 1** calls for the formation of macrosegments based on organisational characteristics such as size, SIC (Standard Industrial Classification) code and product applications.

(b) **Stage 2** involves dividing these macrosegments into microsegments based on the distinguishing characteristics of decision-making units. They identify five general segmentation bases moving from the outer towards the inner in the following sequence: demographic, operating variables, purchasing approaches, situational factors and personal characteristics of the buyer.

Jobber (2009) describes a microsegmentation stage based on six variables:

(a) **Buyer's choice criteria**. Buyers are likely to use different criteria and priorities when making purchase decisions. Cost quality and service and their relative importance are important choice criteria.

(b) **Decision-making unit (DMU) structure**. The composition of the DMU is likely to vary as is the influence wielded by the various stakeholder groups involved.

(c) **Decision-making process**. The time taken to make the purchased decision is linked to the size and structure of the DMU. An extended and complex decision process requires greater marketing effort.

(d) **Buy class**. Purchases by organisations are of three types:

(i) The **straight rebuy** is a repeat purchase from an approved supplier.

(ii) The **new task** occurs when a need for a new type of product arises and there is little experience of its purchase.

(iii) The **modified rebuy** requires the purchase of a standard product and the various sources of supply are well-known, but there has been a problem that has led to a modification of the standard purchasing procedure.

Buy class thus affects the complexity of the purchasing behaviour.

(e) The structure of the **purchasing organisation** within the customer entity influences the purchasing decision. The basic distinction is between centralised and decentralised purchasing. Centralised purchasing tends to be in the hands of internally influential, specialist buyers who know the market in detail and buy in bulk, obtaining significant price discounts as a result. Such purchasing organisations are best dealt with by a national account sales force, while less expert decentralised buying, where the buyers have less influence, can be handled by local territory representatives.

(f) A high degree of **innovation** in the customer organisation makes it a good target for the launch of new products.

The more bases for segmentation that is used therefore, the stronger the overall case will be evidenced.

Once the segmentation bases have been selected, we must apply them and segment the population under question (Tables 7.1 and 7.2).

Whenever we have our population segmented, we need to score the clusters or segments for attractiveness. Here, we set a hierarchy of attractiveness criteria, which in turn becomes our central case for targeting.

The Henley Centre for Forecasting has outlined four different kinds of consumers in the market for technological and media products.

(a) **Technophiles** (24% of the population) 'are enthusiastic about technology in a general sense and also show a high level of interest in applications of new technology. They are concentrated among the under-35s, are more likely to be male than female, and are more likely to belong to social grade C1 than AB'.

(b) **Aspirational technophiles** (22% of the population) 'are excited in a general sense about technology but are much less interested in its applications. They are more likely to be male than female, and are concentrated in the AB social grade'.

(c) **Functionals** (25% of the population) 'claim to be uninterested in technology but are not hostile to its applications, especially those areas which offer an enhancement of existing services. These consumers are more likely to be family... and are most numerous among the over 45s'.

(d) **Technophobes** (29% of the population) 'are hostile to technology at all levels and are sceptical about whether technology can offer anything new. Technophobes are concentrated in the over-60 age group, are more likely to be female than male, and are distributed fairly evenly through the social grades'.

4 Targeting

4.1 Segment validity

A market segment will only **be valid** if it is worth designing and developing a **unique marketing mix** for it. The following questions are commonly asked to decide whether or not the segment can be used for developing marketing plans.

Table 7.8 Segment validity table

Criteria	Comment
Can the segment be measured?	It might be possible to conceive of a market segment, but it is not necessarily easy to measure it. For example, for a segment based on people with a conservative outlook to life, can conservatism of outlook be measured by market research?
Is the segment big enough?	There has to be a large enough potential market to be profitable.
Can the segment be reached?	There has to be a way of getting to the potential customers via the organisation's promotion and distribution channels.
Do segments respond differently?	If two or more segments are identified by marketing planners but each segment responds in the same way to a marketing mix, the segments are effectively one and the same and there is no point in distinguishing them from each other.
Can the segment be reached profitably?	Do the identified customer needs cost less to satisfy than the revenue they earn?
Is the segment suitably stable?	The stability of the segment is important, if the organisation is to commit huge production and marketing resources to serve it. The firm does not want the segment to 'disappear' next year. Of course, this may not matter in some industries.

 The Chartered Institute of Marketing

4.2 Segment attractiveness

A segment might be valid and potentially profitable, but is it potentially **attractive**?

(a) A segment which has **high barriers to entry** might cost more to enter but will be less **vulnerable to competitors**.

(b) For firms involved in **relationship marketing**, the segment should be one in which **viable relationship** between the firm and the customer can be established.

Segments which are most attractive will be those whose needs can be met by building on the company's strengths and where forecasts for demand, sales profitability and **growth** are favourable.

4.2.1 A checklist of factors to consider when evaluating segment attractiveness

Hooley *et al* (2007) give a comprehensive list of factors for evaluating market attractiveness.

Table 7.9   Segment attractiveness scorecard

Factors	Characteristics to examine
Market	■ Size of the segment ■ Segment growth rate ■ Stage of industry evaluation ■ Predictability ■ Price elasticity and sensitivity ■ Bargaining power of customers ■ Seasonality of demand
Economic and technological	■ Barriers to entry ■ Barriers to exit ■ Bargaining power of suppliers ■ Level of technology ■ Investment required ■ Margins available
Competitive	■ Competitive intensity ■ Quality of competition ■ Threat of substitution ■ Degree of differentiation
Environmental	■ Exposure to economic fluctuations ■ Exposure to political and legal factors ■ Degree of regulation ■ Social acceptability

If a market segment is both valid and attractive, it may be accepted as a target market. This is an important strategic decision and will be taken at a high level. If the decision is taken to target a particular segment, further decisions must then be taken about implementing the project.

The scoring criterion again is defined by the project to which the process refers, and will vary from project to project. Having defined the criteria fully, we can proceed to score (Table 7.3).

As a result of our scoring mechanisms, identifiable targets present themselves via a fully quantifiable and justified process. The robustness of our case becomes manifest (Table 7.4).

Now we are presenting a case grounded in fundamental techniques, having introduced a scientific approach to our justifications. The final aspect of the case in this instance is to always remember our approach to positioning.

5 Positioning

5.1 Problems with positioning

How much do people remember about a product or brand?

(a) Many products are, in fact, very similar, and the key issue is to make them distinct in the customer's mind.

(b) People remember 'number 1', so the product should be positioned as 'number 1' in relation to a valued attribute.

(c) Cosmetic changes can have the effect of repositioning the product in the customer's mind. To be effective, however, this psychological positioning has to be reinforced by real positioning.

As positioning is psychological as well as real, we can now identify positioning errors.

Table 7.10 Positioning review table

Mistake	Consequence
Underpositioning	The brand does not have a clear identity in the eyes of the customer
Overpositioning	Buyers may have too narrow an image of a brand
Confused positioning	Too many claims might be made for a brand
Doubtful positioning	The positioning may not be credible in the eyes of the buyer

5.2 Positioning strategy checklist

Table 7.11 Positioning statements

Positioning variable	Comment
■ Attributes	■ Size, for example
■ Benefit	■ What benefits we offer
■ Use/application	■ Ease of use; accessibility
■ User	■ The sort of person the product appeals to
■ Product category	■ Consciously differentiated from competition
■ Quality/price	■ One should support and validate the other, so that it makes sense to the customer and he understands what he is buying. For example, low quality at a high price is unlikely to sell.

ACTIVITY 7.2

Identify examples of positioning strategies relevant to the positioning variables in the table above.

5.3 Perceptual maps

One simple perceptual map that can be used is to plot brands or competing products in terms of two key characteristics such as price and quality.

The Chartered
Institute of Marketing

Figure 7.1   Perceptual positioning map

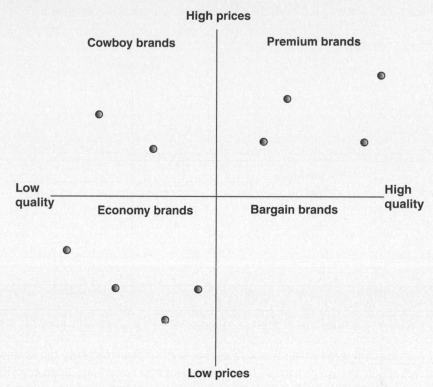

A perceptual map of market positioning can be used to **identify gaps in the market**. The example map we have shown suggests that there could be potential in the market for a low-price high-quality 'bargain brand'.

5.4 Mapping positions

Kotler (1996) identified a 3 × 3 matrix of nine different competitive positioning strategies.

Table 7.12   Product positioning matrix

Product price			
Product quality			
	High price	**Medium price**	**Low price**
High	Premium strategy	Penetration strategy	Superbargain strategy
Medium	Overpricing strategy	Average-quality strategy	Bargain strategy

Once selected, the needs of the targeted segment can be identified and the marketing mix strategy developed to provide the benefits package needed to satisfy them. Positioning the product offering then becomes a matter of matching and communicating appropriate benefits.

5.5 Steps in positioning

Step 1   Identify differentiating factors in products or services in relation to competitors

Step 2   Select the most important differences

Step 3   Communicate the position to the target market

All that needs to be established here is the mindset of the population and any competing entities or variables. Figure 7.2, below, gives a typical B2C commercial positioning statement.

Figure 7.2   Positioning map

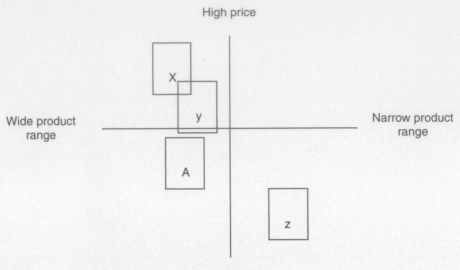

We must always remember that a process of segmentation, targeting and positioning for building and justifying cases should always go hand-in-hand and cannot be a stand-alone approach. That is, it is not just about segmentation – it is about segmentation, targeting and positioning.

This sequential and consequential approach to building a business case in support of our proposed marketing projects also needs to recognise that different scenarios and situations will demand changes to how we manage our marketing tools and techniques in the face of specific undertakings. Integration is, of course, the key and we need to recognise and identify the indicators within our case-building activities.

6 Business cases and the marketing mix

The **marketing mix** is a fundamental concept which you are probably already familiar with. It is appropriate to consider it here because, as noted above, it is through the marketing mix that the firm attacks the target market it has chosen. It is absolutely necessary that the marketing mix is properly managed. For example, the elements of the marketing mix must be properly **integrated** so that they are mutually supporting. Also, elements in the marketing mix can, to some extent, act as **substitutes for each other**. For example, a firm can raise the selling price of its products if it also raises product quality or advertising expenditure. Equally, a firm can perhaps reduce its sales promotion expenditure if it is successful in achieving a wider range and larger numbers of sales outlets for its product.

There are four elements in the fundamental marketing mix:

- Product
- Place
- Promotion
- Price

6.1 The product

From the firm's point of view, the product element of the marketing mix is what is being sold, whether it be widgets, power stations, haircuts, holidays or financial advice. From the customer's point of view, a **product is a solution to a problem or a package of benefits**. Many products might satisfy the same customer need. On what basis might a customer choose?

(a) **Customer value** is the customer's estimate of how far a product or service goes towards satisfying his or her need(s).

(b) Every product has a price, and so the customer makes a **trade-off** between the **expenditure** and **the value offered**.

(c) According to Kotler a customer must feel he or she gets a better deal from buying an item than by any of the alternatives.

6.1.1 The nature of the product

(a) The **core product** is the most basic description of the product – a car is a means of personal transport. The **actual product** is the car itself, with all its physical features such as a powerful engine, comfortable seats and a sun roof. The **augmented product** is the car plus the benefits which come with it, such as delivery, servicing, warranties and credit facilities for buyers.

(b) The **product range** consists of two dimensions.

   (i) **Width**. A car maker may have products in all parts, known as segments, of the market: luxury cars, family cars, small cheap cars, and so on.

   (ii) **Depth**. It may then offer a wide variety of options within each segment – a choice of engines, colours, accessories and so on.

(c) **Benefits offered to the customer**. Customers differ in their attitudes towards new products and the benefits they offer.

   Product issues in the marketing mix will include such factors as:

   - Design (size, shape)
   - Features packaging
   - After-sales service (if necessary)
   - Quality and reliability

Always remember to define this in relation to the offer that is made available for consumption. Business case justifications will concentrate on new product development or the reigniting of the product life cycle.

6.2 The price

The price element of the marketing mix is the only one which brings in revenue. Price is influenced by many factors.

(a) **Economic influences**: supply and demand; price and income elasticities.

(b) **Competitors' prices**. Competitors include other firms selling the same type of product, as well as firms selling substitute products. Generally, firms like to avoid price wars.

(c) **Quality connotations**. High price is often taken as being synonymous with quality, so pricing will reflect the product's image. (Stella Artois lager was once marketed in the UK as being 'reassuringly expensive'.)

(d) **Discounts**. These can make the product attractive to distributors.

(e) **Payment terms** (eg offering a period of interest-free credit).

(f)   **Trade-in allowances**.

(g)   The stage in the **product life cycle**

    (i)   **Penetration pricing** is charging a low price to achieve early market share advantages.

    (ii)   **Skimming pricing** is charging high prices early on to reap the maximum profits.

Always remember to define this as the consideration necessary to transact the consumption. Justifications will concentrate on skimming and penetration.

6.3 The place

Place deals with how the product is distributed, and how it reaches its customers.

(a)   **Channel**. Where are products sold? In supermarkets, corner shops, online? Which sales outlets will be chosen?

(b)   **Logistics**. The location of warehouses and efficiency of the distribution system is also important. A customer might have to wait a long time if the warehouse is far away. Arguably, the **speed of delivery** is an important issue in **place**, and delivery is becoming increasingly important as customers buy more goods online.

A firm can distribute the product itself (direct distribution) or distribute it through intermediary organisations such as retailers. Key issues are:

(a)   **Product push**: the firm directs its efforts to distributors to get them to stock the product.

(b)   **Customer pull**: the firm persuades consumers to demand the product from retailers and distributors, effectively pulling the product through the chain.

Defined as a location or a distribution process or making available what is on offer for consumption. The justification here is normally about extracting transactions out of the channels.

6.4 The promotion

Many of the practical activities of the marketing department are related to **promotion**. Promotion is the element of the mix over which the marketing department generally has most control. A useful mnemonic is AIDA which summarises the aims of promotion.

- Arouse Attention
- Generate Interest
- Inspire Desire
- Initiate Action (ie buy the product)

Promotion in the marketing mix includes all marketing communications which inform the public of the product or service.

- Advertising (newspapers, billboards, TV, radio, direct mail, internet)
- Sales promotion (discounts, coupons, special displays in particular stores)
- Direct selling by sales personnel
- Public relations

Defined as communicating what is on offer for consumption. Our business cases here concentrate on push, pull and profile aspects of our integrated marketing communications mix.

In addition, the elements of People, Processes and Physical evidence will also need to be moulded to determine the extent to which the mix needs to be amended or adjusted for any particular project case. We will look at the People aspect here in more depth.

The Chartered
Institute of Marketing

7 The extended marketing mix

This is also known as the service marketing mix because it is specifically relevant to the marketing of **services** rather than **physical products**. The intangible nature of services makes these extra three Ps, as outlined above, particularly important.

7.1 People

The importance of employees in the marketing mix is particularly important in **service marketing**, because of the **inseparability** of the service from the service provider: the creation and consumption of the service generally happen at the same moment, at the interface between the server and the served. Front-line staff must be selected, trained and motivated with particular attention to customer care and public relations.

In the case of some services, the **physical presence** of people performing the service is a vital aspect of customer satisfaction. The staff involved are performing or producing a service, selling the service and also liaising with the customer to promote the service, gather information and respond to customer needs.

7.2 Processes

Efficient **processes** can become a marketing advantage in their own right. If an airline, for example, develops a sophisticated ticketing system, it can offer shorter waits at check-in or wider choice of flights through allied airlines. Efficient order processing not only increases customer satisfaction, but cuts down on the time it takes the organisation to complete a sale.

Issues to be considered include the following:

- Policies, particularly with regard to ethical dealings (a key issue for many consumers)
- Procedures, for efficiency and standardisation
- Automation and computerisation of processes
- Queuing and waiting times
- Information gathering, processing and communication times
- Capacity management, matching supply to demand in a timely and cost effective way
- Accessibility of facilities, premises, personnel and services

Such issues are particularly important in service marketing; because of the range of factors and people involved, it is difficult to standardise the service offered. Quality, in particular specifications, will vary with the circumstances and individuals.

Services are also innately **perishable**: their purchase may be put off, but they cannot be stored.

This creates a need for process planning for efficient work.

7.3 Physical evidence

Services are **intangible**: there is no physical substance to them. This means that even when money has been spent on them the customer has no **evidence of ownership**. These factors make it difficult for consumers to perceive, evaluate and compare the qualities of service provision, and may therefore dampen the incentive to consume.

Issues of intangibility and ownership can be tackled by making available a physical symbol or representation of the service product or of ownership, and the benefits it confers. For example, tickets and programmes relating to entertainment; and certificates of attainment in training are symbolic of the service received and a history of past positive experiences.

Physical evidence of service may also be incorporated into the design and specification of the service environment by designing premises to reflect the quality and type of service aspired to. Such environmental

factors include finishing, decor, colour scheme, noise levels, background music, fragrance and general ambience.

8 Managing dynamics

There are often many changes over the period of the project. These changes are referred to as 'dynamics'. Irrespective of the methodology, managing project dynamics is key to a project's successful completion. Changes can result from:

External market dynamics – such as changes in competitors, the size and value of the market, the potential media or routes to market.

The business dynamics – such as business priorities, resource levels, personnel, interactions with stakeholders, including suppliers and customers.

Project dynamics – such as the interaction of factors influencing costs and schedules on the specific project, and the interaction of the people within the project.

Managing dynamics is central to the agile project approaches. However, even process methodologies will have to manage some aspects of project dynamics.

9 Managing people

Project process and methodology rely on people to work towards the conclusion. While agile approaches take more account of the individual's views, both are dependent on people working together.

Here, we will look at some key elements of people issues in project management. First, we look at the role and skills of the project manager, then we look at managing the team.

9.1 Project manager

The most central role in the project is that of the project manager. Some organisations have identified the specific requirements for this role through skills/competency analysis. Table 7.5 summarises those identified in research across sectors linked with the problems that can arise when these skills and competencies are not in place.

Table 7.13   Project management skills and project management problems

Project management skills	Project management problems
Communications skills Listening Persuading	Breakdowns in communications
Organisational skills Planning Goal setting Analysing	Insufficient planning Inadequate resources
Team building skills Empathy Motivation *Esprit de corps*	Team members uncommitted Weak inter-unit integration

Project management skills	Project management problems
Leadership skills Setting an example Energetic Vision (the big picture) Delegates Positive	Unclear goals/direction Interpersonal conflicts
Coping skills Flexibility Creativity Patience Persistence	Handling changes
Technological skills Experience Project knowledge	Meeting ('unrealistic') deadlines

Note: These generic categories of project management skills are identified in order of importance, based on a survey of project managers. (Pozner, 1987.)

9.2 The project team

Once the project manager is in place, the next manpower challenge is of forming the project team. Ideally, the project manager and the team should gel. However, problems may exist in this:

- The different backgrounds and experiences of team members.

- The availability of team members, especially where these are on temporary secondments or working part-time on the project.

- The levels of commitment to the project, which may not be central to their main work.

Often, projects are formed on the basis of who is available for the projects. Ideally, these people should also be willing to work on this, but often this is not the case. This is an issue that can cause major problems and, indeed, may be a key area for risk management review in the project.

Team roles may be defined within projects. These can be across the different functional disciplines or created from people with similar backgrounds to create synergy. There may be levels of teams for larger projects, with a core team, which is led by the project manager, and comprises the heads of key activity areas, or subteams, which are led by the heads of key activity areas, and which report to the project manager.

Ideally, team profiling, using for example Belbin (1981), should be applied to the team. This is most appropriate for larger team projects, but it often identifies problems when appointing team members from within a marketing department (who may all have been appointed for similar roles within the marketing team).

Many consultants recommend an initial team-building activity when a project is first launched. However, this is not exclusive to the project launch – team-building events can help sustain a strong, motivated team. Remember that this can include team members from external agencies.

9.3 Managing team problems

Kezsbom (2001) reports that there are seven sources of conflict in managing teams. These are:

- **Project priorities** – team members view the importance and flow of activities and tasks differently.

- **Administrative procedures** – team members often have conflicting views over how the project should be managed or run.

- **Technical problems** – team members disagree over technical matters, such as specifications, performance and priorities.

- **Resources** – such as getting staff and computers from functional departments, and having access to shared services.

- **Cost** – project manager and team members disagree over the costs of the WBS activities and tasks.

- **Schedules** – project manager and team members disagree over the order and timing of project tasks.

- **Personality** – managing interpersonal behaviour to create a culture of collaboration and respect.

10 Managing resources

When considering a marketing project, the estimation of project time and costs is dependent upon the resources that are to be used. The project manager needs to identify specific skills and materials, equipment and facilities required. The availability, cost, quantities required and possible resource constraints must all be accounted for.

It is important to assess company capability when evaluating attractiveness and targeting a market. This can help determine the appropriate strategy, because once the attractiveness of each identified segment has been assessed it can be considered together with relative strengths to determine the potential advantages the organisation would have. In this way preferred segments can be targeted. Jobber (2009) describes four categories of relevant organisational capability.

Exploitable marketing assets. Current marketing assets, such as brands and distribution networks, should be exploited in order to achieve synergy. However, the impact of the proposed target market on those assets must also be considered. For example, would stretching a successful brand into an unrelated market damage the brand's values?

Cost advantages. A cost advantage relating to any aspect of the business will bring significant commercial benefits. These include the possibility of a high promotional budget, the use of penetration pricing, the ability to survive an economic downturn and the possibility of competing on price.

Technological edge. Technological superiority also confers commercial advantages, especially where it takes the form of legally protected intellectual property.

Managerial capability and commitment. Management's abilities should be assessed against that of competitors, as evidenced by their record in the target segment. Marketing success depends on the existence of significant management capability; similarly, it will not be achieved if there is insufficient commitment.

11 Investment and income

It stands to reason that no business case can be complete without fully quantified budgets. These are the 2I (Investment and Income) budgets that will highlight all the necessary financial resource required to be invested and have this detailed on a line-by-line basis and, second, show the expected and projected return on such investments over time.

If we assume the mantra of investing resources as opposed to being defined as a cost centre, we will never lose sight of the fact that it is a business case we are constructing and presenting.

These issues are examined in much more depth in your Managing Marketing course book and will aid your knowledge when developing robust cases.

The major investment measurement and proposal tools that you should be familiar with include:

- Accounting rate of return (ARR)
- Payback
- Discounted cash flow
- Net present value (NPV)
- Internal rate of return
- Return on investment (ROI)

List examples of resource management metrics.

12 Cost benefit analysis

Cost benefit analysis is a general approach of adding up the benefits, taking away the costs and seeing whether what is left is worth the original investment in time and resources, including the opportunity cost of doing something else instead. The alternatives and the 'do nothing' option should always be qualified and quantified. This is not always as easy to do as it sounds. Not all costs and benefits arise in one go and often accrue over time, possibly over many years. Techniques such as payback analysis and discounted cash flow technique attempt to group all of these costs and benefits together in order to make an overall appraisal. This carries the health warning that future cash inflows and outflows are harder to predict the further ahead in time they are set to occur.

In simple models of cost benefit only the financial items are included. In more sophisticated models other, less tangible, factors are taken into account, including social and environmental costs and benefits. In essence, managers need to understand the relationships between performance, costs and revenues and so evaluate the overall value of marketing projects.

The simplest form of cost benefit analysis lists all of the costs and all of the benefits. This makes the assumption that it is possible to assign a financial value to costs and benefits. Imagine, for example, that an organisation wishes to appraise a proposal for investing in a new customer database. The marketing manager could begin to assess its value by identifying and analysing all the relevant items. Often the costs are easier to quantify than the benefits.

Costs:

- Initial purchase of commercial off-the-shelf software: £65,000
- Annual licence: £4,000 pa
- Customisation of software to meet specific organisational needs: £18,000
- Additional annual support licence: £1,300 pa
- Staff training and development: £2,800
- Upgrade of hardware: £11,000
- Installation: £1,700
- Testing: £820
- Data transfer: £3,400

Total cost: £108,020 in the first year, £5,300 in each following year.

Benefits:

- Shorter processing time of membership applications (calculated as a percentage of data input staff time): £4,500 pa

- Savings from reductions in system down time (calculated from emergency call out charges): £800 pa

- Improvements to targeted marketing, reductions in mail out costs and increases in sales: £31,200 pa

- Disposal of old equipment less costs of disposal: £22,000

Total benefits: £58,500 in the first year and £36,500 in each following year.

In this case it would not be until the third year that the project had recovered the initial outlay and ongoing additional costs. It is the addition of a cost benefit analysis to all the other elements of the business case that completes a robust piece of work around a business need and lays the foundations for any subsequent or related project.

▶ **Assessment tip**

Results and accountability are the defining terminology of marketing operations in the 21st century. You must demonstrate your appreciation of this and show that you are fully aware of the operational implications and outcomes of the proposals and decisions you make around functional and resource management.

CHAPTER ROUNDUP

- In this chapter we were able to establish that the central core of our business cases will deal in a robust manner with a situation-specific population.

- We also established that fundamental aspects of segmentation, targeting and position will always be central to any business case we present.

- The management and metamorphosis of our marketing mix will be ever changing.

- Core human and financial resources need to be managed within the confines of organisational capacity.

FURTHER READING

Doyle, P. (2003) 'Strategy as Marketing'. *In*: Cummings, S. and Wilson, D. (eds) (2003) *Images of Strategy*. London, Blackwell Publishing Limited.

REFERENCES

Belbin, M. (1981) *Management Teams*. London, Heinemann.

Hooley, G. *et al* (2007) *Marketing strategy and competitive positioning*. 4th edition. Harrow, Prentice Hall.

Jobber, D. (2009) *Principles and Practice of Marketing*. 6th edition. Maidenhead, McGraw-Hill.

Kezsbom, D. (2001) People Issues. *ACCE International, Transactions 2001*, 1-2.

Kotler, P. (1996) *Marketing Management: Analysis, Planning and Control*. 9th revised edition. Harlow, Pearson.

Plummer, J. (1974) The Concept and Application of Lifestyle Segmentation. Journal of Marketing, January, pp33-37

Pozner, B. (1987) What It Takes To Be A Good Project Manager. *Project Management Journal*, March, pp51-54.

UK National Statistics. Publication Hub. http://www.statistics.gov.uk/hub/index.html [Accessed 23 June 2012].

Wilson, A. (2006) *Marketing Research: An Integrated Approach*. 2nd edition. London, Financial Times/Prentice Hall.

Wind, Y. and Cardozo, R. (1974) Industrial Marketing Segmentation. *Industrial Marketing Management*, March, pp153–166.

QUICK QUIZ

1   What is the importance of having a number of segmentation bases?

2   Which segmentation deals with the stages households pass through?

3   What categories have been traditionally used to segment industrial customers?

4   What criteria must be satisfied if a market segment is to be valid?

5   How do barriers to entry affect segment attractiveness?

6   What four categories of organisational capability does Jobber identify as of importance when assessing segment attractiveness?

7   What are the features of mass customisation?

8   What are the three policy options in selecting target markets?

9   What is positioning?

10   What is underpositioning?

11   What did Kotler call a positioning strategy that combines medium price with low quality?

12   What are the three extra Ps present in the extended marketing mix used for services?

ACTIVITY DEBRIEFS

Activity 7.1

(a)   Adult education

- Age
- Sex
- Occupation
- Social class
- Education
- Family life cycle
- Lifestyle
- Leisure interest and hobbies

(b)   Magazines and periodicals

- Sex (*Woman's Own*)
- Social class (*Country Life*)
- Income and class aspirations (*Ideal Home*)
- Occupation (*Marketing Week*, *Computer Weekly*)
- Leisure interests (*Railway Modeller*)
- Political ideology (*Spectator*, *New Statesman*)
- Age

(c)   Sporting facilities

- Geographical area (rugby in Wales, skiing in parts of Scotland, sailing in coastal towns)
- Population density (squash clubs in cities, riding in country areas)
- Occupation (gyms for office workers)
- Education (there may be a demand for facilities for sports taught at certain schools, such as rowing)
- Family life cycle or age (parents may want facilities for their children, young single or married people may want facilities for themselves)

Activity 7.2

Table 7.14

Positioning strategy	Example
Attributes	Ads for PCs emphasise 'speed', what sort of chip they have (eg Pentium III)
Benefit	Holidays are advertised as offering relaxation or excitement
Use/application	'Easy to use' products (eg hair tints that can be 'washed' in)
User	Reflect user characteristics, to appeal to the target audience and confirm their choice. May use celebrity endorsement, such as David Beckham in Vodafone advertisements
Product category	The Natural History Museum is fundamentally educational, but is moving towards a 'theme park' image for the schools market
Quality/price	'Value for money' advertisements

Activity 7.3

Other resource management metrics include, effectiveness, efficiency, productivity, stock turn, return on capital employed, asset utilisation and brand equity.

QUICK QUIZ ANSWERS

1   One basis will not be valid for every market and sometimes two or more bases might be valid at the same time.

2   The family life cycle.

3   Location, type of business, use made of the product, type and size of organisation.

4   Measurability, size, accessibility, response, profitability, stability.

5   Entry might require significant investment, but the barriers then provide some protection against other potential entrants.

6   Exploitable marketing assets, cost advantages, technological edge and managerial capability and commitment.

7   Economies of scale and tailoring of products to individual requirements.

8   Differentiated, undifferentiated and concentrated marketing.

9   Designing the offer to achieve a distinct and valued place in the customer's mind.

10 Failure to achieve a clear position in the customer's mind.

11 Shoddy goods strategy.

12 People, processes and physical evidence.

BPP LEARNING MEDIA

CHAPTER 8

The case report

Introduction

The case now needs to be presented and illustrated in a manner that enhances the case to its fullest extent, and invariably this will be both in written and verbal forms.

The structure and format for reporting outlined in Section 1 remains as the template here, but now needs to assume the personality of the constructor.

So, our concentration here will be on the use of illustrations and models and hints and tips for verbal presentations. The report or presentation (or both) can be required during any part of the project's life cycle. As with project management itself, they are merely mechanisms and techniques that support the work of the marketing effort – whatever that is at each stage.

Topic list

Don't write it up, draw it up   (1)

Presentation tips   (2)

Maintaining control of the presentation   (3)

- The marketing report
- A structured presentation
- Knowing the audience
- Key impact indicators
- Findings, prioritisation and conclusion

---

1 Don't write it up, draw it up

▶ Key terms

Audio-visual: refers to work with both a sound and a visual component, the production or use of such work, or the equipment used to create and present such work.

Presentation software: is a computer program used to display information, normally in the form of a side show. It typically includes three major functions: an editor that allows text to be inserted and formatted, a method for inserting and manipulating graphic images, and a slide show system to display the content.

Through whatever visual medium the report appears Word or PowerPoint, the more hard-hitting illustrations we can introduce, the better.

So without further ado, let us practice what we preach. Shown following are a series of simple diagrams that illustrate the range and type of diagram that is available to the marketing practitioner (Figures 8.1 to 8.4).

Illustrations bring our reports and presentations to life and every picture paints a thousand words.

Figure 8.1   Value delivery systems and relationships

Physical process sequence

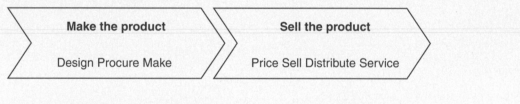

Value delivery system and relationships

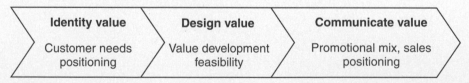

(Adapted from Bower and Garda 1985)

Figure 8.2 Supply chain management

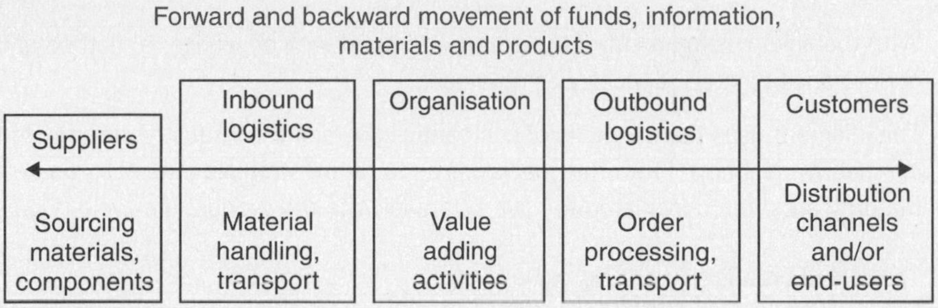

Forward and backward movement of funds, information, materials and products
Suppliers
Sourcing materials, components
Inbound logistics
Material handling, transport
Organisation
Value adding activities
Outbound logistics
Order processing, transport
Customers
Distribution channels and/or end-users

Figure 8.3 Product life cycle

Different patterns of cycles
Fad
Conventional
Growth-slump-maturity
Cycle-recycle
Introduction Growth
Maturity
Decline
Time

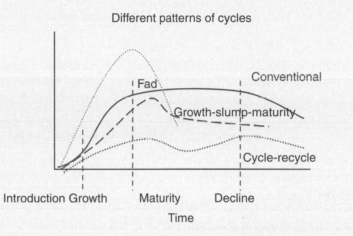

Figure 8.4 Shell directional policy matrix

Multifactor matrix shell directional policy matrix
Prospects for sector profitability
Unattractive
Average
Attractive
Weak
Average
Strong
Company's competitive capabilities

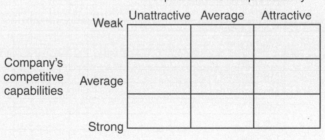

ACTIVITY 8.1

What presentations, conferences, or speech-making occasions have you attended recently? For each, note:

- The style of speech (formal/informal etc)
- The length of the speech
- Any visual aids used

How effective was the speaker in targeting each of these elements to:

(a) The purpose of the speech
(b) The needs of the audience?

A further series of examples of the more popular type of graphics that can be used (amongst many others) is shown below.

With the acknowledgement of the growth in importance of service, a method of measuring gaps in the performance of such services was developed.

This diagram uses the elements of competitive position and industry maturity to help determine the current competitive position. From this, decisions as to future strategic direction can be based. The stages of industry maturity are often considered to have a parallel with the product life cycle (Figure 8.5).

Figure 8.5 The role of branding in adding value

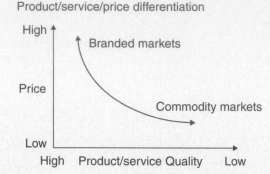

This type of diagram gives a simple, visual picture of how important the brand is within the overall value creation by plotting specified products or services onto the chart. Rapid comparison of those products can be carried out (Figure 8.6).

Figure 8.6 Mapping progress and responsibility

Task	Responsibility	Jan	Feb	Mar	Apr	May	Jun	Jul	Aug	Sep	Oct	Nov	Dec
Get funding													
Suppliers selection													
Plant													
Recruitment													
Skimming													
Product													
Marcomms													
Distribution													
Mkis													
Decor													
Feedback													

The diagram shows a very simple approach where stages are struck through as they are completed. More typically, they may be in the form of a Gantt chart, where the predicted schedule is shown as a bar on the calendar section, showing when and how long it is expected to take. Against that, a further bar shows the actual progress that has been made. Modern software allows for a great deal of 'drilling down' for more detail, but the higher level chart is still useful for giving a snapshot of what has happened and what remains to be done.

A simple pulling together of key accounting values in a table can help understanding, but further detailed investigation can be triggered from it.

2 Presentation tips

Wilson (2006) offers some handy tips, hints and techniques as outlined below.

- Meet your objectives. State them early on and show throughout how your presentation contributes to their achievement. You might even ask the audience what their objectives are at the beginning of the presentation, note them on a flip chart and at the end of the presentation tick them off.

- Know your audience; what do they want to hear? How many will be present? Who are they? What positions do they hold?

- How will you dress? Is it formal or informal or will you be overdressed in a suit and a tie? What do your audience expect?

- Keep it brief and to the point, use a balanced mixture of words and images and keep to time.

- Be prepared for interruptions and stop presenting if your audience are distracted. Do not plough on.

- If using PowerPoint technology, make sure that it is compatible with the projection system. Make sure that your slides do not contain too much information and that tables and graphics can be read.

2.1 Audience

The audience's **motivations** and **expectations** in attending a presentation will influence their perceptions of you and your message. Why might they be at your presentation?

(a) **They need specific information from the presentation**. An audience which is deliberately seeking information, and intending to use it to further their own objectives, is highly motivated. If their objectives match the speaker's (say, in a training seminar, where both trainer and trainees want improved job performance as the outcome), this motivation aids the speaker. It is therefore important to gauge, as far as possible, what this highly-motivated group **want** to hear from you, and **why**.

(b) **They are interested in the topic of the presentation**. The audience may have a general expectation that they will learn something new, interesting, or useful on a topic that they are predisposed to gather information about: it is up to the speaker to hold their attention by satisfying the desire for relevant information. They may also have some prior knowledge, on which the speaker can build: there will be a fine line to tread between boring the audience by telling them what they already know, and losing them by assuming more knowledge than they possess.

(c) **They are required to be there**.

    (i) Attendance may be **compulsory**, whether or not those attending are motivated or interested in the subject matter. In this case, you can at least find out the size and composition of your audience, but unless motivation and interest can be stimulated by the presentation, compulsory attendance may simply create resistance to the message.

    (ii) Attendance may be **recommended by a superior**, in which case even if the participants are not interested in the subject matter, they may be motivated to pay attention because they perceive it to be in their own interest to do so.

    This is known as a **captive audience**. Note that it is a double-edged sword: the audience may be compelled to listen to you, but they are actually **less** likely to listen attentively, co-operatively and with positive results, unless you can motivate them to do so once you have them in front of you.

(d) **They expect to be entertained**. The topic of the presentation may be entertaining or the audience may expect the speaker to put information across in an entertaining manner – using humour, illustration and so on. The organisation culture may encourage the idea that attending meetings and conferences is equivalent to rest and recreation: a bit of a 'day out' for the participants, more useful for the networking in the coffee breaks than the technical content of the presentations. As a speaker, you will have to ensure that you do not fulfil such expectations at the expense of your primary objectives – but be aware

that the entertainment-seekers are also a potential audience for your message: it may be possible to arouse more motivated interest.

Taking into account any **specific** audience needs and expectations, your message needs to have the following qualities.

(a)   **Interest**. It should be lively/entertaining/varied or relevant to the audience's needs and interests, or preferably both.

(b)   **Congeniality.** This usually means positive, supportive or helpful in some way (eg in making a difficult decision easier, or satisfying a need).

(c)   **Credibility**. It should be **consistent** in itself, and with known **facts**, apparently **objective,** and from a source perceived to be **trustworthy**.

(d)   **Accessibility**. This means both:

- **Audible/visible**. (Do you need to be closer to the audience? Do you need a microphone? Enlarged visual aids? Clearer articulation and projection?)

- **Understandable**. (What is the audience's level of knowledge/education/ experience in general? and of the topic at hand? What technical terms or **jargon** will need to be avoided or explained? What concepts or ideas will need to be explained?)

2.2 Physical preparation

At the planning stage, you might also consider physical factors which will affect the audience's concentration: their ability and willingness to *keep* listening attentively and positively to your message. Some of the these may not be in your control, if you are not planning the meeting or conference, arranging the venue and so on, but as far as possible, give attention to the following.

(a)   **Listening conditions**. Try and cut out background noise – conversations outside the room, traffic, loud air conditioning or rattling slide projector, say. (There may be a trade-off between peace and quiet, and good ventilation, also required for alertness: be sensible about the need to open a door or window or switch on a fan.)

(b)   **Freedom from interruption and distraction**. Do not let the focus shift from the speaker and his message to outside views of people passing by and so on. Arrange not to be disturbed by others entering the room. Announce, if appropriate, that questions and comments will be invited at the end of the session.

(c)   **Ventilation, heating and lighting**. A room that is too stuffy, or draughty, too hot or cold, too bright or dim to see properly, can create physical malaise, and shifts attention from the speaker and his message to the listener and his discomfort.

(d)   **Seating and desking**. Excessive comfort can impair alertness – but uncomfortable seating is a distraction. Combined with inadequate arrangements for writing (since many people may wish or need to take notes), it can cause severe strain over a lengthy talk.

(e)   **Audibility and visibility**. Inadequate speaking volume or amplification is a distraction and a strain, even if it does not render the message completely inaccessible. Excessive volume and electronic noise is equally irritating. Visibility requires planning not just of effective visual aids (clear projection in suitable light, adequately enlarged etc) but also of seating plans, allowing unobstructed 'sight lines' for each participant.

(f)   **Seating layout**. Depending on the purpose and style of your presentation, you may choose formal classroom-like rows of seating, with the speaker in front behind a podium, or informal group seating in a circle or cluster in which the speaker is included. The formal layout enhances the speaker's credibility, and may encourage attention to information, while the informal layout may be more congenial, encouraging involvement and input from the whole group.

The Chartered Institute of Marketing

(g) **Time**. Listeners get tired over time – however interesting the presentation: their concentration span is limited, and they will not be able to listen effectively for a long period without a break.

   (i) If you have the choice (and a limited volume of information to impart), a ten-minute presentation will be more effective than a one-hour presentation.

   (ii) If the volume of information or time allotted dictate a lengthy talk, you will need to build in reinforcements, breaks and 'breathers' for your listeners, by using repetition, summary, jokes/anecdotes, question-and-answer breaks and so on.

   (iii) Bear in mind, too, that the time of day will affect your listeners' concentration, even if your presentation is a brief one: you will have to work harder if your talk is first thing in the morning, late in the day (or week), or approaching lunch-time.

(h) **The speaker's appearance**. It should already be obvious that the appearance of the speaker may sabotage his efforts if it is uncongenial or unappealing, lacks credibility or the authority expected by the audience, is distracting in some way, and so on.

ACTIVITY 8.2

In what other research circumstances besides the final presentation might the researcher find it useful to think about physical factors that will affect his or her audience's concentration?

2.3 Content

Armed with your clearly-stated objectives and audience profile, you can plan the **content** of your presentation.

One approach which may help to clarify your thinking is as follows:

Table 8.1   Presentation checklist

Prioritise	Select the **key points** of the subject, and a **storyline** or theme that gives your argument a unified sense of 'direction'. The **fewer** points you make (with the most emphasis) and the clearer the **direction** in which your thoughts are heading, the easier it will be for the audience to grasp and retain your message.
Structure	Make notes for your presentation which **illustrate** simply the **logical order** or **pattern** of the key points of your speech.
Outline	Following your structured notes, **flesh out** your message. ■ **Introduction** ■ **Supporting evidence, examples and illustrations** ■ **Notes** where **visual aids** will be used ■ **Conclusion**
Practise	Rehearsals should indicate difficult logical leaps, dull patches, unexplained terms and other problems: adjust your outline or style. They will also help you gauge and adjust the **length** of your presentation.
Cue	Your outline may be too detailed to act as a cue or **aide-memoire** for the talk itself. **Small cards**, which fit into the palm of the hand may be used to give you: ■ **Key words** for each topic, and the logical links between them ■ Reminders for when to use **visual aids** ■ The **full text** of any detailed information you need to quote

An effective presentation requires two key structural elements.

(a) An **introduction** which:

- Establishes your credibility.

- Establishes rapport with the audience.

- Gains the audience's attention and interest (sets up the problem to be solved, uses curiosity or surprise).

- Gives the audience an overview of the **shape** of your presentation, to guide them through it: a bit like the scanning process in reading.

(b) A **conclusion** which:

- **Clarifies and draws together** the points you have made into one main idea (using an example, anecdote, review, summary).

- **States or implies what you want/expect your audience to do** following your presentation.

- Reinforces the audience's **recall** (using repetition, a joke, quotation or surprising statistic to make your main message **memorable**).

2.4 Clarity

Your structured notes and outline should contain cues which clarify the **logical order**, shape or progression of your information or argument. This will help the audience to **follow you** at each stage of your argument, so that they arrive with you at the conclusion. You can signal these logical links to the audience as follows:

(a) **Linking words or phrases**

Therefore … [conclusion, result or effect, arising from previous point]
As a result …
However … [contradiction or alternative to previous point]
On the other hand …
Similarly … [confirmation or additional example of previous point]
Again …
Moreover … [building on the previous point]

(b) **Framework**: setting up the structure

'Of course, this isn't a perfect solution: There are advantages and disadvantages to it. It has the advantages of … . But there are also disadvantages, in that … '

(c) You can use more elaborate devices which summarise or repeat the previous point and lead the audience to the next. These also have the advantage of giving you, and the listener, a 'breather' in which to gather your thoughts.

Other ways in which content can be used to clarify the message include the following.

(a) **Examples and illustrations** – showing how an idea works in practice.

(b) **Anecdotes** – inviting the audience to relate an idea to a real-life situation.

(c) **Questions** – rhetorical, or requiring the audience to answer, raising particular points that may need clarification.

(d) **Explanation** – showing how or why something has happened or is so, to help the audience understand the principles behind your point.

(e) **Description** – helping the audience to visualise the person, object or setting you are describing.

The Chartered
Institute of Marketing

(f)   **Definition** – explaining the precise meaning of terms that may not be shared or understood by the audience.

(g)   The use of **facts, quotations or statistics** – to 'prove' your point.

Your **vocabulary and style** in general should contribute to the clarity of the message. Remember to use short, simple sentences and non-technical words (unless the audience is sure to know them): avoid jargon, clichés, unexplained acronyms, colloquialisms, double meanings and vague expressions (like 'rather', 'good'). Remember, too, that this is **oral** communication, not written: use words and grammatical forms that you would **normally use in speaking** to someone – bearing in mind the audience's ability to understand you, the formality of the occasion and so on.

Visual aids will also be an important aspect of content used to signal the structure and clarify the meaning of your message. We discuss them specifically later.

2.5 Adding emphasis

Emphasis is the 'weight', importance or impact given to particular words or ideas. This can largely be achieved through delivery – the tone and volume of your voice, strong eye contact, emphatic gestures and so on – but can be reinforced in the content and wording of your speech. Emphasis can be achieved by a number of means:

(a)   **Repetition:**   'If value for money is what the market wants, then value for money is what this brand must represent.'

'One in five customers has had a quality complaint. That's right: one in five.'

(b)   **Rhetorical questions:**   'Do you know how many of your customers have a quality complaint? One in five. Do you think that's acceptable?'

(c)   **Quotation:**   'Product quality is the number one issue in customer care in the new millennium. That's the conclusion of our survey report.'

(d)   **Statistical evidence:**   'One in five of your customers this year have had a quality complaint: that's 10% more complaints than last year. If the trend continues, you will have one complaint for every two satisfied customers – next year!'

(e)   **Exaggeration:**   'We have to look at our quality control system. Because if the current trend continues, we are going to end up without any customers at all.'

2.6 Adding interest

Simple, clear information often lacks impact, and will only be interesting to those already motivated by the desire for the information. The speaker has to balance the need for clarity with the need to get the key points across. All the devices discussed so far can be used for impact.

Here are some further suggestions:

(a)   **Analogy, metaphor, simile** etc – comparing something to something else which is in itself more colourful or interesting.

(b)   **Anecdote or narrative** – as already mentioned, telling a story which illustrates or makes the point, using suspense, humour or a more human context.

(c)   **Curiosity or surprise** – from incongruity, anticlimax or controversy. Verbatim quotes from customers can be very useful in this respect.

(d)   **Humour**. This is often used for entertainment value, but also serves as a useful 'breather' for listeners, and may help to get them on the speaker's side. (Humour may not travel well, however: the audience may not be on the speaker's wavelength at all, especially in formal contexts. Use with caution.)

2.7 Controlling nerves

Stage-fright can be experienced before making a phone call, going into an interview or meeting, or even writing a letter, but it is considerably more acute, for most people, before standing up to talk in front of a group or crowd of people. Common fears are to do with **making a fool of oneself**, forgetting one's **lines**, being unable to answer **questions**, or being faced by blank incomprehension or **lack of response**. Fear can make vocal delivery hesitant or stilted and **body language** stiff and unconvincing.

A **controlled amount of fear**, or stress, is actually **good for you**: it stimulates the production of **adrenaline**, which can contribute to alertness and dynamic action. Only at excessive levels is stress harmful, degenerating into **strain**. If you can **manage your stress** or stage-fright, it will help you to be **alert** to feedback from your audience, to think 'on your feet' in response to questions, and to project vitality and enthusiasm.

(a)   **Reduce uncertainty and risk**. This means:

- **Preparing thoroughly** for your talk, including rehearsal, and anticipating questions.

- **Checking** the venue and facilities meet your expectations.

- **Preparing** whatever is necessary for your own confidence and comfort (glass of water, handkerchief, note cards etc).

- **Keeping your notes to hand**, and in order, during your presentation.

(b)   **Have confidence in your message**. Concentrate on the desired outcome: that is why you are there. Believe in what you are saying. It will also make it easier to project enthusiasm and energy.

(c)   **Control physical symptoms**. Breathe deeply and evenly. Control your gestures and body movements. Put down a piece of paper that is visibly shaking in your hand. Pause to collect your thoughts if necessary. Smile, and maintain eye contact with members of the audience. If you **act** as if you are calm, the calm will **follow**.

2.8 Non-verbal messages

Any number of body language factors may contribute to a speaker **looking confident and relaxed**, or nervous, shifty and uncertain. **Cues** which indicate confidence – without arrogance – may be as follows.

(a)   An upright – but not stiff – **posture**: slouching gives an impression of shyness or carelessness.

(b)   **Movement** that is purposeful and dynamic, used sparingly: not constant or aimless pacing, which looks nervous.

(c)   **Gestures** that are relevant, purposeful and flowing: not indecisive, aggressive, incomplete or compulsive. Use gestures **deliberately** to reinforce your message, and if possible keep your hands up so that gestures do not distract the audience from watching your face. In a large venue, gestures will have to be exaggerated – but practise making them look **natural**. Watch out for habitual, irrelevant gestures you may tend to make.

(d)   **Eye-contact** with the audience maintains credibility, maintains the involvement of the audience and allows you to gather audience feedback as to how well you are getting your message across. Eye-contact should be **established immediately**, and **re-established** after periods when you have had to look away, to consult notes or use visual aids.

The most effective technique is to let our gaze wander (purposefully) across the whole audience, **involving** them all, without intimidating anybody: establish eye-contact long enough for it to be registered, to accompany a point you are making, and then move on.

The Chartered Institute of Marketing

2.9 Visual aids

The term **visual aids** covers a wide variety of forms which share two characteristics:

(a) They use a visual image.

(b) They act as an aid to communication. This may seem obvious, but it is important to remember that visual aids are not supposed to be impressive or clever for their own sake, but to support the message and speaker in achieving their purpose.

A number of media and devices are available for using visual aids. They may be summarised as follows.

Table 8.2 Presentation media

Equipment/medium	Advantages	Disadvantages
Slides: photographs, text or diagrams projected onto a screen or other surface	▪ Allow colour photos: good for mood, impact and realism ▪ Preprepared: no speaker 'down time' during talk ▪ Controllable sequence/ timing: pace content/audience needs	▪ Require a darkened room: may hinder note-taking ▪ Malfunction and/or incompetent use: frustration and distraction
Film/video shown on a screen or TV monitor	▪ Moving images: realism, impact: can enhance credibility (eye witness effect)	▪ Less flexible in allowing interruption, pause or speeding-up to pace audience needs
Overheads: films or acetates (hand drawn or printed) projected by light box onto a screen behind/above the presenter	▪ Versatility of content and presentation ▪ Low cost (for example, if hand written) ▪ Clear sheets: can be used to build-up images as points added	▪ Require physical handling: can be distracting ▪ Risk of technical breakdown: not readily adaptable to other means of projection
Presentation software: for example, Microsoft PowerPoint. PC-generated slide show (with animation, sound) projected from PC to screen via data projector	▪ Versatility of multi-media: impact, interest ▪ Professional design and functioning (smooth transitions) ▪ Use of animation to build, link and emphasise as points added	▪ Requires PC, data projector: expensive, may not be available ▪ Risk of technical breakdown: not readily adaptable to other means of projection ▪ Temptation to over-complexity and over-use: distraction
Flip charts: large paper pad mounted on frame – sheets are 'flipped' to the back when finished with	▪ Low cost, low-risk ▪ Allows use during session (for example, to 'map' audience views, ideas) ▪ Can be preprepared (for example, advertising 'story boards') ▪ Easy to refer back	▪ Smaller, still, paper-based image: less impact ▪ Hand-prepared: may lack perceived quality (compared to more sophisticated methods)
Handouts: supporting notes handed out for reference during or after the session	▪ Preprepared ▪ Audience doesn't need to take as many notes: reminder provided	▪ Audience doesn't need to take as many notes: may encourage passive listening.
Props and demonstrations: objects or processes referred to are themselves shown to the audience	▪ Enhances credibility (eye witness effect) ▪ Enhances impact (sensory solidity)	▪ May not be available ▪ Risk of self-defeating 'hitches'

Whatever medium or device you are using, visual aids are **versatile** with regard to **content**: maps, diagrams, flowcharts, verbal notes, drawings, photographs and so on.

When planning and using visual aids, consider the following points:

(a)   Visual aids are **simplified and concrete**: they are easier to grasp than the spoken word, allowing the audience to absorb complex relationships and information.

(b)   Visual aids are **stimulating** to the imagination and emotions, and therefore useful in gaining attention and recall.

(c)   Visual aids can also be **distracting** for the audience – and for the presenter, who has to draw/write/organise /operate them. They can add complexity and ambiguity to the presentation if not carefully designed for relevance and clarity.

(d)   Visual aids impose **practical requirements**.

- The medium you choose must be **suitable** for the needs of your **audience**. Demonstrations, or handing round a small number of samples, is not going to work for a large audience. A flipchart will not be visible at the back of a large room; a slide projector can be overwhelming in a small room. A darkened room, to show video or slides, will not allow the audience to take notes.

- **Skill, time and resources** must be available for any prepreparation of aids that may be required in advance of the presentation.

- **The equipment, materials and facilities** you require must be available in the venue, and you must **know** how to **use** them. (No good turning up with a slide projector if there is no power source, or film when there is no overhead projector, or without proper pens for a particular type of board.)

The following are some **guidelines** for effective use of visual aids.

(a)   Ensure that the aid is:

- **Appropriate** to your message, in content and style or mood
- **Easy to see** and understand
- Only used when there is **support** to be gained from it

(b)   Ensure that all **equipment** and materials are **available and working** and that you can (and do) operate them efficiently and confidently. This includes having all your slides/acetates/notes with you, in the right order, the right way up and so on.

(c)   Ensure that the aid does not become a **distraction**.

(i)   Show each image **long enough** to be absorbed and noted, but not so long as to merge with following idea.

(ii)   Maintain **voice and eye contact** with your audience, so they know that it is you who are the communicator, not the machine.

(iii)   **Introduce** your aids and what they are for, placing the focus on the verbal presentation.

(iv)   Hand out **supporting material** either well before the presentation (to allow reading beforehand) or at the relevant point: if you hand it out just before, it will distract or daunt the audience with information they do not yet understand.

(v)   **Write or draw**, if you need to do so during the presentation, as quickly and efficiently as possible (given the need for legibility and neatness).

The look of presentation slides (or other visual aids) is very important. Make sure that they are:

- Simple: not too many points
- Visually appealing: use graphics and type styles to create an effect
- Neat: especially if you are preparing them by hand

2.10 Handling questions

Inviting or accepting questions is usually the final part of a presentation.

(a) In informative presentations, questions offer an **opportunity to clarify any misunderstandings**, or gaps that the audience may have perceived.

(b) In persuasive presentations, questions offer an opportunity to address and overcome specific doubts or resistance that the audience may have, which the speaker may not have been able to anticipate.

The manner in which you 'field' questions may be crucial to your **credibility**. Everyone knows you have prepared your presentation carefully: ignorance, bluster or hesitation in the face of a question may cast doubt on your expertise, or sincerity, or both. Moreover, this is usually the last stage of the presentation, and so leaves a lasting impression.

The only way to tackle questions effectively is to **anticipate** them. Put yourself in your audience's shoes, or, more specifically, in the shoes of an ignorant member of the audience, a hostile member and a member with a particular axe to grind: what questions might they ask and why? When questions arise, listen to them carefully, assess the questioner's manner, and draw the questioner out if necessary, in order to ascertain exactly what is being asked, and why. People might ask questions to:

(a) **Seek additional information** of particular interest to them, or to the group – if you have left it out of your talk

(b) Seek **clarification** of a point that is not clear

(c) **Add information** of their own, which may be relevant, helpful and accurate – or not

(d) **Lead the discussion into another area** (or away from an uncomfortable one)

(e) Display their **own knowledge or cleverness**

(f) **Undermine** the speaker's authority or argument, to 'catch him out'

If you have anticipated questions of the first two kinds (a) and (b) in the planning of your talk, they should not arise: incorporate the answers in your outline.

The important points about **answering questions** are as follows:

(a) You may **seek feedback** throughout your talk, as to whether your message is getting across clearly – and it is common to invite the audience to let you know if anything is unclear – but by and large, you should encourage questions only at the *end* of your presentation. That way, disruptive, rambling, hostile and attention-seeking questions will not be allowed to disrupt your message to the audience as a whole.

(b) You should **add or clarify** information if required to achieve your purpose. An honest query deserves a co-operative answer.

(c) You need to **maintain your credibility** and authority as the speaker. Strong tactics may be required for you to stay in control, without in any way ridiculing or 'putting down' the questioner.

    (i) If a question is based on a **false premise** or incorrect information, **correct it**. An answer may, or may not, then be required.

    (ii) If a question is **rambling**: interrupt, clarify what the question, or main question (if it is a multiple query) is, and answer that. If it is completely irrelevant, say politely that it is outside the scope of the presentation: you may or may not offer to deal with it informally afterwards.

    (iii) If a question is **hostile or argumentative**, you may wish to show understanding of how the questioner has reached his conclusion, or why he feels as he does. However, you then need to reinforce, repeat or explain your own view.

(iv)   If a question tries to **pin you down** or 'corner' you on an area in which you do not wish to be specific or to make promises, be straightforward about it.

(v)   If a question exposes an area in which you do not know the answer, **admit your limitations** with honesty and dignity, and invite help from members of the audience, if appropriate.

(vi)   Try and answer all questions with **points already made** in your speech, or related to them. This reinforces the impression that your speech was in fact complete and correct.

(d)   **Repeat** any question that you think might not have been **audible** to everyone in the room.

(e)   **Clarify** any question that you think is lengthy, complex, ambiguous or uses jargon not shared by the audience as a whole.

(f)   **Answer briefly**, keeping strictly to the point of the question (while relating it, if possible, to what you have already said). If your answer needs to be lengthy, structure it as you would a small talk: introduce what you are going to say, say it, then confirm what you have said!

(g)   Keep an eye on the **overall time-limit** for your talk or for the question-and-answer session. Move on if a questioner is taking up too much time, and call a halt, courteously, when required. 'I'll take one more question … ' or 'I'm afraid that's all we have time for' is standard practice which offends few listeners.

3 Maintaining control of the presentation

The following points will help you maintain control of your presentation:

- During the presentation, maintain eye contact with your audience. Try to avoid having a physical barrier between you and your audience.

- Be aware of your body language, relax your shoulders, smile and try to project enthusiasm.

- Relax and use natural movements. Engage with your audience but do not invade their personal space.

- Make eye contact with all the people in the room early in the presentation – get them on your side.

- Face your audience rather than the screen. If you are able to, determine where each member of the team presenting and the audience will sit.

- Never turn your back to the audience.

- Do not hide behind lecterns and A4 notes.

- Use cue cards if necessary, do not try to ad-lib unless you are well rehearsed. Be aware of your strengths and limitations and do not let your ego conflict with professionalism.

- Provide handouts for your audience of the slides, tables and graphs that may be hard to read.

- If working with a team of presenters, make sure that you support them. When you are not presenting, maintain a positive attitude and listen to the rest of the team. If a team member falters or technology is causing problems, act to sort out the situation. Do not sit there thinking, 'thank goodness that is not me'. You will be judged by the performance of the team as a whole.

- Keep to time and take responsibility for your own timings. Some audiences for competitive pitches will stop a presentation if it overruns.

- Use pictures, video and audio clips to enliven and add variety to the presentation, but do not make a presentation overbusy.

- Research has shown that people forget 30% of what they are told after just three hours and 90% is forgotten after only three days. Visual aids can help and variety is the key. The combination of verbal

and visual material has been shown to deliver 85% recollection after three hours and up to 65% after three days.

- Almost all presentations are made using PowerPoint, and the lack of pacing and variety often creates a very flat atmosphere and passive audience. This is often the case as projection equipment may mean that the lights have to be dimmed and the audience sink into a soporific state. Popcorn might be a more appropriate snack than the executive biscuit selection. Liven it up by using a variety of support and dynamic pacing through the presentation – rather than trying to compensate by overly using graphics (slide transitions, animations etc).

- Practise, practise, practise, and remember 'fail to prepare, prepare to fail'.

- Make sure you carry out a 'dress' rehearsal. Practise speaking out loud.

- Practise all aspects of the presentation including the transition between speakers and the use of supporting technology or audio-visual aids.

- It may help to record your rehearsal and pick up your verbal tics, the 'you knows', the 'hums' and the 'yes's'. Knowing that you have these verbal tics can help control them. Practise volume and pace and the use of silence.

- Tell them what you will tell them, tell them and tell them what you have told them.

- Structure the presentation by using staging posts and summarising slides to close sections and introduce new sections.

- Always start and finish on a high note.

ACTIVITY 8.3

Aside from PowerPoint, what other presentation software is available?

▶ **Assessment tip**

On occasion an assignment task will ask for a PowerPoint presentation and accompanying speaker notes. These should be compelling in their own right but ultimately convincing when viewed and read together. Take on board and apply all of the hints, tips and techniques outlined above here.

CHAPTER ROUNDUP

- If our cases are written in a report or presented in person, we must remember that we are pitching for the initiation of our projects.

- Care, dedication and rigour must be employed and aligned with confidence, ambition and passion.

FURTHER READING

Collier, P.M. (2006) *Accounting for Managers*. 2nd edition. Chichester, Wiley.

Peter, J.P. and Olson, J.C. (2010) *Consumer Behaviour and Marketing Strategy*. 9th edition. London, McGraw-Hill.

REFERENCES

Bower, M. and Garda, R. A. (1985) The Role of Marketing in Management. *The McKinsey Quarterly*, Autumn, pp34-46.

Wilson, A. (2006) *Marketing Research, An Integrated Approach*. 2nd edition. Harlow, Prentice Hall.

QUICK QUIZ

1   List five reasons why people might ask questions when attending a presentation.

2   Name five models that could be used to present data or findings.

3   Name three reasons that may motivate audience members to attend a presentation.

4   Name four qualities that any presentation should have.

5   How can content be used to clarify a core message?

ACTIVITY DEBRIEFS

Activity 8.1

The answer to this depends upon your own experiences.

Activity 8.2

We had in mind a situation when the researcher is conducting qualitative research, particularly focus groups and also when an agency first presents its proposal to a client in a beauty parade.

The Chartered
Institute of Marketing

Activity 8.3

A simple browser search will identify the following open source presentation software: Corel, Google Docs, Kingsoft Office, LibreOffice, OpenOffice, SlideRocket, Apple Keynote and Prezi.

QUICK QUIZ ANSWERS

1   To seek additional information, to seek clarification, to add information, to lead the discussion into another area, to display their own cleverness, to undermine the speaker.

2   Product life cycle, Porter's five forces, Shell Directional, Ansoff matrix and diffusion of innovation.

3   They need specific information, they are interested in the topic or they may be obliged to be in attendance.

4   Interest, congeniality, credibility and accessibility.

5   Practical examples, anecdotes, rhetoric, explanation and definition.

Section 2:

Senior Examiner's comments

This section of the syllabus develops the case further by assessing the organisational potential and the impacts and implications on capabilities and resources. Whereas, at Level 3, the emphasis is on introducing the notion of control and then at Level 4, developing the imperative further, here we go much deeper. Building cases from a project management perspective is the ultimate control mechanism.

Candidates need to understand now that practicing marketers are judged by their decision-making and recommendations and are accountable for the associated outcomes. This is all about rigour and the courage of conviction. Marketing students and practitioners can be ultimately more courageous when in possession of a justified case.

Students must recognise and define via SMART criteria the deliverables to be achieved while at the same time recognising that control mechanisms are introduced from the outset and not as a 'bolt-on'. It is, therefore, necessary to express the vision in core terms of customers, management and profit. A point of note here is that 'profit' can be defined from a number of perspectives and does not exclusively relate to financial standards. What determines the definition is the nature and scope of the project.

Within the section, a framework exists for building the case and a sequenced approach maintains the mantra of 'limiting the risk of failure'. In other words, the evidence has been collected and synthesised. Now, it must be prepared and cross-examined. If a case exists, it can be presented. If it does not, more evidence is required.

Candidates are expected to evaluate relevant customer segments and clusters, critically rank and identify where the greatest impact exists and ensure that any given project fits within the mindset of the customer relative to the competition.

There needs to be recognition of the availability of scant resources, and the aspect here is to examine the structure, competence and capability of the organisation to implement and deliver. Having determined this, the student can recommend an operational fit that becomes the vehicle by which the objectives are met. This will necessitate the adaptation of the extended marketing mix to be compatible with the proposed project.

With this in place, operational budgets can be formulated that outline the resources required and projected returns. It is important here to be as accurate and detailed as possible. The detail of this analysis will justify the case.

At this level, there is no option for sitting on the fence and the examining team will be looking for a structured approach to building business cases.

As in Section 1, the presentation of the case is key and the formalised report should reflect this in a highly professional document.

From an assessment perspective, there are two aspects that are important.

First, where customers, management and profit are concerned, it is essential that formal SMART objectives are developed and associated projections and budgets presented. Without these value creating statements (both operational and financial), it is unlikely that any case would be justified or acceptable.

Second, but not exclusively, core recommendations should be grounded in the fundamental principles of segmentation, targeting and positioning. Value-creating solutions must be interdependent and compatible with context and resources. A cohesive and coherent operational fit within these core areas will be rewarded.

A core understanding of, and the ability to apply, traditional forecasting, extrapolation and budgeting tools for both investment and income/profit in any given context is imperative here.

Section 3:

Assessing, managing and mitigating risk associated with marketing projects (weighting 25%)

CHAPTERS

Chapter 9 – Identifying risk

Chapter 10 – Risk assessment and evaluation

Chapter 11 – Risk management and mitigation

LEARNING OBJECTIVES

By the end of this section, you will be able to:

- Evaluate risk assessments across a variety of marketing project contexts
- Evaluate different types of organisational risk
- Analyse and assess the sources and impacts of risk
- Develop a risk management programme
- Evaluate different approaches to mitigate risk
- Develop a range of methods for controlling risk

SYLLABUS REFERENCES

3.1 Critically evaluate the importance of developing an understanding of risk assessments in organisations in order to protect long-term stability of a range of marketing projects

3.2 Critically evaluate the differences between the common types of organisational risk

3.3 Analyse and assess the potential sources of risk, of both internal and external origins, directly related to a specific case and consider the impact of these risks on the organisation

3.4 Design a risk management programme appropriate to measuring the impact of risk in the context of marketing projects

3.5 Undertake risk assessments on marketing projects and assess the impact of short/long-term tactical changes to the marketing plan

3.6 Critically evaluate the different approaches organisations can take to mitigate risk in order to reduce its potential to harm the organisation or its reputation

3.7 Critically assess the strategic impact of implementing proposed risk control measures versus the strategic impact of taking no action

3.8 Develop a range of methods for monitoring, reporting and controlling risk on an ongoing basis for project implementation

CHAPTER 9

Identifying risk

Introduction

Risk is an inevitable part of life. To remove risk from our life and to live life fully is impossible. For most of us, the assessment and management of risk occurs almost subconsciously and draws on our experience and the application of commonsense.

In the world of business, future events cannot be foretold with certainty. The confidence with which forecasts can be made varies from very high to nil, depending on the matter under consideration. Nevertheless, plans must be made. A consideration of possible future events is thus fundamental to management. Some of the variation in potential outcomes is taken for granted in the normal process of business planning and budgeting. For example, circumstances and business conditions may result in a 5 or 10% difference between actual sales and the budgeted sales without any major consequences for the sales team or the organisation. However, a difference of 60 or 70% would be likely to have major consequences and it would be appropriate for the Sales Director to understand in advance the circumstances that might bring about such a difference, their likely further implications and what, if anything, should be done about them.

Thus, if the occurrence of a possible future event is capable of statistical or mathematical evaluation, we may reasonably speak in terms of risk. If no such evaluation is possible, we are dealing with uncertainty.

This definition of risk is clearly most relevant where clear statistical records of past events can be used. Also, it assumes that the future will resemble the past, an idea that should always be treated with caution. In practice, the distinction between risk and uncertainty is not clear. Major insurance losses demonstrate that assessments of risk have been undermined by unexpected events such as floods, and health claims arising from the use of asbestos in the past.

Despite the use of the term 'risk', businesses actually operate under uncertainty. A marketing team that only proposed strategies with precisely quantifiable risk would not launch new products, enter new markets, or develop new technologies.

Topic list

What is risk?	1
Risk in the context of project management	2
Risks versus threats	3
Perspectives on risk	4
Risk and management culture	5
Types of risk	6
Overall risk	7
Risks and the marketing plan	8

Syllabus references

3.1	Critically evaluate the importance of developing an understanding of risk assessments in organisations in order to protect long-term stability of a range of marketing projects:
	■ Definition of risk
	■ Risk perspective
	■ Probability management
	■ Risk culture
	■ Strategic management
3.2	Critically evaluate the differences between the following types of organisational risk:
	■ Strategic
	■ Operational
	■ Financial
	■ Knowledge
	■ Compliance
	■ Project-based areas of risk

> ▶ **Key terms**
>
> **Risk** is measurable by considering the way in which past data varies. For example, records will tell us the number of life assurance policyholders that survive beyond the age of 65.
>
> **Uncertainty** is not quantifiable in this way. For example, we cannot say whether a given policyholder will survive beyond the age of 65, or even until next week.
>
> **Risk perspective** simply means taking a **measured view** of both the probability of an undesirable future event and its potential impact as already outlined. In broad terms, it is only if both probability and potential impact are of significant magnitude that extensive risk management effort becomes appropriate.
>
> **Business risk** is about the variability of returns traceable to the way a business operates.

In marketing and business, the ability to assess, manage and mitigate risk has never been more important. Over the next few years, as we leave a period of high growth in many sectors, during which many of us have seen marketing budgets increase alongside sales, and enter a recession widely feared to be the worst for several generations, the need to manage the risks that might threaten the successful delivery of marketing projects becomes more important. There are many examples of the failure to manage risks effectively.

Remember that the ability to assess risk and to react effectively is fundamental, not just within project management, but as a basic prerequisite for business survival.

Let us look at a few examples of what can go right and what can go wrong.

The example below (The Real World) refers to a promotional campaign where the purchase of a new Hoover vacuum cleaner gave 'free flights'. The value of such flights was often greater than the cost of the cleaner, and many bought them simply to reduce their travel costs. The company was taken to court when it tried to find legal loopholes that reduced its liability, but the courts found in the favour of those who had bought the product in good faith.

Hoover Sucks

'The Hoover promotion has been described as "Britain's worst marketing disaster" and one that promoters should have learned from. The results of this promotion could have and should have been easily avoided if the risk management industry's advice had been adhered to and the promoter had incorporated necessary risk management steps when the promotion was first put together'.

(Brand Republic, 2004)

The web link in the References section of this chapter leads to a short article that looks at the lack of even basic risk management at the time. The consequences were that Hoover eventually spent '£48 million' in response to thousands of irate customers (Chan, 2004).

Ask yourself the following: What went wrong? Why?

ACTIVITY 9.1

The records of Palindrome Limited indicate that its fleet of delivery vans has suffered the total loss of 14 vehicles over the last seven years. During that period, turnover has increased by 350%, road vehicle registrations in its region have increased by 84% and annual average mileage per van has increased by 35%.

How many total losses should the transport manager budget for in the coming year?

HBOS

In the years leading up to the global financial crisis of 2008, the mistakes made at HBOS were much simpler than the complicated array of toxic assets amassed in the profligate years. The business seems to have failed because it had inadequate corporate governance and a malfunctioning risk control process.

Lloyds Banking Group who purchased Bank of Scotland at the height of the crisis had to write off £20bn as a consequence of the absence of suitable risk assessment, mitigation and control.

Bank of Scotland broke a key corporate governance role that states organisations must have adequate risk management systems. In fact, a Financial Services Authority report into the affair highlighted the fact that risk management seemed to be a constraint to the firm as opposed to an integral part of its management systems. This went even further to suggest that senior management treated risk management with derision.

The results are still impacting the sector and the wider economy to the present day.

(Telegraph, 2012)

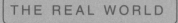

1 What is risk?

Chapman and Ward tell us that 'all projects involve risk – the zero risk project is not worth pursuing...some degree of risk is likely to yield a more desirable and appropriate level of return for the resources committed to the venture' (Chapman and Ward, 2003).

Risk can be defined simply as hazard, or the possibility of experiencing loss or harm.

While this is common sense, it is clear that the level of risk and the nature of the rewards from risk avoidance or management will vary according to the project that is being undertaken. There are degrees of risk, and the ability or willingness to experience risk occurs often in relation to the reward that is available from exposing ourselves to that risk.

The risk attached to crossing the road is far less than a tightrope walker using a tightrope to cross the same road. Equally, if I was crossing the road to ask a stranger for the time, I would be less inclined to take that risk than if the person on the opposite side were a friend I had not seen for ages and who owed me money!

This can be expressed graphically in a simplistic form (Figure 9.1).

Figure 9.1   Risk and return

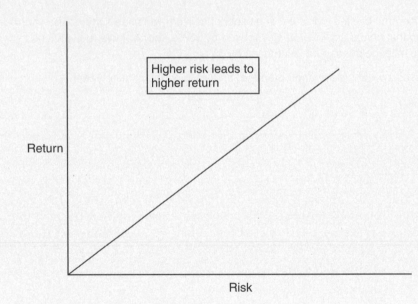

However, this is an oversimplification of the facts; there is always an optimal balance between the rate of return and risk. The representation below comes closer to the truth (Figure 9.2).

Figure 9.2 Risk and relative return

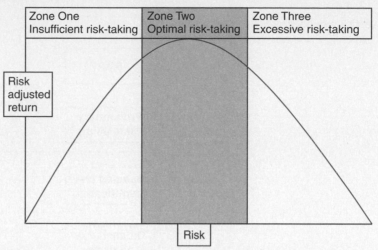

(Adapted from Lam, 2003)

So, a clear principle is established early on. We need to assess risk and weigh up the impact of that risk in accordance with the likelihood of the perceived risk being actually experienced and in the light of the potential rewards available to us.

Lewis (2007) defines risk simply as 'anything that can go wrong with a project'.

Gardiner in his book on project management contrasts between two definitions; the first his own:

'An event with an undesirable outcome for the project that may happen sometime in the future' (Gardiner, 2005).

He contrasts this with the Project Management Institute's (PMI) definition that describes risk as:

'An uncertain event or condition that, if it occurs, has a positive or negative effect on a project outcome' (PMI, 2000 cited in Gardiner, 2005).

This can be set against the Association of Project Management's (APM) definition of risk as 'an uncertain event or set of circumstances that should it occur will have an effect on the achievement of the projects objectives' (APM, 2007 cited in Chapman and Ward, 2003).

---

2 Risk in the context of project management

Risk is inevitable in projects and needs to be managed in a positive way. There are some specific factors that are commonly associated with high risk.

- Organisational issues (such as attitude to change)
- Management structure (poor communications, undefined responsibilities for example)
- Team composition and level of expertise
- Type of project (R&D and IT projects are particularly risky)
- Projects involving unproven technology
- Inadequate resources
- Fast-tracked projects (timescale involved)
- Complex projects with inherent risks (eg legal, political, safety)

The following diagram illustrates the process of project management and how risk is managed throughout it.

Figure 9.3   Project risk management

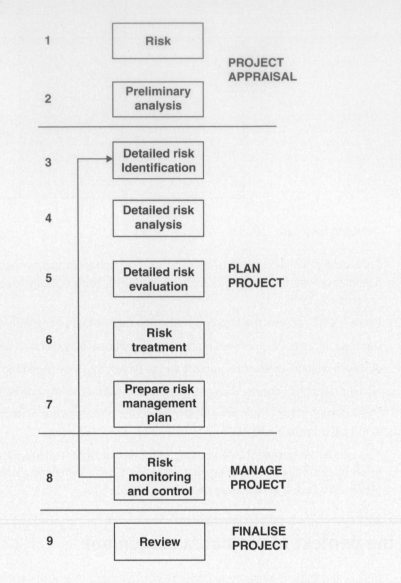

3 Risks versus threats

Earlier in the workbook, you will have seen the use of SWOT. Lewis reminds us that there is a difference between threats and risk. 'Risks are things that can happen without having any deliberate intention to cause harm' (Lewis, 2007). This means that threats are something that is done by a competitor to interfere actively to compromise your business goals. Risks may include acts of God, fire, flood etc, accidents, financial problems, staffing issues, the impact of technology breakthroughs or the output of political change.

ACTIVITY 9.2

List three specific threats and three specific risks relevant to your organisation.

4 Perspectives on risk

The perception of risk varies according to organisational culture and the markets in which they operate. In the last six months, we have seen companies like RBS and HBOS reaping the effects of a bullish approach to the identification and acceptance of risk. The commentary has focused on the failure of risk management in these organisations in comparison with other companies operating in the same sector.

To be fair, these organisations were responding to a variety of factors operating in the market and with the benefit of hindsight, it is easy to say that they were reckless. Six months ago however, the same commentators were praising the strategies pursued by these companies and marking their share prices up to record levels.

The process of identifying, assessing and managing risk works at many levels and risk can be experienced at any level within the organisation.

It is tempting to try to proceed on the basis that risk and, therefore, undesirable events can be entirely avoided. This is, however, unrealistic: some risk will always be present no matter what precautions may be taken. Also, the avoidance of risk imposes costs and it is a simple principle that costs and benefits should be balanced. Simple precautions will generally have a major impact on risk but the law of diminishing returns is likely to apply: each further reduction in risk is likely to be more expensive to achieve than the previous one. It is important, therefore, that both organisations and individuals should establish a realistic **risk perspective**.

In a business context it is important to remember that risk and reward are usually linked: projects offering higher potential rewards are usually riskier than those offering more modest returns (though high risk linked to low return is not unknown).

A company's desire to increase the returns it achieves may incline it to take on extra risk. We may thus say that risk appetite or risk tolerance varies.

5 Risk and management culture

Miles and Snow (2003) analysed a sample of large corporations. They suggest that superior performance is associated with consistency in mission and values; strategies; and characteristics and behaviour. Attitude to risk is relevant to all of these things. Miles and Snow concluded that there are four types of business, defined by the ways in which their management approach strategic challenges.

- Defenders
- Prospectors
- Analysers
- Reactors

Of the four types identified, the first three may exhibit superior performance. Reactors tend to perform less well.

5.1 Defenders – low risk tolerance

Defenders concentrate on a single core technology and a specific product or service They are often vertically integrated. They tend to have strong finances and a stable structure. The efficiency of their internal processes gives them a competitive advantage, which they maintain by incremental improvements.

Defenders perform best in stable markets with high barriers to entry. They grow cautiously and incrementally. They have a narrow area of operations and tend not to look for business opportunities outside their sphere of expertise, preferring to increase the depth of their skills within their current markets.

The risk tolerance of such businesses is consequently quite low.

5.2 Prospectors – seeking risk

Prospectors are very different from defenders. They are entrepreneurial innovators and pursue new products and markets aggressively. They continually search for potential responses to emerging trends and maintain a flexibility to respond to change. Their innovations cause change and uncertainty to which their competitors must respond.

Prospectors are risk-seekers, willing to take on the risks associated with new developments in order to benefit from them.

5.3 Analysers – balancing risk and return

Analysers balance the risk-avoidance attitude of the defenders and the risk-seeking attitude of prospectors. They innovate more deliberately than prospectors, observing market reaction to new developments and analysing the key success factors of any new opportunity before committing themselves. When they launch new products, they aim to achieve a high level of efficiency in order to build and maintain market share. It is these products that tend to be the major revenue generators.

Analysers operate in two product/market areas. In the stable areas, analysers perform as defenders, using efficient structures and processes to achieve high returns. In the changing area they act more like prospectors, adapting to any promising changes.

Analysers cannot be said to be risk-averse, but they minimise risk where they can.

5.4 Reactors – inconsistent attitude to risk

Reactors do not have any consistent or clearly defined strategy or effectively managed supporting technology, structure, and processes. They are inconsistent and ineffective in their responses to environmental developments, seldom making changes until forced to do so.

Reactors generally fail to manage risk sensibly, avoiding the obvious risks, which undermines their strategic development, and failing to detect more fundamental and threatening risks.

5.5 Other influences on risk appetite

Other factors may influence the organisation's risk appetite:

- **Expectations of shareholders**: a long history of stable performance will attract risk-averse investors.

- **National origin of the organisation**: the appetite for change and desire for stability vary somewhat from place to place.

- **Regulatory framework**: many organisations must implement a wide range of regulations designed to minimise various aspects of risk. Airlines are an example: they must minimise the exposure of passengers to risk.

- **Nature of ownership**: managers of state-owned enterprises gain little from successfully making risky ventures but they will lose heavily if they make unsuccessful ones. Similarly, a family firm may be prevented from risk-taking by the influence or dependence of family members.

- **Personal views**: surveys suggest that managers obtain emotional satisfaction from successful risk-taking. This has been attributed in part to the fact that, unlike shareholders, they will not suffer a loss of wealth if their gambles fail.

Under each of these factors, outline the prevailing culture and appetite on risk within your organisation.

THE REAL WORLD

Ultimately, all harmful events have financial consequences. For example, the oil leak from the Deepwater Horizon rig in the Gulf of Mexico in 2010 has cost BP dearly, both in terms of financial resources and its reputation. The oil leak was triggered by an explosion at the rig. Before the explosion, senior managers at Transocean (from whom BP leased the rig) had complained BP was taking short cuts in some of its operating routines and in doing so increasing the risk of such a disaster occurring.

(BBC, 2012)

---

6 Types of risk

Business risk can be analysed into three main areas: strategic, operational and financial.

6.1 Strategic risks

Strategic risks are those relating to projects concerning the strategic orientation of the organisation within its environment, and are concerned with the management of the long-term direction of the organisation.

You should be familiar with the Ansoff matrix. At the heart of this strategic tool is an assessment of the risk relating to strategic options (Table 9.1).

Table 9.1   Risk and the Ansoff matrix

	Existing markets	New markets
Existing products	Market Penetration Lower risk 1	Market Development Higher risk 4
New products	Product Development Higher risk 2	Diversification Highest risk 16

(Adapted from Ansoff growth matrix, 1957)

The evidence here is that for one of the most basic tools for determining the marketing strategy, risk is at its heart. However, the strategic management of risk is not often seen as a key marketing skill.

Strategic risk is associated with wider environmental factors that affect the long-term strategic objectives of the business. The business is vulnerable to developments relating to, for instance, competitors, customers, reputation, law, regulation, economic conditions and politics. Strategic risk also encompasses risk relating to knowledge resources, including intellectual property, key personnel and production technology.

A strategic approach to risk should have the following impacts:

- Speed-up the process of delivery of new marketing initiatives.
- Enhance upside value of marketing projects.
- Provide a case for budget allocation.
- Improve the process and output of planning at strategic, tactical and operational level.

6.2 Operational risks

Operational risk arises from the effectiveness of day-to-day management and control systems and structures in dealing with such matters as health and safety, consumer protection and data security. **Compliance risk** is the kind of operational risk associated with non-compliance with laws or regulations. This includes breaches by both the company and by a stakeholder, such as a customer or supplier, that have consequences for the company.

6.3 Financial risks

Financial risk arises from the way the business is financed. Its level of **gearing** (the ratio between loan capital and share capital) is particularly important, since interest on loans must be paid even when times are hard, while dividends on shares can be reduced or missed altogether. Also important are exposure to credit risk; interest and exchange rates; and liquidity risks. Financial risk tends to amplify the inherent business risk at low levels of gearing, and at higher levels may directly contribute to the risk of business failure. Other associated risks can also become apparent.

6.4 Knowledge risks

The ability to capture and act on knowledge relating to the successful delivery of the project is central to its successful implementation.

6.5 Compliance risks

Risks may relate to compliance with regulatory framework, codes of conduct or legislation.

6.6 Project-based risks

There is a range of risks relating to the planning process itself.

The Chartered Institute of Marketing

7 Overall risk

The *International Risk Standard* shows these types of risk diagrammatically.

Figure 9.4   Risk management standard

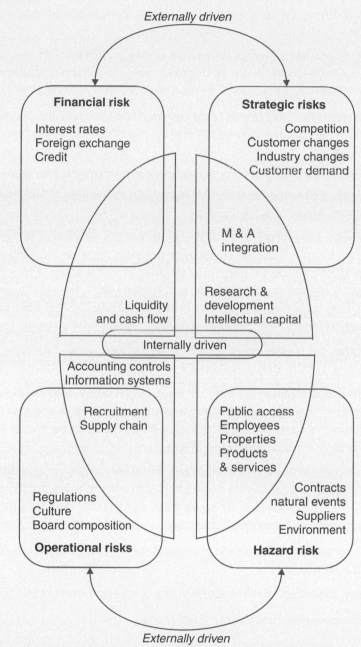

(Institute of Risk Management – A risk management standard)

8 Risks and the marketing plan

The creation, execution, control and monitoring of the marketing plan has the characteristics of a major project. Risk can be identified, assessed and controlled at all stages of the plan, from the analysis of the environment, its impact on objective setting, the development of strategy and the tactical mix around this to the key areas of monitoring control and contingency. The ability to manage this process is a core competence for marketing managers.

Typically, the planning process is managed to deliver value to customers who give us something in return, often money, but occasionally we are looking for a change in behaviour or attitudes. For example, governments spend money on marketing to get people to live a healthier lifestyle, to pay their taxes and drive safely.

Planning reconciles the interests of the customer base, the activities of the management responsible for execution of the plan and delivers the desired output from this interaction, typically expressed in terms of profit or value creation.

These phrases may bring to mind the definition of marketing by CIM and the American Marketing Association: 'Marketing is the management process responsible for identifying, anticipating and satisfying customer requirements profitably' (CIM, 2010).

CIM describes marketing as both a concept dedicated to meeting customer requirements and a range of techniques, which enables the company to determine those requirements and ensure that they are met. The output of these processes is a mutually satisfying exchange of value. This is better expressed in the AMA's (American Marketing Association's) definition: 'Marketing is the activity, set of institutions, and processes for creating, communicating, delivering, and exchanging offerings that have value for customers, clients, partners, and society at large'.

The fact that risk is experienced at many different levels, as we have seen above, means that the classification of risk under those related to customer, management and the outcome in terms of profit is useful.

Risks affecting the interaction with customers can be experienced at all levels within the planning process. At a strategic level, they may be related to the effort to exploit new markets or develop new products, rebranding or repositioning the brand. At a tactical level, it may relate to an element of the mix, for example, a failure in service delivery or inappropriate use of data.

The assessment of risk within the plan and the implementation of contingency plans are assessed later in this module. Clearly, changes to the marketing plan in order to avoid or mitigate risk place demands on the resource base of the business. This may mean that financial resources are needed to mitigate the effects of risk or that different management skills are required to manage the issues that emerge.

Risk assessment should also include an assessment of the competences of the management team required to deliver the plan.

Ultimately, the impact of risk is assessed in a commercial environment in terms of impact on the bottom line.

As the Financial Reporting Council (FRC) states:

> 'A company's objectives, its internal organisation and the environment in which it operates are continually evolving and, as a result, the risks it faces are continually changing. A sound system of internal control therefore depends on a thorough and regular evaluation of the nature and extent of the risks to which the company is exposed. Since profits are, in part, the reward for successful risk-taking in business, the purpose of internal control is to help manage and control risk appropriately rather than to eliminate it' (FRC, 2005).

We will see later the techniques for assessing the profit impact of risk assessment and the impact of management and mitigation.

The Chartered
Institute of Marketing

Risk can therefore be assessed at many different levels and because of organisational complexity, a range of services exist to help the risk assessment planning process. For example, Price Waterhouse Cooper has a bespoke system for providing risk analysis for its customers.

▶ **Assessment tip**

It is always important to highlight the shortfalls in organisational appreciation and understanding of risk. Classification of the different types of risk will often be sought and it is imperative that candidates have a sound understanding and appreciation in this area.

CHAPTER ROUNDUP

- In this chapter we concentrated on the very important aspect for organisations of risk awareness.

- We looked at the core elements involved in the identification of risk and the different types and nature of risk.

- We also highlighted the fact that a culture of risk understanding must be nurtured and promoted within the modern organisation.

FURTHER READING

Chapman, C.B. and Ward, S.C. (2011) *How to Manage Project Opportunity and Risk: Why Uncertainty Management Can be a Much Better Approach Than Risk Management*. 3rd edition. Chichester, John Wiley and Sons.

REFERENCES

Aldrick, P. (2012) *The HBOS horror story is a grim read*. TNG, http://www.telegraph.co.uk/finance/newsbysector/banksandfinance/9135277/The-HBOS-horror-story-is-a-grim-read.html# [Accessed 30 May 2012].

Anon. (2012) *BP must cover some Transocean liabilities for oil spill*. BBC, http://www.bbc.co.uk/news/business-16753061 [Accessed 13 June 2012].

Ansoff, I. (1957) Strategies for Diversification. *Harvard Business Review*, Sept-Oct, pp113-124.

Chapman, C.B. and Ward, S.C. (2003) *Project risk management: Process, techniques and insights*. 2nd edition. Chichester, John Wiley and Sons.

Chan, A. (2004) *Hoover's free flights fiasco recalled*. BBC, http://news.bbc.co.uk/1/hi/business/3704669.htm [Accessed 23 June 2012].

Gardiner, P.D. (2005) *Project Management*. Hampshire, Palgrave Macmillan.

Kimber, M. (2004) *Still a lot to learn from the Hoover free flights fiasco*. Brand Republic. www.brandrepublic.com/News/210917/lot-learn-Hoover-free-flights-fiasco/ [Accessed 23 June 2012].

Lam, J. (2003) *Enterprise Risk Management: From incentives to controls*. New Jersey, Wiley Hoboken.

Lewis, J.P. (2007) *Mastering Project Management, Applying Advanced Concepts to Systems Thinking, Control & Evaluation, Resource Allocation*. 2nd edition. New York, McGraw Hill.

Miles, R. and Snow, S. (2003) *Organisation Strategy, Structure and Process*, Stanford, Stanford Business Classics.

The Chartered Institute of Marketing

1   What are the main categories of risk identified in the International Risk Standard?

2   Identify the four descriptions of management attitudes to strategic risk identified by Miles and Snow.

3   Define a realistic risk perspective.

4   What other types of risk can you categorise?

5   In terms of risk and the marketing planning process, what can a plan reconcile?

ACTIVITY DEBRIEFS

Activity 9.1

This is a very difficult question to answer. There is wealth of statistical information that would permit the calculation of past rates of loss, but they all produce different answers. The most useful pieces of information, which are the number of losses, the average size of the fleet and the average mileage per vehicle in the preceding year are not given. Presumably the transport manager would have these figures available. We do not, so, despite the information given, we can do no more than guess.

Activity 9.2

Threats might include any significant change in the political, economic or social dynamic and risks might include any significant change in the operational finances, human resources or internal systems and processes within your organisation.

Activity 9.3

This will be specific to your choice of organisation.

1   Hazard risk
       Strategic risk
       Financial risk
       Operational risk

2   Prospectors
       Defenders
       Analysers
       Reactors

3   Taking a measured view of both the probability of an undesirable future event and its potential impact.

4   Project, compliance and knowledge.

5   Interests of customers, management activities and desired outcomes.

CHAPTER 10

Risk assessment and evaluation

Introduction

Whatever the risks an organisation experiences, they all have certain characteristics:

- They exist in the future and we can moderate the future effect by analysis of past events.
- They are wholly or partially unknown.
- They are not constant in that they change over time and in relation to context.
- Their impact may be managed, moderated, removed or controlled.
- They are ubiquitous to all projects.

Risk management has become an important area for marketing. The nature of marketing projects as we have seen has changed and many of these involve a very high degree of resource commitment, for example, the development of a Customer Relationship Management (CRM) system or the development of international operations. The need for marketing to be accountable at all times has become paramount, and calculating and managing exposure to risk and the potential returns on activity is a characteristic of good marketing management.

The management of risk has been described as the new Total Quality Management (TQM), and it is true to say that the management of risk and the attendant benefits from the effective delivery of risk management is a key criterion against which effective marketing management is assessed.

The management of risk is a key driver of financial performance and can drive shareholder and stakeholder value. In doing so, it creates opportunities and stability for all those involved in the organisation.

Topic list

The risk management process	①
Other risk factors	②
Techniques for risk identification	③
Risk evaluation	④
Probability analyses	⑤

3.3	Analyse and assess the potential sources of risk, of both internal and external origins, directly related to a specific case and consider the impact of these risks on the organisation:
	■ Internal strategic, operational, financial and hazard
	■ External social, legal, economic, political and technological

1 The risk management process

> ▶ **Key terms**
>
> **Risk evaluation** is the process by which a business determines the significance of any risk and whether that risks needs to be addressed.
>
> **Risk assessment** is the determination of risk related to a concrete situation and a recognised threat (also called hazard).
>
> **Probability analysis**: the analysis of random phenomena.
>
> **Event tree analysis**: forward logic to construct a graphical representation of subsequent consequences.
>
> **Scenario planning** is a process of projecting what future conditions or events are probable, what their consequences or effects would be, and how to respond to, or benefit from them.

Gardiner (2005) says that risk planning can be divided into two phases: risk assessment and risk control.

Risk assessment includes:

■ Risk identification
■ Risk analysis
■ Risk prioritisation

Risk control includes:

■ Risk response planning
■ Risk resolution
■ Risk monitoring and reporting

Other frameworks are more complex, but they all involve the following stages:

■ The monitoring, identification of risk or risk audit

■ The evaluation, classification and assessment of risk

– Qualitative assessment
– Quantitative assessment

■ The management or treatment of risk

■ Risk review and reporting

THE REAL WORLD

PWC

From a risk assessment perspective, PWC's web based Risk Culture Survey (RCS), allows for the identification and consideration of key attributes of effective risk management in the following areas:

Leadership and strategy – In terms of ethics, values and corporate communications
Accountability and reinforcement – In terms of responsibility, review and reward
People and development – In terms of recruitment, training and knowledge transfer
Risk management and infrastructure – In terms of evaluation, mitigation and control

Here are some of the common issues uncovered by client RCS:

1 Risk awareness
2 Understanding risk
3 Impact of risk
4 Lack of control
5 Lack of training

 The Chartered Institute of Marketing

1.1 Identifying sources of risk, the risk auditing process

Where does risk come from? There are several useful frameworks that can be applied to the identification and assessment of risk in marketing projects. Chapman and Ward use the 6Ws framework as a starting point to help the identification of risks (Table 10.1).

Table 10.1   Chapman and Ward 6Ws framework

Who:	Are the parties involved?
What:	What are the parties interested in?
Wherewithal:	What resources are required?
Why:	What do they want to achieve?
Which way:	How is it to be done?
When:	When does it have to be done?

(Chapman and Ward, 2003)

Each of these aspects fits within the broader project management process that we have seen earlier in the workbook. At its simplest, the three-stage SHAMPU model, **Shape**, **Harness** and **Manage**, highlights risks of different types with different degrees of severity and with a different range of potential outcomes (Figure 10.1).

Figure 10.1   Uncertainty and risk at each stage of the project life cycle

Conception	Level of project definition Definition of appropriate performance objectives Stakeholder expectations
Design	Novelty of design and technology
Plan the execution strategically	Regulatory constraints Milestone management and concurrency of activities Capturing dependency relationships Errors and omissions
Allocate resources tactically	Adequate resource estimates
	Estimating resources required Defining responsibilities Defining contractual terms and conditions Selection of capable participants
Execute production	Exercise adequate co-ordination and control Determine level and scope of control systems Ensuring effective communications between partners Ensure effective leadership Ensure continuity in personnel and responsibilities
Deliver the project	Adequate testing Adequate training Managing stakeholder expectations Obtaining licences
Review the process	Capturing corporate knowledge Learning Understanding success
Support the ongoing implementation	Organise Identity liabilities Manage expectations

A risk plan will take in to account the following risk categories:

- Risks that exist and are controlled and managed within the project being undertaken

- Risks in the external environment, whose resolution depends on decisions being taken that rest largely outside our immediate control

- Risks that are wholly uncontrollable such as natural disasters

In 2011, Ernst & Young published a survey on sources of risk. It consolidated these into strategic risk radar, and this is summarised in the table below

Table 10.2

Macro threats
Energy shocks
Global financial shocks
Operational threats
Poor execution of strategic decisions
Cost inflation
Sector threats
Inability to respond to sector consolidation or transition
Regulatory and compliance risk
Inability to capitalise on emerging market opportunity
Ageing consumers and workforce
Radical greening
Consumer demand shifts
The next five years
War for talent
Pandemic
Private equity rise
Inability to innovate
China setback

(Ernst & Young, 2011)

Of course, this table focuses on the potential sources of risk for larger businesses; however, some of the categories are relevant for all businesses including SMEs.

Risks that relate to marketing projects may include the above and perhaps some of the following:

1.1.1 Political risks

Political risk is largely concerned with the possibility of a change of government. Most developed nations offer a reasonably stable political environment, though they may present important risks in relation to such matters as tax rates; building and other development policy and regulation; and labour law. Less developed countries may present enhanced risk of rapid change in government policy. The areas of policy that most commonly present risk are discussed below.

- **Import quotas** limit the quantity of goods that a subsidiary can buy from its parent company and import for resale.

- **Import tariffs** make imports more expensive and domestically produced goods, therefore, become more competitive.

- **Exchange control regulations** can complicate or prevent the remittance of profits.

- **Nationalisation** of foreign-owned companies and their assets, with or without compensation, may be a threat.

- **Legal standards** relating to safety or quality can be deliberately used as non-tariff barriers to imports.

- **Laws relating to ownership** could restrict the ability of foreign companies to buy domestic companies, even on a partnership or minority basis. This is especially relevant to companies that operate in politically sensitive industries such as defence contracting, communications, energy supply and so on.

1.1.2 Business and economic factors

Business operations are heavily influenced by economic fundamentals such as the availability of resources and the operation of market forces. Linked to this is the effect of government attempts at macro-economic management. Several sources of risk can be identified. Developments in any may create sources of risk.

- The **economic cycle** typically varies between benign and difficult trading conditions. Different countries may be at different stages of the cycle at any one time.

- **Monetary, fiscal and exchange rate policies** differ both internationally and from time-to-time within a single nation.

- **Labour force** capability, mobility and cost vary widely.

- **Economic infrastructure** such as transport links, training facilities and capital markets may or may not be adequately developed.

1.1.3 Trading risks

All traders will face trading risks, although those faced by companies trading internationally will generally be greater because of the increased distances and times involved.

- **Physical risk** is the risk of goods being lost or stolen in transit, or of the accompanying documents being lost.

- **Credit risk** is the possibility that the customer will fail to pay.

- **Trade risk** is the risk that the customer may refuse to accept delivery of the goods or cancel the order during transit.

- **Liquidity risk** is the risk of being unable to finance the trade credit required.

1.1.4 Social and cultural risk

Risks may need to be managed in connection with trends and developments relating to socio-cultural elements such as those listed below.

- Age and sex distribution of the population
- Geographic concentration of the population
- Ethnicity and religion
- Household and family structure: the accepted roles of the sexes may be particularly important
- Class
- Employment patterns
- Wealth distribution

 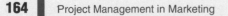

How might the geographic distribution of the population present risk?

1.1.5 Legal risk

Companies may be confronted with legislation or legal action that affects its activities. Some important topics are given below.

- The **general legal framework** relating to such matters as tort, agency and contract and product liability

- **Criminal law**, especially relating to such matters as insider trading, deception, product safety and industrial espionage

- **Monopolies, mergers, competition and restraint of trade** legislation

- **Property rights** including law relating to intellectual property

- **Taxation**

- **Marketing communications**, including restrictions on promotional messages, methods and media

Companies may also be at risk from inadequate legislation (or poor enforcement of legislation) that fails to protect them.

Legal penalties and accompanying bad publicity may have severe effects on businesses that fail to comply with the law. Legal standards and costs are particularly significant for companies trading internationally. Companies may relocate to countries with lower legal costs and regulatory burdens.

1.1.6 Technology

Technological change can present sources of risk affecting commercial organisations. The risks generally are of being too fast or too slow in exploiting the new technology. The most successful companies allow others to take the risks associated with breaking the new ground and move in when a successful launch seems likely. Risk arises from sources such as those shown below.

- The type of products or services that are made and sold.

- The way in which products are made (consider robots, new raw materials).

- The way in which services are provided. For example, companies selling easily transportable goods, such as books and CDs can offer much greater consumer choice and are enjoying considerable success over the internet.

- The way in which markets are identified. Database systems make it much easier to analyse the market-place.

- The way in which firms are managed. IT encourages delayering of organisational hierarchies, home working, and better communication.

- The means and extent of communications with external clients. Many services are now provided by telephone and online.

How might risk arise in connection with the way in which products are made?

1.1.7 Risks from IT systems

IT systems are particularly important sources of risk because of their vulnerability and importance to the organisation.

- **Natural threats** include fire, flood and electrical storms.

- **Human threats**: may be malicious or accidental. Politically inspired cyber-terrorism is a major risk.

- **Data systems integrity** may be compromised by such problems as incorrect entry of data, use of out-of-date files and loss of data through lack of back-ups.

- **Fraud** may be perpetrated by the dishonest use of a computer system.

- **Deliberate sabotage**

- **Viruses** and other malware can spread to all of the organisation's computers through the internet or through its own internal network. **Hackers** may be able to steal data or damage the system.

- **A denial of service attack** is an attempt by attackers to prevent legitimate users of a service from using it.

- **Non-compliance with regulations**: the use of IT systems, and the data they contain, is subject to close legal supervision in most countries.

THE REAL WORLD

Data Theft

In a digital era, all aspects of IT and web based security are imperative. The risk of systems infiltration, malware, viruses, and the increasing use of cloud based storage systems continues to keep the hackers salivating.

Risks such as 'denial of service' attacks that render a site useless with a bombardment of bogus requests, or cyber-attacks that kidnap home and information pages, continue to proliferate.

When this is also added to by careless use of social media, these manifest threats can be devastatingly effective. Mobility and tablet computing trends aggravate the situation also by placing data in circumstances that are poorly protected by most organisations. Consequently, the following risks are on the increase:

- Malicious sites hosting on compromised hosts
- Over 50% of all data theft is web based
- Malicious streaming media within social networks
- Incentivised lures
- Website redirects

(Websense, 2012)

The Chartered
Institute of Marketing

2 Other risk factors

- Business impact and benefits, for example, the strategic impact of projects, the level of stakeholder support and engagement.

- Risks may relate to standing or reputation, a loss of confidence in the organisation may seriously damage our ability to meet project objectives.

- Risks that relate to the organisation itself and the impact of the project on the organisation, which departments are involved, how well do they communicate, the level of political conflict and cultural issues.

- Risks inherent in the project itself, running overtime, poor-quality outputs, staff skills base, stakeholder attitudes.

- Testing, compliance and standards issues.

- Acts of God or natural disasters like floods, fires etc.

- Competitive threats, new entrants or supplier dominance may have a significant impact.

Identification of these risks is obviously project specific and the list above is not exhaustive. Once the risks have been identified, it is then necessary to evaluate the risks, and the first stage is to establish where and if they apply. Is the project particularly vulnerable to any of the risks identified and if so at what stage and to what extent? The precise evaluation and quantification of risk comes later in this section.

ACTIVITY 10.3

For any particular project you are familiar with, use one of the frameworks above to identify the risks that may affect the ability to complete the project.

3 Techniques for risk identification

The process of risk identification should follow a set procedure in a proactive way and be as comprehensive as possible. All relevant sources should be considered. These may include:

- Past project files
- Project planning documentation
- Risk checklists
- Feasibility reports
- Expert interviews
- Trade-off analyses

The major techniques for risk identification are listed below.

- Team briefings or risk clinics/brainstorming
- SWOT analyses
- Cause and effect diagrams
- Risk concepts mapping

3.1 Team briefings or risk clinics/brainstorming

Lewis in his book on project management talks about the technique he advises clients to use when trying to identify the risk attached to certain projects:

'I have them brainstorm a list of potential pitfalls and record them on a flip chart with no discussion or evaluation…I simply ask, What could go wrong that could impact schedule, cost performance or scope in the project' ? (Lewis, 2007)

The rules for successful brainstorming are:

- Facilitators should be chosen carefully
- All relevant parties should attend, this may mean 5–30 participants
- Have clear objectives without narrowing or biasing the scope of enquiry
- No idea is wrong; leaders should create a sense that everything is on the table and be inclusive
- Never judge at this stage
- Quantity is a virtue at this stage
- Build on discussions, make links and try to reach a position where every aspect of the issue has been explored
- Have an independent scribe to record the discussion
- Create a good physical environment – consider the room layout, a circle may be appropriate, heat, light and refreshments

Even at this stage, it may be helpful to begin the process of risk classification. Lock (2007) suggests that risks might be usefully grouped under the following headings:

1 Risks most likely to occur at the start of the process
2 Risks most likely to occur during execution
3 Risk that may affect the final stages of the project
4 Risks that occur on implementation
5 Risks that may affect the project at any stage

3.2 Cause and effect diagrams

Cause and effect diagrams are a useful way of looking at the range of risks and beginning to classify their potential impacts on the organisations concerned (Figure 10.2).

Figure 10.2   A cut down cause and effect diagram

Possible causes		Effect
Human Skills base lacking Skills shortage Limited training	**Organisational** No senior involvement in decision-making Interdepartmental conflict Poor briefing of external suppliers	Project overspend
Operational Failure to communicate Poor project management control systems Diverse teams	**Financial** Inadequate financial controls Poor management information	

The Chartered Institute of Marketing

The most common form of cause and effect diagram is the Ishikawa fishbone analysis. The diagram above could be presented in this way, with ever-increasing levels of analysis. For example, the Poor Management Information entry might have its own subsidiary causes, but ultimately, this produces a complex diagram (Figure 10.3).

Figure 10.3   Ishikawa fishbone diagram

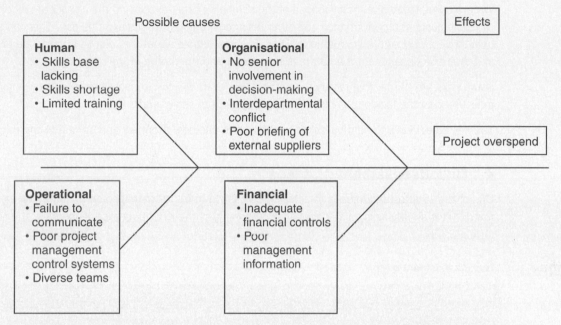

The strengths of the fishbone analysis are that they represent graphically and accessibly the drivers of risk.

The weakness is that they look at the output first and then try to understand what has caused this. In reality, the management of risk implies that we start by trying to isolate and manage the causes.

3.3 Risk concepts maps

A risk concept map is defined as 'a flow diagram designed to show in one picture the total risk scenario of a project or programme' (Bartlett, 2002 cited in Gardiner, 2005).

A risk concept map will contain key risk drivers, which create individual risk situations and associated impacts. Assumptions and reactions can also be included.

For example, the launch of a new international database system may include the following:

- The risk driver might be national cultural differences
- The risk situation might be inconsistencies in data capture and maintenance

The impacts may be:

- Marketing managers lose faith in the system
- Replica systems set up
- Data protection rules are broken

4 Risk evaluation

Once risks have been identified, then they need to be analysed for their impact, and there is a range of tools to help us with this task.

We are trying to predict the likelihood of the risk being experienced and the impact of risk on the project schedule costs and performance and other resources required to manage this risk. This can involve both qualitative and quantitative methods. There is some debate about the relative importance of these approaches and their use depends on the nature of the project and the nature of the risks.

Some risks are harder to quantify than others. For example, the impact of cost overruns maybe easier to measure than the lack of commitment to a project from senior staff.

The key objective is to help us prioritise risk and to allocate resources appropriate to the mitigation of that risk.

4.1 Risk assessment matrices

One of the simplest techniques to achieve the basic aim of risk management is to develop a risk assessment matrix. This simply assigns a score to the probability of the risk being experienced and the impact of this risk (Table 10.3).

Table 10.3   Risk assessment matrix

Probability		Impact		
		Low 1	Medium 2	High 3
Low	1	1	2	3
Medium	2	2	4	6
High	3	3	6	9

Each risk is put in one of the nine boxes; this is best done as a team as individuals will perceive risk differently.

The output helps assess the vulnerability of the project to risk. A high-risk project may have one or more risks evaluated at 9; a lower-risk project may have the majority of risks at fewer than 3.

The output of this is a simple formula:

risk exposure = probability of risk × impact.

4.2 Risk quantification

There are a number of quantification techniques for risk assessment.

The most commonly used are:

- Expected value
- Sensitivity analysis
- Monte Carlo simulations
- Failure mode effect criticality analysis
- PERT

4.2.1 Expected value

This is a technique for helping us assess the output of a project and mitigating this against the risk or likelihood of occurrence.

If the development of a new product line has a 66% chance of generating a profit of £10 million, then the expected value is 0.66 × £10,000,000 or £660,000.

Expected value can be used to allocate resources to alternative projects taking into account the level of return and the impact of risk in terms of the likelihood of successful delivery of the project.

4.2.2 Sensitivity analysis

This analysis allows us to evaluate the impact of a range of risks and the financial impact of these risks, for example, in the context of the cost of inputs into the project, which are likely to change over time. Over the last few years, for example, we have seen major changes in the price of energy inputs and raw materials.

An expected value of the main inputs into the project is calculated and a sensitivity analysis is applied for example at 615% (Table 10.4). In the example below, we have the following figures:

Revenue	£1,000,000
Materials	£400,000
Labour	£100,000
Overheads	£200,000 constant

Table 10.4 Sensitivity analysis

	−15%	Materials expected	115%
−15%	1,000,000	1,000,000	1,000,000
	340,000	400,000	460,000
	85,000	85,000	85,000
	200,000	200,000	200,000
	375,000	**315,000**	**255,000**
Labour expected	1,000,000	1,000,000	1,000,000
	340,000	400,000	460,000
	100,000	100,000	100,000
	200,000	200,000	200,000
	360,000	**300,000**	**240,000**
115%	1,000,000	1,000,000	1,000,000
	340,000	400,000	460,000
	115,000	115,000	115,000
	200,000	200,000	200,000
	345,000	**285,000**	**225,000**

4.2.3 Monte Carlo simulation

This is a computer-generated model providing data on a range of variables with different values and distribution, for example costs timings, input costs and shows the impact on a range of outputs, for example financial outputs.

It is available on Excel as well as in many bespoke project management software products. It is linked to Project Evaluation and Review Techniques (PERT) in that it deals with a range of possible outcomes. A consideration of the PERT technique is given below.

4.2.4 Failure, mode and effect analysis

This is a useful approach as it takes into account all possible risks and also tries to outline their possible effects. This may be quantified although often no priority is given to the risks described (Table 10.4).

Table 10.5   Failure, mode and effect matrix

	Risk item	Failure mode	Cause of failure	Effect	Remedial action
1	Product	Product contamination	Faulty cleaning Contaminated ingredients	Illness Litigation Reputation Brand values Product withdrawal	Institute crisis planning
2	Etc				
3					

The failure, mode and effect analysis may be quantified. Table 10.6 illustrates how this is done with a score entered for the key risk variables identified by the project team. Again, there may be many risk items considered within the table.

Table 10.6   Failure mode and effect criticality matrix

	Risk item	Failure mode	Cause of failure	Effect	Remedial action	Probability	Impact	Detection	Total
1	Product	Product contamination	Faulty cleaning Contaminated ingredients	Illness Litigation Reputation Brand values Product withdrawal	Institute crisis planning	1	5	3	9
2	Etc								
3									

4.2.5 PERT

Project Evaluation and Review Techniques (PERT) deal with the fact that the estimated time for completion on any project will almost certainly vary. Instead of taking one value, the techniques deals with three values:

1   O = Optimistic time, if conditions are perfect, the time taken to complete a task
2   M = Most probable time under expected conditions
3   P = Pessimistic time if we experience some of the things that could go wrong

The distribution of these figures will vary; there may be little difference or a large difference in the range of figures. However, we cause the figures entered to work out the expected time that a task will take.

For example, look at the following figures with the implication being that the expected time is the average time the task would require if it were repeated on a number of occasions (4), over an extended period of time (6 months).

O = 3, M = 5 and P = 7

Using the formula we arrive at the expected time E.

$$E = [O + 4M + P]/6$$

Therefore, for this activity, the expected time is:

$$E = [3 + (4 \times 5) + 7]/6 = 5$$

We can do this for any number of tasks and work out the expected time of the entire project in this way.

The Chartered Institute of Marketing

In reality, for most large projects, the computer will complete the analysis (Figure 10.4).

Figure 10.4 A PERT-based chart for the production of mailing

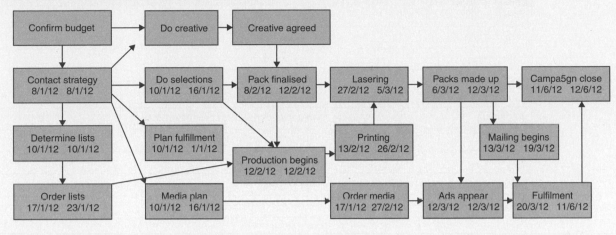

5 Probability analyses

As we have seen that the identification of risk is only one small part of the risk management process, what concerns the marketing project manager is the probability of that risk being experienced. This can be combined with a measure of the severity of the impact and our ability to detect this risk to produce an overall risk probability score. Lewis (2007) suggests the use of a logarithmic scale to estimate the probability of occurrence (Table 10.7).

Table 10.7 Probability of occurrence

Probability	Possible rate of occurrence	Score
Very high	>1 in 2	10
	1 in 3	9
High	1 in 8	8
1 in 20	7	1 in 20
Moderate	1 in 80	6
	1 in 400	5
	1 in 2,000	4
Low	1 in 15,000	3
	1 in 150,000	2
Remote	<1 in 1,500,000	1

The second area to consider is the impact of the risk being experienced (Table 10.8).

Table 10.8   Assessing impact

Effect	Impact	Score
Severe unforeseen	Terminal	10
Severe foreseen	Severe implication	9
Very serious	Delay and/or financial repercussion	8
Serious	Significant impact; project delivered but significantly below expectations	7
Moderate	Noticeable impact on desired outputs	6
Low	Limited impact to deliverables	5
Very low	Very limited impact	4
Insignificant	Minor impact	3
Very insignificant	Little or no impact	2
Zero	No impact	1

Clear probability is of little consequence on its own. If an event is likely to occur but is of limited consequence, then it may be ignored.

The final area to consider is the ability to detect the risk before its impact is felt (Table 10.9).

Table 10.9   Capability of detection

Detectable	Score
Unknown	10
Very unlikely	9
Unlikely	8
Very low	7
Low	6
Moderate	5
Reasonably high	4
High	3
Very high	2
More or less certain	1

Again, this can be given a score.

These elements can be combined into a final risk analysis schedule of the project. The outcome of this process is a risk probability number for the risk attached to any specific projects. We can see this for selected risk relating to an industry conference (Table 10.10).

Table 10.10   Selected risk analysis, industry conference

Risk	P	I	D	Risk probability number
Power fails	3	10	8	240
Projection fails	5	8	3	120
Loss of key speaker	3	8	5	120

5.1 Scenario planning

It is a technique that can be used to determine the risks and opportunities relating particularly to the long-term strategic direction of the organisation. It is a complex process and normally involves experts from a range of related areas or departments within the organisation. The use of external consultants is common.

In her book *Scenario Planning*, Gill Ringland (2006) identified several outputs of the scenario planning process.

- Erste Allgemeine Versicherung, the Austrian insurance company, anticipated the fall of the Berlin Wall and entered new markets in central Europe.

- KRONE, the wiring and cable supplier, developed 200 new product ideas.

- Unilever decided on marketing strategies for Russia and Poland.

- United Distillers (now Diageo) set market strategies for India, South Africa and Turkey.

- Electrolux spotted new consumer markets.

Shell's scenario planning is world renowned, as it seeks to manage the volatility around the politics of global energy management.

The process is:

- Define the scenario
- Identify the risks relating to that scenario
- Create a plan to identify early warning indicators and identify management responses
- Communicate this plan to all parties involved in resolving the scenario
- Review regularly

5.2 Event tree analysis

Event trees are diagrammatic representations of the range of outputs that occur in response to any event, including risks that can happen within a project. With the increase in the number of outputs, the diagram grows to look like the branches of a tree.

We always start with what is known as the initiating event, and the event tree helps us to analyse the potential results of a range of alternative reactions to this initial event, whether they successfully resolve the issues or exacerbate it.

The example below draws on the risk of fire (Figure 10.5). There are two systems that are designed to deal with this: a fire extinguishing system and an automated call to the fire brigade.

Figure 10.5   Event tree

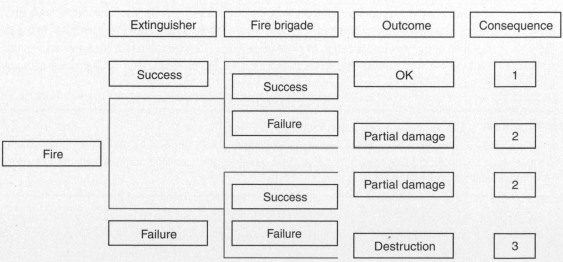

It is possible to enhance this process through a variety of additional activities. For example, we can add probabilities impact assessment scores and values to outcomes to create a graphical representation of the projects and related picture of the risks and opportunities (Figure 10.6).

Figure 10.6   Risk tree

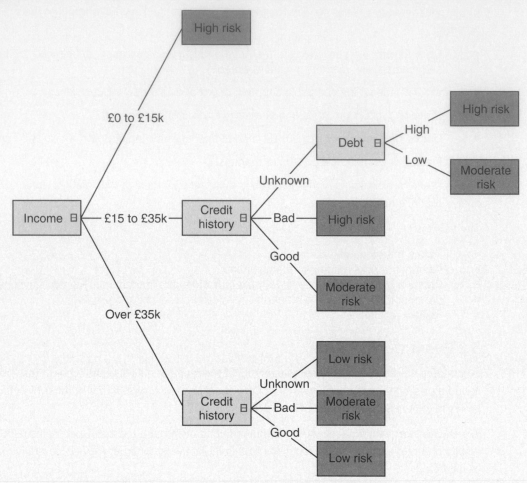

5.3 Assumptions analysis

Assumptions analysis is an important technique that is used to minimise risks involved in making assumptions.

Interested parties and team members should list the assumptions that have been made and built into the project planning process. For each of these assumptions, risks should be identified on the basis of potential mistakes or incorrect application of the assumption. The team should assess the assumption for validity and if it is believed that the assumption is not valid, it should be reassessed. This process is ongoing through the project planning process.

> ▶ **Assessment tip**
>
> Evaluation techniques have been consistently criticised as an area of extreme weakness among candidates taking this unit and across the level as a whole. It is imperative that evaluative variables and qualified commentary are utilised to the full when dealing with risk assessment and evaluation.

 The Chartered Institute of Marketing

- In this chapter, we concentrated on the core fundamental aspects of risk assessment and evaluation using industry benchmark, illustration and case examples and activities.

- We looked at how risk can be identified through teamwork, concept maps and cause and effect analysis.

- We identified how risk can be quantified through:

  - Expected value

  - Sensitivity analysis

  - Monte Carlo simulations

  - Failure mode effect criticality analysis

  - PERT

- We also looked at the probability of risk through techniques such as scenario planning, event tree and assumptions analysis.

FURTHER READING

Lynch, G.S. (2008) *At Your Own Risk*. New Jersey, Wiley Hoboken.

REFERENCES

Chapman, C.B. and Ward, S.C. (2003) *Project Risk Management: Process, Techniques and Insights*. 2nd edition. Chichester, John Wiley and Sons.

Ernst & Young (2010) Eleven risks for consumer products companies. http://www.ey.com/GL/en/Industries/Consumer-Products/Eleven-risks-for-consumer-products-companies [Accessed 23 June 2012].

Gardiner, P.D. (2005) *Project Management*. Hampshire, Palgrave Macmillan.

Lewis, J.P. (2007) *Mastering Project Management*. 2nd edition. New York, McGraw Hill.

Lock, D. (2007) *Project Management*. 9th edition. Aldershot, Gower.

PWC. (2009) The Risk Culture Survey. http://www.pwc.com/us/en/risk-culture/assets/2009_RCS_Brochure.pdf [Accessed 30 May 2012].

Ringland, G. (2006) *Scenario Planning*. 2nd edition. Chichester, John Wiley & Sons.

Sinclair, V. (2012) Websense Security Threats Report 2012. Phoenix, http://www.phoenixs.co.uk/phoenixblog/?tag=/data+theft [Accessed 30 May 2012].

1   What is credit risk?

2   What is a denial of service attack?

3   What are the stages in the process of scenario planning?

4   What is PERT an acronym for?

5   What are the major techniques for risk identification?

ACTIVITY DEBRIEFS

Activity 10.1

Distribution systems must deal specifically with geography. Where the population is evenly spread over a wide area or perhaps distributed in a linear fashion, distribution costs may be greater than expected where the population is more concentrated.

Activity 10.2

New methods might give competitors a cost saving that would increase their ability to compete on price. However, adoption of new methods might impose unacceptable capital and training costs and interruption to production. There may be hazards associated with new machinery or processes and there may be legal complications involving disputes over intellectual property.

Activity 10.3

This will be specific to the example that you use.

The Chartered
Institute of Marketing

1   The risk that a customer may default on payment

2   An attempt to prevent legitimate users of an internet service from using it

3   ■   Define the scenario
     ■   Identify the risks relating to that scenario
     ■   Create a plan to identify early warning indicators and identify management responses
     ■   Communicate this plan to all parties involved in resolving the scenario
     ■   Review regularly

4   Project evaluation and review techniques

5   ■   Team briefings or risk clinics/brainstorming
     ■   SWOT analyses
     ■   Cause and effect diagrams
     ■   Risk concepts mapping

CHAPTER 11

Risk management and mitigation

Introduction

So far we have seen how risks can be identified, categorised and assessed. We are now going to look at the ways in which risk can be managed and mitigated.

Of course, there are other facts that help any successful project to completion and many of these have been covered earlier in the workbook. These include effective project planning system and policies, employing skilled project managers and other staff, management and leadership skills, sound and effective reporting and information systems and financial control.

Identifying and understanding risk are only the first steps toward dealing with it in an appropriate way. Organisations must also make suitable arrangements to avoid, reduce or transfer risk where possible and appropriate. Normally, only a small proportion of significant risk will be retained.

Risk management is becoming an imperative that ranks alongside the quest for profits and business growth as strategic imperatives. Many business strategies, such as outsourcing, diversification and simplification back to core businesses are aimed as much at risk reduction as they are at cost reduction or revenue enhancement.

Here, we are talking about the management of identified risks. There are several broad approaches and we will consider each of them.

Topic list

Risk management   ①

Generic risk management strategies   ②

Generic risk mitigation strategies   ③

Risk reduction   ④

Risk retention   ⑤

Developing the risk management process   ⑥

Risk reporting and documentation   ⑦

3.4	Design a risk management programme appropriate to measuring the impact of risk in the context of marketing projects:
	■ Risk audit
	■ Risk evaluation
	■ Risk report
	■ Risk treatment
	■ Risk monitoring
3.5	Undertake risk assessments on marketing projects and assess the impact of short/long-term tactical changes to the marketing plan:
	■ Customer assessment
	■ Management assessment
	■ Profit assessment
3.6	Critically evaluate the different approaches organisations can take to mitigate risk in order to reduce its potential to harm the organisation or its reputation:
	■ Organise for risk
	■ Incorporate risk management
	■ Risk avoidance
	■ Risk transfer
	■ Risk financing
3.7	Critically assess the strategic impact of implementing proposed risk control measures versus the strategic impact of taking no action:
	■ Business impact analysis
	■ Event tree analysis
	■ Threat analysis
	■ Scenario analysis and planning
	■ Assumption analysis
	■ Probability analysis
3.8	Develop a range of methods for monitoring, reporting and controlling risk on an ongoing basis for project implementation:
	■ Risk audits
	■ Risk management objectives
	■ Risk reporting
	■ Risk awareness
	■ Risk response
	■ Industry benchmarking

The Chartered
Institute of Marketing

1 Risk management

1.1 The role of management

According to the **Turnbull Report** on corporate governance, a company's directors should do two things in the context of risk management. They should acknowledge their responsibility for the company's internal controls and they should explain to stakeholders that they are designed to **manage rather than eliminate** risk. This approach is notable for the following reasons.

(a) It is open, requiring appropriate disclosures to stakeholders about the risk.

(b) It does not seek to eliminate risk, but companies must understand and manage the risks they accept.

(c) It requires regular, integrated review and management of risk throughout all business units and a common terminology of risk.

(d) It is closely related to business objectives and takes a strategic view of, particularly, the need for the company to adapt to its changing business environment.

(e) It requires durable risk management that that can evolve as the business and its environment change.

Risks change and risk management must be a continuous process involving continuous identification, assessment, treatment, monitoring and review. Though it is convenient to discuss risk management as a linear process, it is actually continuous and iterative with the identification, assessment and treatment processes never ceasing and the results of any monitoring and review feeding back into the system so as to refine its response.

Effective **risk management** enables a business to:

- Reduce business threats to acceptable levels
- Make informed decisions about potential opportunities

This allows stakeholders to have confidence in the business and its future prospects.

The role of management in dealing with risk is to set an appropriate **risk management policy** and keep it current. This policy should provide effective measure to achieve the following.

(a) **Identify** the risks to which the organisation and its operations are subject.

(b) **Evaluate** the risks identified.

(c) **Address the risks** in an appropriate way.

(d) **Monitor** the risks identified, the risk environment and the success of the methods adopted to deal with them.

The risk of longevity, the possibility that those people retiring now will exhaust all of the fund built up in their private pension schemes long before they die, is one of the biggest threats to the sustainability of the pensions industry going forward.

A survey of 76 pension scheme managers by Aberdeen Asset Management identified this risk as second only now to that of investment risk and a much greater risk than the threat of high inflation and interest rates. 80% of respondents stated that this was the current case. Furthermore, while methods for mitigating against investment, inflation and interest rate risk are well practised and mature, techniques for hedging longevity risk are very much in their infancy.

In essence, the health and wherewithal of a pension scheme is now inextricably linked with the health and wherewithal of its members and this is becoming increasingly inversely correlated.

(The Financial Times, 2009)

1.2 Terminology

The processes of identifying, evaluating, addressing and designing methods of monitoring risk are commonly included in the concept of a **risk assessment**. We will avoid using this term as it is generally understood to be a fairly low-level activity carried out as subsidiary activity in the management of health and safety. Another term commonly used is that of the '**risk audit**', the purpose of a risk audit is to identify where an organisation's risks come from; the sources of risk.

1.3 Risk management policy

The organisation's risk management policy describes its approach to and appetite for risk, together with the way it proposes to comply with any legal requirements such as health and safety legislation. Risk appetite may vary according to risk type. For example, it would be unusual for an organisation to have a large appetite for risk in health and safety or other legal compliance matters. More particularly, risk appetite may vary for different aspects of financial, operational and strategic risk. For example, a firm in a poor financial position may be extremely averse to any risk to its ability to satisfy the terms of its bank covenants while it might accept enhanced operational risk (of, say, machine breakdown because it has reduced maintenance spending) in order to stay in business.

An effective system for risk management, reporting and communication is needed in order to implement any risk management strategy. Also, all levels in the business should be involved.

- **The board of directors** should take an overall business view and should require that approved policies are implemented and enforced.

- **Managers of business units** should assess risks from the perspective of their business units and implement the board's risk management policies.

- **Individuals** must be aware of risks and may be responsible for managing some of them.

Risk management *strategy* should be a top-down process integrated across the entire business. However, it is important that everyone in the organisation should be able to contribute to the *processes* of risk management, so a combination of bottom-up and top-down approaches is valuable, particularly in such areas as risk identification and monitoring. As far as possible, approved processes for dealing with risk should become an integral part of the businesses' culture and systems. Senior management's role is to break down the overall risk management strategy into operational policies; managers and other employees should then be made responsible for implementing them and given the requisite authority to do so.

Risk management policies for a large corporation would include:

- **Corporate codes of conduct** regulate how managers and staff deal with each other and with outsiders and seek to control risks from discrimination, bribery, anti-social behaviour and so on.

- **Environmental policies** deal with issues such as emissions, recycling and waste disposal.

- **Health and safety policies** establish H&S officers at all levels, set up committees, provide for routine risk assessments and lay down fire procedures.

- **Financial controls** include budgetary control of income and spending, authorisation procedures for capital expenditure, credit control procedures, cash management procedures and so on.

- **Information systems controls** include the appointment of information officers at all levels, regulations to control use by staff, password and access controls, requirements for back-ups and stand-by systems, institution of firewalls and other security precautions.

- **Personnel controls** include policies on identity and background checks on new recruits, discipline and grievance procedures, door entry controls and attendance monitoring. Appraisals of staff and management can provide early warnings of stress or potential inability to perform vital tasks.

These policies can mitigate the risk of **financial loss** arising from occurrences such as:

- Personal injury litigation.

- Loss of assets to theft or damage.

- Costs arising from internal errors such as those involved in replacing lost data, apologising to injured parties, restoring damaged public image.

- Revenues lost as a result of breakdowns or regulatory action.

ACTIVITY 11.1

Risk management policy of your college

You are probably taking classroom tuition as part of your preparation to pass this exam. Therefore having you on its premises represents one part of the risks being managed by the college or training firm offering you the classes.

Suggest the elements of a risk management policy that your college should adopt to treat the risks of having you in its classrooms.

ACTIVITY 11.2

Outsourcing

The management of a state-funded hospital is considering outsourcing the cleaning of its premises. This will mean private firms taking over as employers of existing cleaning staff and assuming responsibility for the cleaning of the areas around beds, corridors and communal spaces.

Increases in incidents of infections during hospital stays by patients, some resulting in death, have been widely attributed by the media to poor hospital hygiene. Several legal cases for compensation have been decided against hospitals on the grounds of negligence by management.

What factors should management consider in evaluating the proposal to outsource its cleaning?

2 Generic risk management strategies

2.1 Avoid the risk

Perhaps, this can be done in situations where a different choice between options results in a safer strategy, but one with fewer rewards.

2.2 Cancel the project

The ultimate way of avoiding risk is not to carry out the project at all. Many projects go ahead because of the mistaken belief that it will never happen. What can go wrong will go wrong, and the courage to take a decision to cancel a project when there is pressure on all members of staff to deliver is very strong. A corporate culture that embeds the acceptance of risk avoidance based on evidence would clearly prevent this. However, there are few rewards available for not doing something.

Effective use of risk assessment tools and the quantification of risk set against the possible returns are the best way of managing this process.

2.3 Fail-safe and risk avoidance systems

The second way of avoiding risk is to build fail-safe systems so that identified risks simply cannot occur. Lock (2007) gives the example of a Japanese car manufacturer who built in a fail-safe system that meant that unless all required components were in place, the machinery designed to fit those components would not work.

2.4 Overspecify

Overspecification at key stages of the project can help avoid risk being experienced. The Forth Bridge is a good example of an overspecified project; designed after the disaster on the Tay Bridge, the engineering specification was significantly more than required.

2.5 Test, pilot and trial

The role of testing and piloting in marketing projects is well known. Testing in direct marketing involves the small-scale sampling of alternatives in order to optimise the outcome of any activity. The use of computer-simulated test marketing of new product launches is now used prior to the actual launch of new products to try to avoid the expense of actually launching the products, an expensive process even on a regional basis.

3 Generic risk mitigation strategies

3.1 Mitigation of risk

Take precautions to prevent or moderate the risk. There are many actions we can take to reduce the impact of risk. These have been covered to some extent earlier in the section but they include some or all of the following, depending on the nature of the risk and its potential impact.

- Training
- Employment strategies
- Leadership and risk culture
- Back-up and security of data
- Excellence management reporting systems
- External inspection and consultancy
- Financial auditing and fraud prevention

The Chartered
Institute of Marketing

3.2 Accept the risk

The fact that certain risks can be accepted is obvious. The key aspect is that the risks are identified, categorised and assessed for impact and those that cannot be accepted are actively managed.

3.3 Share the risk

Risk can be spread and managed through the use of multiple partners in a project.

3.4 Limit the risk over time

Risk can be limited by completing tasks stage by stage and reassessing risk after the completion of each intermediate stage. It is, therefore, possible to limit the downside risks after the completion of each stage and to cancel the project should the assessment of the impact of risks outweigh the advantages from the completion of the task.

3.5 Managing risk through insurance

The transfer or spread of risk is something that is very much in the news. The use of insurance to transfer and control the impact of risk, however, has been around since Edward Lloyd started his coffee house in the City of London in 1688. Here, traders and merchants came together to exchange information to manage the risk involved in importing and exporting goods by sea.

There are four main types of insurance:

- Insurance relating to legal obligations or liabilities
- Insurance against loss or damage
- Insurance relating to personnel performance and activities
- Insurance against financial loss

In many cases, insurance can be a legal obligation. These relate to laws and regulations as well as to conditions that are laid down in commercial contracts. It may be that a company that is employing a sales promotion agency will want to build in insurance against overredemption, for example.

Other liability insurance may cover failure to meet expected professional standards, resulting in negligence claims, environmental damage and loss relating to property, compensation for bodily harm due to accidents and professional liabilities.

All parties involved in the project should be adequately covered for any liability.

Insurance that is required by legislation includes those relating to health and safety at work. With much of this, professional advice should be sought from internal legal counsel or external lawyers and insurance advisors. Professional bodies may also be able to offer advice and access to preferential rates.

3.6 Latent defects risk insurance

This insurance will cover damage relating to problems in design or materials.

3.7 Accident and sickness insurance

This will cover sickness or injury relating to key staff.

3.8 Key person insurance

This covers loss relating to illness, injury or death of named personnel.

3.9 Pecuniary insurance

This covers financial loss relating to a variety of causes, for example, late completion of projects. Export credit insurance is an example of this.

4 Risk reduction

Risk reduction is applied when it is appropriate to retain an activity. It requires the undertaking of actions and precautions to reduce the risk to acceptable levels. Methods may be directed at reducing the probability of the risk event or its consequences. Good examples of risk reduction appear in the realm of safety precautions and procedures such as fire alarms and drills.

Risk reduction controls include:

(a)   **Preventative controls** minimise the probability that an undesired event will occur. Many financial procedures such as limits on the authorisation of expenditure are preventative controls. A non-financial example is a no smoking rule, which reduces the chance of fire.

(b)   **Corrective controls** deal with the effects of a risk event: an example is a sprinkler system to control fire if it occurs.

(c)   **Directive controls** are policies and procedures intended to ensure a particular risk outcome is achieved, especially in the context of security or Health and Safety. For example, a team undertaking an inherently hazardous operation may have to include a nominated first aider.

(d)   **Detective controls** identify the occurrence of risk events that did not lead to downside consequences. Various financial audit procedures fall into this category.

5 Risk retention

Risk retention means that the loss is accepted and absorbed if it occurs. This is a reasonable way of dealing with minor risks where the cost involved in other approaches would be greater than the total losses they would avoid. Some uninsurable risks such as the effects of war can only be dealt with in this way. Risk retention will normally be supplemented by planning means to deal with the implied contingencies.

Where risk is transferred by means of insurance, it is likely that there will be an 'excess' that represents a retained risk, as would any loss in excess of the sum insured.

ACTIVITY 11.3

Managing risks in a mining company

A large mining company is considering exploiting the mineral reserves in a developing country. The board is concerned that the country's government has in the past effectively expropriated significant foreign assets and profits by adjustments to licensing and ownership regulations.

Suggest strategies that the company could use to manage this area of risk.

6 Developing the risk management process

Like any other aspect of management in a dynamic environment, it would be inappropriate to regard risk management as something that can be done once and for all. Risk management should be understood as a continuing, iterative process. Known risks themselves; measures to address them and detect new ones; and the management process itself must all be subject to attention aimed at improving the organisation's principles and practice. Proper regard must therefore be paid to the matters discussed below.

6.1 Risk monitoring

The organisation's risk profile must be monitored and reported on to establish if is changing. The probability and potential impact of risk events are likely to change and new risks may emerge, just as existing ones may disappear. As a result, the measures taken to address risk must also be reviewed to establish whether they are still appropriate and adequate.

Risk management monitoring and reporting may be embedded in the normal management control reporting system alongside other aspects of routine reporting such as monthly management accounting reports. Also, there should be regular reviews of the overall risk profile and risk management assumptions. A comprehensive review will be particularly important if a risk event, such as a fire or loss of a major customer, does actually occur.

6.2 Examples of risk monitoring processes

(a)   Reporting systems, possibly anonymous, should be established for prompt notification of incidents and near misses.

(b)   Proper management of projects will include periodic review of projects against targets for progress, cost and quality.

(c)   Internal audit is often considered to be an aspect of the financial control system, but it can usefully be expanded to include other aspects of risk, such as health and safety.

(d)   Practical measures can be taken to ensure readiness, such as fire drills and rehearsals of moves to alternate sites.

(e)   Information can be gathered on occurrences elsewhere, such as frauds, equipment failures, and experience of legal actions.

THE REAL WORLD

When the German firm Edscha, a manufacturer of component car parts, ran into financial difficulty and was forced to file insolvency applications, BMW was faced with a crisis. The luxury automotive company was poised for the launch of its new high end model the Z4 convertible and Edsha supplied the car's roof. No other supplier was an option given the timescale and therefore BMW had to make the decision to effectively prop their supply chain up.

Edscha is still trading today but the lessons learned forced BMW to invest further in their own risk monitoring department so as to pre-empt any potential disruption to their supply chain in the future.

(The Financial Times, 2009)

J P Morgan

Risk Management

At J P Morgan, risk management is now a fundamental part of the business and its regulatory and governance frameworks. The systems and processes are essentially broken down into five essential components that construct and validate a robust risk management process.

- Corporate governance – This is now all about a positive risk culture which develops policy and strategy for risk tolerance from a corporate perspective. This in turn then permeates down through the business creating a positive and accountable organisational culture.

- Corporate procedures – This is what maps competence to accountability and allows for the top down delegation outlined above. It is the procedures that create empowerment and therefore nurture and promote the culture of positive risk management.

- Data integrity – With policies and strategies, systems and processes, comes data. Therefore, data capture, manipulation and utilisation is at the core of information processing *per se*, but arguably even more so when dealing with risk. Technology is increasingly allowing for real-time data automation and such resources are now forming the centrepiece of current and future investment in risk management systems.

- Metrics – Risk must be assessed, evaluated, measured and quantified. Such metrics as size, degree, exposure and volatility are historically and statistically plotted and projected with increasingly sophisticated scenario and simulation models emerging. The all-encompassing Value-at-Risk (VAR) metric is used to calculate the total worst case scenario across the entire risk portfolio which is continuously back and forward tested. The mantra is 'accountability'.

- Monitoring – This is all about control and allows for built in review, audit and independent external validation.

As risk is intrinsically linked to the operation of the business, having a risk management function in place is crucial to the on-going success and long-term sustainability of any business.

(JP Morgan, 2012)

▶ **Assessment tip**

There will always be a question on general or specific risk management and/or risk mitigation, be prepared to apply in context.

---

7 Risk reporting and documentation

7.1 Documentation

The process of recording the outcome of projects and the risks attached to them is a key aspect of risk management systems. As Chapman and Ward (2003) state in their excellent book on risk management, documentation provides six core benefits:

1   **Clearer thinking**: writing clarifies thinking.

2   **Clearer communications**: documentation including risk reports and audits provides a valuable means for communication between remote parties to a project.

3   **Familiarisation**: documentation helps new project team members to come up to speed with project issues.

4   **A record of decisions**: documentation should explain the rationale behind key decisions.

5   **A knowledge base**: the knowledge gained from one project can help the efficient implementation of subsequent projects.

6   **A framework for further data acquisitions**: analysis helps organisations understand better the information requirements for project management.

There is also an obligation for effective risk reporting for Public Limited Companies (PLCs).

7.2 Addressing risk

Once the project is underway, there are a range of tools that are employed to monitor and to report on the risks identified. A **risk log** is maintained and regularly updated by the project team. New risks that might emerge through the project are also logged and assessed using the range of tools outlined above. If an identified risk occurs, then this is also is recorded together with the outcomes. If an identified risk does not occur, then this too is recorded, as the avoidance of identified risk is clearly a vital part of the risk management plan. The management of the risk log is an active process and forms a key element of the risk management documentation.

7.2.1 Risk register

Risks that have been identified and assessed should be recorded in a **risk register**. A risk description should include the following detail:

(a)   **Name** and **identification number**.

(b)   **Risk type** – financial, strategic, operational, hazard and so on.

(c)   **Scope** of the risk – a description of the possible future events involved.

(d)   **Quantification** of the risk – the probability and scale of any losses or gains, possibly including 'Value at Risk' assessments.

(e)   Possible **indicators and symptoms** that may indicate enhanced likelihood that the risk event may occur.

(f)   Risk **tolerance/appetite** – level of risk considered acceptable for this matter.

(g)   **Parties affected** – both internal and external parties and how they will be influenced.

(h)   Risk **treatment and control** – the means by which the risk is managed at present and an assessment of the current risk controls in force.

(i)   Potential **action for improvement** – recommendations about further risk reduction options.

(j)   Risk **owner** – this person monitors the risk event.

7.2.2 Communication and learning

A learning approach is particularly relevant to the development of the risk management process.

Everyone capable of making an input into the risk management process should be familiar with its importance, with the risks they are exposed to and the ways in which the organisation intends to deal with them. This will improve the implementation of the chosen measures and their integration into business systems.

Mangers should be regularly updated on current risk management strategy as it affects their areas of responsibility and should monitor its adequacy and completeness.

Knowledge obtained or created by one area of the business and any lessons learnt from experience should be incorporated into the business-wide risk management strategy and shared with other areas of the business.

Communication with external stakeholders such as suppliers, customers and regulators is also required. This will help to ensure that the organisation is on top of its risk management problems and that it can take its

partners' risk management strategies into account. It will also assist in the management of stakeholders' expectations on the subject of risk management.

7.3 Risk review

The review process can be broken down into four distinct phases:

1   Immediate reactions, success and failure should be quickly assessed and analysed
2   Immediate action to counter negative outcomes
3   Long-term review and evaluation
4   Systems and strategy review and evaluation

The reasons for review are many, and most are commonsense.

A risk review within the project enables us to:

- Assess personal or team performance
- Prevent future risks being experienced
- Identifying training needs to help avoid future risks
- To identify issues with processes and systems

Risk review can be done by:

- Members of the project team
- Staff independent of the project
- External audit teams

Finally, risk-aware companies might choose to work towards BS 31100. This is a key Standard for risk management and gives a clear view on how to develop and sustain effective risk management.

BS 31100 gives an understanding on how to develop, implement and maintain effective risk management within your business.

Using BS 31100 effectively can help increase a company's effectiveness.

(Information about the standard can be obtained from the British Standards Institute at http://www.bsigroup.com/en/Standards-and-Publications/Industry-Sectors/Risk/Project-risk-management/)

7.4 Contingency planning

Another important document is the contingency plan. Should risks occur, then such a contingency or crisis management plan will be implemented. The plan should identify:

- Alternative actions relating to key risk events occurring
- Resource allocation to implement remedial activity
- An alternative project timeline

Contingency plans should be regularly rehearsed: this may reveal issues with the plan and allow corrections to be made before they are tested in reality. All partners involved in the business should also be involved in testing.

Testing may be paper-based using a workshop environment or may involve quasi-live testing using communications cascading to test the efficiency of communications between those involved in implementing the contingency at all levels. Finally, a full-dress rehearsal can be used; this is expensive but may be useful.

▶ **Assessment tip**

There will always be a question on general or specific risk control mechanisms, be prepared to apply in context.

The Chartered
Institute of Marketing

- Here, we were able to concentrate our thinking and exposure to ways of protecting our organisations and ourselves by mitigating risk via: insurance finance and transfer.

- We established that organisations need to incorporate risk management policies into their business operations.

- We also identified other ways of mitigating risk through reduction and retention.

- We concluded by recognising that risk management is an ongoing process that requires consistent and constant monitoring.

- We have seen the value of risk planning within the overall project plan. It could be argued that in today's difficult business conditions, assessment and mitigation of risk is a core business function.

- We looked at the risk management process and established that this involves:

  — Risk audit

  — Risk evaluation

  — Risk report

  — Risk treatment

  — Risk monitoring and reporting

- We looked at the range of techniques that marketers could use within this framework to boost the upside opportunities that exist within a project and to counter and manage the downside risks.

FURTHER READING

Charrel, P-J. and Galarreta, D. (eds) (2007) *Project Management and Risk Management in Complex Projects: Studies in Organisational Semiotics.* Dordecht, The Netherlands Springer.

Reuvid, J. (2008) *Managing Business Risk.* 5th edition. London, Kogan Page.

REFERENCES

Berry, R. (2012) Setting Up A sound Risk Management Framework. J P Morgan, http://www.jpmorgan.com/tss/General/Risk_Management/1159351270285 [Accessed 30 May 2012].

Chapman, C.B. and Ward, S.C. (2003) *Project risk management: Process, techniques and insights.* 2nd edition. Chichester, John Wiley and Sons.

Johnson, S. (2009) Early solutions to the risk of long life. FT, http://www.ft.com/cms/s/0/a96dbc44-050d-11de-8166-000077b07658.html#axzz1wQ1YzNr5 [Accessed 30 May 2012].

Lock, D. (2007) *Project Management.* 9th edition. Aldershot, Gower.

Milne, R. (2009) Early warnings in the supply chain. FT, http://www.ft.com/cms/s/0/cfaf418e-1813-11de-8c9d-0000779fd2ac.html#axzz1wQ1YzNr5 [Accessed 30 May 2012].

1   To what extent can risk management be regarded as a project to be completed to specification.

2   Is it likely that an organisation's appetite for risk will vary from risk to risk?

3   What are the two broad approaches to identifying risk?

4   Name two quantitative risk evaluation methods.

5   What methods are used to address risk?

ACTIVITY DEBRIEFS

Activity 11.1

Elements of a risk policy for a college offering classroom courses would include:

Policies to control admission

The college probably has door entry and identification systems to ensure only those entitled to attend classes can do so. This provides protection for its assets and its revenues. It can also stop undesirables disturbing students and staff.

Health and safety policies

There will be policies to minimise accidents, ensure cleanliness and alleviate occupational stress, among others.

Identity and data security

Course and individual records will be safeguarded and examinations administration standardised.

Course quality

There should be policies in place to make sure that materials you study are appropriate and that tutors are competent both as teachers and in the subjects they present.

Activity 11.2

The list of factors will be very large and will include:

Costs and benefits from outsourcing

- Fees charged by contractors
- Cost presently incurred by using own staff
- Financial returns from transfer of assets to contractor (floor polishing machines, vacuum cleaners etc)
- Potential redundancy costs of staff not transferred
- Costs of writing and agreeing suitable contracts and service level agreements
- Costs of monitoring compliance of contractors with service agreements

Risks from outsourcing

- Financial stability and robustness of the contractor

- Track record of contractor in delivering suitable service elsewhere

- Availability of controls over performance (eg whether staff will take instructions from hospital managers, performance indicators, regular meetings, legal redress mechanisms)

The Chartered
Institute of Marketing

- Potential staff and media criticism of decision

- Extent of proof of link between hospital cleanliness and acquired infections

- Extent of public hostility to outsourcing as a source of increased infections

- Will legal liability for negligence claim pass to the contractor or stay with the hospital?

Risks from continuing to provide cleaning in-house

- Operational risks from cleaners not being available (eg strike action)
- Employment risks of having own staff (eg claims for industrial injury, discrimination etc)
- Rising wages and other employment costs
- Legal costs of negligence claims resulting from poor cleaning
- Potential fines for inadequate monitoring of staff (work permits, benefit fraud, health and safety)

Risk environment and appetite

- Potential changes in government policy resulting in contract penalties

- Extent of pressure on hospital to cut costs

- Management's previous experience of outsourcing agreements

- Relative risks of other cost-cutting measures under consideration

- Degree of support management enjoys from influential stakeholders (eg media, governors, doctors, nurses)

- Potential personal consequences for management of bad decision (eg personal liability, career impact, stress of dealing with problems)

Activity 11.3

Risk avoidance

Don't invest in the country

Risk reduction

- Obtain public undertakings from the government that it will not expropriate
- Ensure the firm has other sources of earnings
- Undertake political lobbying in order to influence the policy of the government
- Keep as much of the operation as possible outside the country
- Invest small amounts incrementally

Risk transfer

- Set up the venture as a separate company with its own sources of finance, preferably local
- Obtain investment and participation from local minerals firms
- Sell the rights to the minerals to third parties as soon as possible

Risk retention

Accept any residual loss when it occurs

1   Not at all: risks change and the risk management process must be continuous.

2   Highly likely. It will tend to accept risks in the areas it considers to be core activities and seek to eliminate risk elsewhere.

3   The risk source approach and the risk problem approach.

4   Breakeven analysis and event trees.

5   Avoidance, reduction, transfer and retention.

Section 3:

Senior Examiner's comments

This section of the syllabus recognises the contemporary and practical alignment of risk management in an applied organisational context and the associated interface with fundamental marketing management. Although alluded to at Level 4, the extent of exposure to these concepts has been limited thus far. Consequently, it was necessary to introduce a relative depth within this unit while at the same time endeavouring to balance the knowledge and application requirements at Level 6. To that end, and with particular reference to the current business environments, it is necessary to explore, appreciate and understand that operating within organisational and environmental dynamics, risk exists.

This is not a new concept. As marketing students, the necessity to audit dynamics is fundamental to the marketing management discipline and from the outset, at all levels, we are introduced to the aspects and elements of risk. At Level 6, a framework for the actual and potential manifestation of these risks is explored.

There is no guarantee for success and a realisation of this dictates the imperative of a rigorous, disciplined and formal control regime.

Therefore, there is a need to incorporate the concept of risk within an organisation's orientation. This is not about negating innovation or implementation but more about assurance in practice.

The students will be expected to assess situational risks, for example, relating to communications projects, Customer Relationship Management, New Product Development to name but a few, within the parameters of marketing projects and therefore should examine these relative to the undertakings in Section 2. So, in essence, the concepts and frameworks that candidates already know and understand from a core marketing perspective should now be applied in relation to risk.

To that end, students will drill down and concentrate their skills in auditing, planning and control.

The additional elements here are in effect around contingency and impact. As a result, a relative examination of mitigation and a critical analysis of recommended actions are sufficient.

We do not want to reinvent the wheel here. This section purely brings to the fore elements of marketing that have been implicit and inherent from the discipline's inception and through its evolution. Commonsense is the order of the day, and given the current business environment, the management of or more importantly the control of risk is even more imperative. We want the student and the practitioner to embrace an enhanced mindset. It is no longer enough to be customer focused and market-oriented. In addition, it is necessary for our analysis and decision-making to fully incorporate a pillar that identifies analyses and plans to control and limit risk.

Therefore, risk is no different to any other aspect of the marketing discipline. In essence, concentrate on identifying the problems and implementing the solutions. Again, these will be specific and in context. An assessment brief will be published, which will highlight the core areas of identification, analysis, mitigation and control.

Relative to the different briefs at each assessment diet, a core element of the risk management process will always be highlighted in context. These will be published at the beginning of each examination board. To reiterate, we are not trying to reinvent the wheel, and industry standards and benchmarks alongside professional models should be used when analysing, evaluating, managing or controlling risk.

Within this element of the assessment, the expectation is on the application of approach to manipulating identified and previously analysed and evaluated risk. This will have already happened within the previous two sections and consequently only summarised. Here, we give the opportunity to elaborate and present these findings in a predirected format that extracts data, information and manipulation for the award of marks.

Where, however, innovative and original approaches to monitoring and measuring risk are presented, these will be rewarded.

A core appreciation of risk assessment and management concepts, principles and techniques is expected here.

Section 4:

Project management for analysis, planning, implementation and control (weighting 40%)

CHAPTERS

Chapter 12 – Foundations of project management

Chapter 13 – Project process

Chapter 14 – Project tools and techniques

Chapter 15 – Project control, termination, review and evaluation

LEARNING OBJECTIVES

By the end of this section, you will be able to:

- Evaluate approaches to developing a project management culture
- Evaluate different types of projects in terms of implementation
- Develop all of the main stages of a project management plan
- Assess the importance of scope within marketing projects
- Utilise tools and techniques for project planning and implementation
- Utilise tools and techniques for project control
- Assess a range of methods for evaluating project success or failure

SYLLABUS REFERENCES

4.1 Critically evaluate different approaches to developing a culture of project planning within the marketing function and the organisation

4.2 Critically evaluate soft and hard projects in the context of marketing and consider the differences in terms of project implementation

4.3 Develop the main stages of a marketing project plan, identifying the activities, estimating time and cost, sequencing of activities, and assess the competency and skills required of the people needed to deliver the project

4.4 Critically assess the importance of, and techniques for, establishing the marketing project's scope, definition and goals relative to the organisational marketing plan

4.5 Utilise a range of tools and techniques to support project planning, scheduling, resourcing and controlling of activities within the project to enable effective and efficient implementation

4.6 Utilise a variety of methods, measurements and control techniques to enable effective monitoring and measuring of progress throughout the project to ensure that it is completed to specification, on time and within budget

4.7 Critically assess the main techniques for evaluating effectiveness, success or failure of a marketing project on its completion.

CHAPTER 12

Foundations of project management

Introduction

Historically, project management (a specific form of management) was given limited attention in academic texts in marketing. However, professional project management has gained recognition, and this is now recognised as a factor impacting on marketing performance. Its importance in effective marketing and business success is reflected in the focus in CIM marketing qualifications.

Project management is an important aspect of strategic implementation. In the first place, many organisations' business consists largely of projects: civil engineering contractors and film studios are two obvious examples. Second, even where operations are more or less continuous, the need for continuing strategic innovation and improvement in the way things are done brings project management to the forefront of attention. Finally, even relatively low-level, one-off projects must be managed with a view to their potential strategic implications.

Marketing is particularly suited to a project-based management approach. Much of the higher direction of marketing revolves around activities that are, essentially projects.

Topic list

Syllabus references

4.1	Critically evaluate different approaches to developing a culture of project planning within the marketing function and the organisation:
	■ Managing dynamics
	■ The marketing/project interface
	■ The project structured organisation
	■ Planning, implementation and control
	■ Policies, strategies and methodologies
	■ Managing the project life cycle
4.2	Critically evaluate soft and hard projects in the context of marketing and consider the differences in terms of project implementation:
	■ Types of project
	■ Strategic context
	■ Operational context
	■ Tactical context
	■ Short/medium/long-term objectives
	■ Quality, investment and delivery

▶ **Key terms**

Project: a temporary endeavour undertaken to create a unique product or service (Project Management Institute, 1996).

Project management is managing non-repetitive activities to ensure that they achieve time, cost and performance objectives.

Project life cycle addresses the time from the initiation of a project (with the start of its planning), through its implementation and then on to termination, when the project ceases to exist.

Strategic project management is the process of managing complex projects by combining business strategy and project management techniques in order to implement the business strategy and deliver organisational breakthroughs.

Managing projects has always been a central part of marketing activity.

Project work in marketing includes planning events, marketing research and campaigns, for example. Further, marketers are commonly involved in strategic, cross-functional projects, such as new product or market development, or implementing change within the organisation. However, until recently, project management was a general part of marketing professionals' management activities.

Marketing gained professional status in the United Kingdom in the 1980s on the basis of the body of knowledge that underpins effective marketing. Project management developed over a similar period, and like marketing, it developed a body of knowledge of best practices and terminology. With the increasing pressure to ensure marketing effectiveness, it is clear that use of the insight from the project management discipline adds to marketing projects. Effective project implementation – regardless of topic – needs good project management.

This first chapter in Section 4 specifically centred on project management provides the foundation for the following chapters. As such, it is focused on understanding about projects and the factors that influence their success. Later chapters will build on this foundation and add more detail on terminology, tools and techniques.

Project Management in Marketing has been incorporated into the new syllabus as an acknowledgement of what happens in much of our everyday lives. It combines a series of skills, tools and disciplines that help guide us to effective outcomes. Many of the ideas and techniques will be familiar as they involve information gathering, analysis, decision-making, implementation and control.

This is still very much a marketing module with a focus on the practical application of learned skills – the project techniques are to support the marketing effort.

Let's look at a typical marketing planning cycle illustrated below (Figure 12.1).

Figure 12.1   The marketing planning cycle

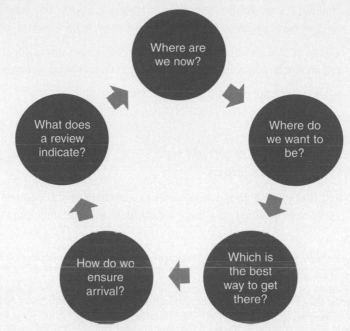

When planning marketing strategy most models will suggest that the first step is to conduct a marketing audit of where we are, what we are capable of, what our comparative position is against our competitors and what our customers want from us. Any strategy must be comaptible with the overall mission statement and corporate strategies that emerge from it.

To consider where we want to be is centred on segmentation, targeting and positioning (both ourselves and our offerings) in the most appropriate way to satisfy our defined target sectors.

Using a variety of tools to help choose the strategic path forward brings us to the point where we must commit resources to progress along that path. Resources are finite and valuable, and whatever they are allocated to means that there is an opportunity cost – those resources are now lost to other opportunities that we may have had.

The marketing mix comprises the traditional set of marketing elements that we use, but there are further decisions to be made to achieve the best return on investment for the resources we have committed. Should we develop a greater online presence and invest further in digital marketing communications? Does our brand need refreshing? Has our corporate image been harmed so that public relations takes on a higher priority? These are the types of questions that may need to be answered before the best mix is agreed.

From this, our most detailed level of plan or campaign is chosen and implemented, but only the most optimistic (or foolish) organisation would imagine that everything will go to plan and at all stages. The situation is monitored and progress charted against pre-defined targets of success.

This monitoring and evaluation feedback cycle is a basic ingredient of most planning methods as it allows you to take corrective action to compensate for flaws in the original plan or unexpected changes in the marketing environment.

When the objectives have been achieved, for example, market research shows that awareness of your brand has increased to the target level, then that plan is completed. This doesn't mean that it is completely forgotten about, but it may move to a different phase where less intensive, periodic reviews are carried out.

If that is marketing planning in a nutshell, what is project management? A project is defined by Wysocki *et al* (2000) as follows: 'A project is a sequence of unique, complex and connected activities having one goal or a purpose and that must be completed by a specific time, within budget, and according to specification.'

Do the elements of that definition seem familiar? When the same authors look at the stages in a project management life cycle they determine the stages to be as shown in Figure 12.2 (Wysocki *et al*, 2000).

Harvey Maylor (2010) abbreviated the stages into 4 Ds:

- Define the project
- Design the project
- Do It! or Deliver the project and
- Develop the project process

He illustrated these four phases with a series of key issues and fundamental questions. For the project definition stage they included organisational strategy and goal definition – what is to be done and why is it to be done?

The design stage included planning, resource analysis and justification – how will it be done, who will do it and when can it be done?

The delivery stage includes control, organisation, decision-making and leadership – how is the project managed on a day-to-day basis?

Finally, the post delivery phase looks at developing the processes and procedures used to gain experience – what can be improved for the future?

Figure 12.2   The project management life cycle

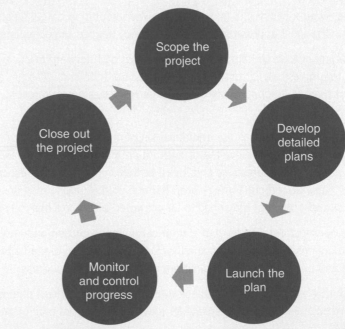

(Adapted from Wysocki *et al*, 2000, p86)

Although many definitions of what comprises a project point out that a project is unique in nature it does not mean that nothing **similar** has been done before. The definition is to distinguish it from routine administrative functions or closed-loop processes where identical output is the desired outcome.

A business may evaluate the level of sales on a particular product or service and choose to run a promotional campaign based on vouchers or coupons that give a financial incentive or discount. This is not the first time that they have done this for that product or service. What makes it unique is that the marketing environment and the organisation itself will have changed in many ways since the previous campaign. For example,

recessionary pressures may make the target customers more price sensitive than when they had a higher margin of disposable income. Perhaps a new competitor has grown with aggressive marketing that needs a rapid response.

What should not be forgotten is what was good and bad about the previous promotional campaign. What can they learn from it to improve the present promotion?

This section of the book will take you through a detailed exploration of how best we can embed the good discipline that effective project management can engender into your marketing operations.

In terms of synergies between marketing and project management, project management techniques have relevance to all aspects of marketing. For example,

- Market research and internal audits give us information to help in deciding what project is most viable.
- Strategic planning tools help decide the overall approach we will take
- Project implementation is through the marketing mix.
- Feedback, control and evaluation are common to both.

This text looks at the use of project management techniques as a continuing framework which include the collection and processing of information, risk assessment, project evaluation and decision-making, through to planning, analysis, implementation and control.

Although quite a lot of the content is new, the fundamental underlying concepts and principles of marketing management remain intact with adaptation where necessary. That adaptation is to align these fundamentals with the fundamentals that exist within other management disciplines. In this instance, project management.

1 Foundations of project management

The Project Management Institute (PMI) define a project as 'A temporary endeavour undertaken to create a unique product or service'.

On the basis of this definition, projects:

- Are transitory or for a determined period of time (ie they are not routine or continuous activities)
- Will achieve a specific, unique output
- Have defined start and end dates (ie they are not open-ended business activities)

At the simplest level, there are three core stages of a project, which are referred to as the project life cycle. Most sources expand these basic three, but they are always there, underpinning more complex models.

1   Beginning (or initiation): A project begins – or is initiated – once its planning starts.

2   Implementation: A project takes place during the implementation stage. This is simplistic. To many people, including the consumers or users, this is a time of more high visibility, but a very significant part of the time can be spent in the planning and design processes.

3   Termination: Once the management process is complete (including the 'shake down' and project review), the project no longer exists and is terminated.

Often, a project's output, such as a new product or a new branch layout, will exist at the end of the life cycle, but this is no longer a project and no longer a project management responsibility. For example, a project to develop a new product would be managed as a project, but the launched product is a marketing management responsibility.

So, project management focuses on managing *non-routine* activities and situations effectively. The unique aspect of projects brings complexity or uncertainty in their management, as the situation is different and needs to be managed in a way that addresses the novelty and complexity.

Projects involve different participants, processes and resources from their beginning to their termination in order to meet their outcomes.

Further, different organisations with similar marketing projects, similar budgets, timescales or performance would result in different project approaches, staff involved etc. The organisations' goals, culture and resources would impact on the nature of the project.

These different elements of projects add to their uncertainty.

1   Input uncertainty: The skills and labour that is available, and the desired mix of skills; the roles, experience, reliability, involvement, availability and solvency of suppliers and subcontractors and material provision.

2   Process uncertainty: The risk involved in the project activities, including the work breakdown, the integration and linking of activities, management of bottlenecks and understanding critical paths; the speed of environmental changes; stakeholders' expectations and interrelationships and even project politics.

3   Output uncertainty: The fit of the results with client and stakeholder requirements, specification changes and market changes during the project.

ACTIVITY 12.1

Consider the list of marketing-related activities below. Which do you consider to be of an operations-like nature and which of a project-like nature?

- Buying advertising space
- Dealing with customer complaints
- Summarising marketing research findings
- Procuring sales support material
- Visiting customers
- Responding to media enquiries

THE REAL WORLD

MasterCard and sports sponsorship

The aim of MasterCard's sponsorship of these globally watched events is to enable themselves and their worldwide partner institutions to develop their existing and new businesses.

MasterCard has sponsored prestigious football events since 1990, when it was the Official Card and Official Product Licensee of Italia 1990. It continued in this World Cup role until the 2006 FIFA World Cup. It is also the Official Payment System of the various PGA (Professional Golf Association) tours and events.

However, VISA card claimed the sponsorship rights for 2010 and 2014 World Cups from FIFA.

(VISA, 2012)

ACTIVITY 12.2

Refer to the MasterCard case and answer the following questions:

The Chartered
Institute of Marketing

MasterCard has considerable experience in sponsoring major football events. Is each event a project or a routine activity? Why could this be so?

VISA has taken over sponsorship for 2010 and 2014 World Cups. Is the uncertainty likely to be higher for VISA than for MasterCard?

Explain your thinking.

2 Organisational context for projects

'Every strategic initiative in a firm involves change management—and that is best accomplished through the tools, tactics and techniques of project management...'

Project management thus becomes the enabler, the vehicle through which all strategic change happens. The project itself is the gap filler, the bridge between what is and what will be' (Baker, 2008).

Projects should be undertaken within the usual corporate and functional (eg marketing) planning processes. The objectives set at different levels will set the foundations of strategy. Project management is often critical in ensuring that required changes are put in place.

Projects can be set at corporate level, departmental level, product level and market level or even across departments or geographies. Top-level projects include culture change throughout the organisation, new market entry or even implementation of an enterprise system. Departmental, product and market levels could include research or promotional projects for marketers, or the roll out of a new sales force reporting system as examples. Projects that span departments and geographies include new product development projects.

It is clear that projects are an essential part of the business activities at all levels. The challenge then is to prioritise and manage these appropriately to meet the organisation's needs.

Organisations and departments typically have many projects at any given time. Projects need to be aligned with the organisation's strategic priorities, and prioritised to ensure that the organisation's resources are focused on the priorities of the organisation. However, Rad and Levin (2008) comment that often projects appear like 'floating' islands and are not best integrated into the organisation.

They recommend the use of Project Portfolio Management (PPM), which enables organisations to select, resource and implement projects to ensure that the right projects are selected on the basis of their benefit to the organisation, and also taking account of the organisation's resources. Most PPM approaches result in a prioritised list of the most important projects. The project at the top of the list should have priority over others, and resourcing decisions should follow.

This PPM approach is not limited to new projects, but places a check on the relevance of projects as the organisation's strategy changes. As the portfolio term implies, this assessment must not only apply in the original selection decision, but also review the project at key stages to test the current alignment with the organisation's objectives and strategy, failing which can result in early project termination.

While the discipline of a PPM approach is perfectly logical, it must be recognised that the outcomes are often not. If a number of projects are competing for approval at a project board or equivalent, then the relative strength of support and positions of power of the project champions will often influence the decision.

External conditions may have an impact – it is much harder to get approval for expenditure during recessionary times, as otherwise important work will be cancelled or postponed.

It is often more difficult to make a case for large-scale in-house projects that do not *directly* relate to profitability. For example, a company may have a series of databases within separate departments that are not integrated. To rationalise them into a consolidated database with much more potential for improving, Customer

BPP
LEARNING MEDIA

Relationship Management could give significant longer-term returns. The problem is that it might be forgotten when a campaign shows good results that it was the refined database that pointed the way to better targeting of new clients.

ACTIVITY 12.3

Make a list of projects in your organisation and marketing department.

Consider whether these are strategic or operational projects, whether they are cross-department or within-a-department activities. Look also at the topics they address (promotions, products, culture, logos etc).

- Who is involved in managing, supporting and working on these?

- What differences can you see between marketing projects and the routine work in marketing?

- Are these projects viewed discretely – ie managed individually – or managed as part of a portfolio approach?

- What are the implications of your findings?

Projects involve estimates of how long and costly the separate elements will be. Estimates can be optimistic or pessimistic. It is hoped that the staff involved in any estimating will try and be as rational as possible, but some subjective opinion is needed. This can colour people's attitudes in deciding on the viability of the respective projects.

THE REAL WORLD

GlaxoSmithKline

GSK is one of the world's largest pharmaceutical companies. Project management is very important in its business success. A recent project has been to establish a global training programme to ensure that project management in Glaxo is at world-class level, with a common commitment to and understanding of company policies, attitudes to risk and discipline for managing projects.

Top management sponsored and championed the training programme, and project 'champions' were also identified within the strategic business units. These 'champions' helped build enthusiasm for the programme, and ensured that training materials were relevant to their SBUs. These approaches helped to reinforce the value of the programme to the company, and in using the materials.

In doing this, the project management training has resulted in relevance throughout the company, which enables cross-functional collaboration across the many GSK businesses.

(Alexander, 2008)

 The Chartered Institute of Marketing

What are the advantages of an organisation-wide approach to project management?

What problems could exist?

Does your organisation have a shared approach to project management?

Who, if anyone, champions a project management approach?

3 Why is project management important?

Professional project management started on major projects, such as new airport developments or major industrial developments. In such instances, project managers were required to co-ordinate and control the development process and the interaction of all players (eg owners, funding agencies, developers, designers, contractors, suppliers, operators, regulatory bodies etc). The complex nature of these projects meant that a formal management was required.

Successful project management in this sphere led to an awareness that organisations with strong project management were more effective than those that did not manage projects well. Project management then developed its 'body of knowledge' that has since spread to all sizes of projects across different functions and throughout organisations.

What is effective project management? Meredith and Mantell (2003) state that success or failure of a project is based on whether they have achieved targets on:

- Required performance (quality)
- Cost (money invested)
- Due date (delivery)

Traditionally, the key measure of success in marketing projects is achieving the *outcome*. A successful project is thus completed within the allocated time and cost and to the desired quality or results (such as achieving a level of awareness or encouraging people to trial or specific sales results).

The three core issues – performance, cost and delivery – are clearly sound commercial issues. A delay in the launch of a movie may mean that it misses a period when demand is traditionally high. A delay in launching the movie in one market may result in pirated copies there. A poor-quality soundtrack or editing of a movie may limit customers' enjoyment and reduce the possibility of word-of-mouth referrals. Failing in one of these areas results in loss of revenue and customer satisfaction. Exceeding the budget will also impact on profitability.

A further criterion is increasingly being added as a requirement for marketing projects – customer satisfaction. In this instance, customer satisfaction may refer to the internal customer – the person who commissions the project – or the organisation's customers.

However, customer satisfaction may be more complex to assess. Consider the following domestic examples.

Family A requires new fitted wardrobes. The joiners say it can be done to time and cost. When these are fitted – on schedule and to the agreed cost – they find that these are not substantial enough to withstand standard family use, and were broken within days.

Family B had the same budget and delivery, but were advised part-way through the contract that the original doors were potentially not going to survive 'normal' family use. They were advised that that they should exceed the budget given the requirements, which resulted in a delay in getting the replacement doors. However, once they were installed, they were glad they had added to the cost, and the late delivery was seen as acceptable.

Where outputs are clear and fixed – such as delivery dates, cost or quality – it is easy to set requirements. However, sometimes other factors may turn out to be more important. This is a problem in marketing projects, where uncertainty and change may require changes in the project definition (or **scoping**). However, this still must be managed well.

ACTIVITY 12.5

Find out about past projects in your organisation. Ideally, you should be able to identify some that are deemed to be successful and others that were unsuccessful.

What criteria are used to define success and failure of these projects?

Many organisations undertake research to calculate the costs of late delivery, or poor performance or monitor the cost/profit levels.

Identify whether this research exists in your organisation. What does this tell you about the importance of these outcomes?

4 Project management and marketing projects

Project management's contribution is now widely recognised as important within the functional areas of organisations. Marketing initiatives, activities and campaigns often fit the above definition of projects. Professional project management gives attention to the various players, tasks and outcomes for their success.

The consideration of project management will first address the types of marketing projects (activities), how these are undertaken (people and processes) and why they do it (strategic goals, competitive position and customer satisfaction). Success results from their effective co-ordination and integration.

4.1 Projects present some management challenges

Table 12.1   Sample project challenges table

Challenge	Comment
Teambuilding	The work is carried out by a team of people often from varied work and social backgrounds. The team must 'gel' quickly and be able to communicate effectively with each other.
Expected problems	Expected problems should be avoided by careful design and planning prior to commencement of work.
Unexpected problems	There should be mechanisms within the project to enable these problems to be resolved quickly and efficiently.
Delayed benefit	There is normally no benefit until the work is finished. The 'lead-in' time to this can cause a strain on the eventual recipient who is also faced with increasing expenditure for no immediate benefit.
Specialists	Contributions made by specialists are of differing importance at each stage.
Potential for conflict	Projects often involve several parties with different interests. This may lead to conflict.

4.2 Project success factors

Projects, small or large, are prone to fail unless they are appropriately managed and some effort is applied to ensure that factors that might contribute to success are present. Here are some of the key factors.

- **Clearly defined mission and goals** effectively communicated to, and understood by, all participants.

- **Top management support** that is visible is important in sending out the right messages regarding the significance of the project.

- **Competent project manager** with the necessary technical and inter-personal skills.

- **Well designed operational process** to ensure that work proceeds efficiently.

- **Competent team members** with the appropriate knowledge, skills and attitudes. A good team spirit helps to smooth the path to completion.

- **Sufficient resources** in terms of finance, materials, people and processes.

- **Excellent communication ethos** to ensure information is shared and there are no misunderstandings.

- **Use of effective project management tools** such as charts, leading edge software and project progress meetings.

- **Clear client focus** so that all work is done bearing in mind the needs of internal and external customers.

Project management ensures responsibilities are clearly defined and that resources are **focused** on specific objectives. The **project management process** also provides a structure for communicating within and across organisational boundaries.

All projects share similar features and follow a similar process. This has led to the development of **project management tools and techniques** that can be applied to all projects, no matter how diverse. For example, with some limitations, similar processes and techniques can be applied whether building a major structure (eg Terminal 5 at Heathrow Airport) or implementing a company-wide computer network.

All projects require a person who is ultimately responsible for delivering the required outcome. This person (whether officially given the title or not) is the **project manager**.

4.3 Why do projects go wrong?

Project planning is fundamental to project success. **Realistic timescales** and resource requirements must be established, use of **shared resources** must be planned and, most fundamental of all, jobs must be done in a sensible **sequence**.

Common reasons for project failure are also:

- Poor project planning (specifically inadequate risk management and weak project plan)
- A weak business case
- Lack of top management involvement and support

However, even if all these aspects are satisfactory there are other potential pitfalls that the project planner must avoid or work around. Here are some examples.

(a) **Unproven technology**

The use of **new technological developments** may be a feature of any project. The range of such developments extends from fairly routine and non-critical improvements, through major innovations capable of transforming working practices, costs and time scales, to revolutionary techniques that make feasible projects that were previously quite impracticable. As the practical potential of a technical change moves from minor to major, so its potential to cause disruption if something goes wrong with it also increases.

(b) **Changing client specifications**

It is not unusual for clients' notions of what they want to evolve during the lifetime of the project. However, if the work is to come in on time and on budget, they must be **aware** of what is **technically feasible**, **reasonable** in their **aspirations**, **prompt** with their **decisions** and, ultimately, **prepared to freeze the specification** so that it can be delivered.

Note that the term 'client' includes *internal* specifiers.

(c)   **Politics**

This problem area includes politics of all kinds, from those internal to an organisation managing its own projects, to the effect of national (and even international) politics on major undertakings. Identification of a senior figure with a project; public interest and press hysteria; hidden agendas; national prestige; and political dogma can all have disastrous effects on project management. **Lack of senior management support** is an important political problem.

---

5 A project-oriented organisation ('POO')

A **project oriented organisation** (POO) is an organisation, which:

- Defines 'Management by Projects' as an organisational strategy
- Applies temporary organisations for the performance of complex processes
- Manages a project portfolio of different project types
- Has specific permanent organisations to provide integrative functions
- Applies a 'New Management Paradigm'
- Has an explicit project management culture
- Perceives itself as project-oriented

A **project-oriented culture** ('POC') is characterised by the existence of an explicit culture of project management. In the POC, project management is considered as a business process, for which there exist specific procedures and a common understanding of the performance of this process.

---

6 Projects and strategy

6.1 Linking projects with strategy

Grundy and Brown (2002) see three links between **strategic thinking** and **project management**.

(a)   Many projects are undertaken as **consequences of the overall strategic planning process**. These projects may change the relationship between the organisation and its environment or they may be aimed at major organisational change.

(b)   Some important projects arise on a bottom-up basis. The need for action may become apparent for operational rather than strategic reasons: such projects must be given careful consideration to ensure that their overall effect is **congruent with the current strategy**.

(c)   Strategic thinking is also required at the level of the **individual project**, in order to avoid the limitations that may be imposed by a narrow view of what is to be done.

6.2 Project managing strategy

Project management in its widest sense is fundamental to much strategy. This is because very few organisations are able to do the same things in the same ways year after year. Continuing **environmental change** forces many organisations to include extensive processes of **adaptation** into their strategies. Business circumstances change and new conditions must be met with new responses or initiatives. Each possible new development effectively constitutes a project in the terms we have already discussed.

The Chartered Institute of Marketing

Gray and Larsen (2010) give examples, some of which have particular relevance to marketing and are noted below.

(a) **Compression of the product life cycle**: product life cycles have fallen to one to three years, on average, and it has become necessary to achieve very short time to market with new products if advantage is to be retained.

(b) **Global competition** emphasises cost and quality; project management techniques are used to achieve the new requirements.

(c) **Increased product complexity** requires the integration of diverse technologies.

(d) **Management delayering** has eliminated routine middle-management posts while much work has been outsourced: such organisational change tends to be continuous and project management techniques are required to get things done in a flexible manner.

(e) **Increased customer focus** in the form of customised products and close service relationships is often achieved through a project management approach.

Grundy and Brown (2002) offer an integrative analysis of this trend and suggest three reasons for taking a project management view of strategic management.

(a) Much strategy appears to develop in an incremental or fragmented way; detailed strategic thinking may be best pursued through the medium of a **strategic project** or group of projects. Project management is a way of making *ad hoc* strategy more deliberate and therefore better-considered.

(b) **Strategic implementation** is more complex than strategic analysis and choice; a project management approach, as outlined above, has an important role to play here, but must become capable of handling more complex, ambiguous and political issues if it is to play it effectively. When an apparent need for a project emerges, it should be screened to ensure that it supports the overall strategy.

(c) Even at the smaller, more traditional scale of project management, **wider strategic awareness is vital** if project managers are to deliver what the organisation actually needs

Of course, not all new developments are recognised as worthy of project management. For example, the installation of a new, shared printer in an office would probably be regarded as a matter of routine, though it would no doubt have been authorised by a responsible budget holder and installed and networked by a suitable technician. There would probably have been a small amount of training associated with its use and maintenance and it might have been the subject of a health and safety risk assessment. All these processes taken together look like a project, if a very small one.

In contrast to the multitude of such small events, modern organisations are likely to undergo significant change far less often, but sufficiently frequently and with developments that have sufficiently long lives for project management to be an **important aspect of strategic implementation**. Project management and **change management** are thus intimately linked.

An atmosphere of change and continuing development will be particularly evident in relation to marketing; information systems and technology; organisation structure; and organisation culture.

6.3 Marketing projects

Marketing as a business activity is, of course, closely linked to strategy and much of what has been said about the relevance of project management to strategy also applies to marketing. A moment's thought will produce many illustrations of this: here are some examples of marketing activities that require a major element of skilled project management.

- Test marketing
- Marketing research
- Creation of a customer database

- New product development
- Promotional campaigns
- Introduction of the various aspects of e-commerce

This is not to imply that all marketing management is project management, for that is simply not the case: there are many aspects of marketing that can be managed as continuing operations. However, the extensive applicability of project management to strategic implementation in general, and to marketing in particular, means that project management skills are a core competence for many organisations and for many marketing managers.

6.4 Project management as a core competence

Project management can be a **core strategic competence** for many companies. This is particularly true for companies working in such industries as consulting and construction, but it is also true of organisations of all kinds that can benefit from Grundy and Brown's (2002) approach outlined above. Such companies must ensure that they maintain and improve their project management abilities if they are to continue to be commercially successful.

Kerzner (2009) describes a five-level **project management maturity model** of continuous organisational improvement in the methodology of project management. Organisations should aspire to progress to the highest level, which is a state of **continuous improvement**. The five levels need not necessarily follow one another in a linear fashion: they may overlap, but the degree of overlap allowed is reflected in the risk associated with the overall process.

Level 1 Common knowledge

The importance of project management to the organisation is understood and training in the basic techniques and terminology is provided.

Level 2 Common processes

The processes employed successfully are standardised and developed so that they can be used more widely, both for future projects and in concert with other methods such as total quality management.

Level 3 Singular methodology

Project management is placed at the centre of a single corporate methodology, achieving wide synergy and improving process control in particular. A separate methodology may be retained for IS matters.

Level 4 Benchmarking

Competitive advantage is recognised as being based on process improvement and a continuing programme of benchmarking is undertaken.

Level 5 Continuous improvement

Benchmarking information is critically appraised for its potential contribution to the improvement of the singular methodology.

Models such as Kerzner's are a guide to progress; in particular they indicate corporate training needs and career development routes for project managers.

6.5 Strategic project management

It is possible to move from the slightly *ad hoc* approach outlined above, where project management is essentially an implementation method, to a more all-embracing theory of strategic development (which will inevitably involve marketing management activities). Grundy and Brown (2002) suggest that it is often appropriate for organisations to combine project management and strategic management into a process that they call **strategic project management**. This envisages strategy as a **stream of projects**.

7 The project-structured organisation

Globalisation, other aspects of rapid environmental change and, above all, the need to **exploit knowledge** make the **structures**, **processes** and **relationships** that compose configurations vital for strategic success.

Johnson, Scholes and Whittington (2008) identify three major groups of challenges for twenty-first century organisation structures.

(a)   The rapid pace of **environmental change** and increased levels of **environmental uncertainty** demand flexibility of organisational design.

(b)   The creation and exploitation of **knowledge** requires effective systems to link the people who have knowledge with the applications that need it.

(c)   **Globalisation** creates new types and a new scale of technological complexity in communication and information systems; at the same time, diversity of culture, practices and approaches to personal relationships bring their own new problems of organisational form.

Of these three sets of issues, the need to capture, organise and exploit knowledge is probably the most pressing for most organisations. An important element of response to this need is therefore an emphasis on the importance of facilitating effective **processes** and **relationships** when designing **structures**. Johnson, Scholes and Whittington (2008) use the term **configuration** to encompass these three elements.

(a)   **Structure** has its conventional meaning of organisation structure.

(b)   **Processes** drive and support people: they define how strategies are made and controlled; and how the organisation's people interact and implement strategy. They are fundamental to systems of control.

(c)   **Relationships** are the connections between people within the organisation and between those internally and those externally.

Effective processes and relationships can have varying degrees of formality and informality and it is important that formal relationships and processes are aligned with the relevant informal ones.

It is very important to be aware that structures, processes and relationships are **highly interdependent**: they have to work together intimately and consistently if the organisation is to be successful. Here we will be concerned with structures and processes: relationships in this model are not really relevant to project management.

7.1 Structure

An organisation's formal structure reveals much about it.

(a)   It shows who is **responsible** for what.

(b)   It shows who **communicates** with whom, both in procedural practice and, to a great extent, in less formal ways.

(c)   The upper levels of the structure reveal the **skills the organisation values** and, by extension, the **role of knowledge and skill** within it.

We are concerned here with the project-structured organisation, but we will approach it via some other forms that are relevant to it.

7.2 The functional structure

In a functional organisation structure, departments are defined by their **functions**, that is, the work that they do. It is a traditional, commonsense approach and many organisations are structured like this. Primary functions in a manufacturing company might be production, sales, finance, and general administration. Sub-departments of marketing might be selling, advertising, distribution and warehousing.

Functionally structured organisations can undertake projects successfully, partly, because they are able to provide in-depth expertise to project managers by allocating expert staff from appropriate functions. However, such staff can suffer from lack of focus if they still have a major functional role to play and it can be difficult to integrate their efforts properly.

Functional structures are simple and almost intuitive in their operation. However, they tend to promote insularity of thought and even distrust between functions. Achieving full co-ordination of the work of the various departments can be very difficult. This sort of problem leads to the matrix structure.

7.3 The matrix structure

The matrix structure imposes an extra layer of cross-functional management on top of the functional structure in order to improve co-operation and integration of effort by granting authority to project managers. Typically, the superimposed structure will be concerned with individual products or product groups. Product or brand managers may be responsible for budgeting, sales, pricing, marketing, distribution, quality and costs for their product or product line, but have to liaise with the R&D, production, finance, distribution, and sales departments in order to bring the product to the market and achieve sales targets.

The product managers may each have their own marketing team; in which case the marketing department itself would be small or non-existent. The authority of product managers may vary from organisation to organisation. The division of authority between product managers and functional managers must be carefully defined. Many decisions and plans will require careful negotiation if there is to be proper co-operation. This can result in stress, conflict and slow progress.

The matrix structure is now regarded as rather old-fashioned, since it is essentially a complex way of retaining the basic functional structure by adding extra resources to overcome its disadvantages. More modern approaches seek fundamental improvements and tend to focus on processes and projects.

7.4 The team-based structure

Both team- and project-based structures use cross-functional teams. The difference is that projects naturally come to an end and so project teams disperse.

A team-based structure extends the matrix structures' use of both vertical functional links and horizontal, activity-based ones by utilising **cross-functional teams**. Business processes are often used as the basis of organisation, with each team being responsible for the processes relating to an aspect of the business. Thus, a purchasing team might contain procurement specialists, design and production engineers and marketing specialists, to ensure that outsourced sub-assemblies are properly specified and contribute to brand values as well as being promptly delivered at the right price.

7.5 The project-based structure

The project-based structure is similar to the team-based structure except that projects, by definition, have a **finite life** and so, therefore, do the project teams dealing with them. Staff are allocated to a project team as

needed to deliver the project end state. This approach has been used for many years by such organisations as civil engineers and business consultants.

A high level of motivation is common and the integration of specialist work is eased by commitment to project delivery. Staff may work on several projects at the same time and thus have responsibilities to several project managers.

This approach is very flexible and easy to use; it tends to complete projects quickly if the discipline of project management is well-understood. In particular, it requires clear project definition if control is to be effective and comprehensive project review if longer-term learning is to take place.

However, there is a downside to project-based organisation:

- It can be expensive in staff and loss of economies of scale.
- Project teams can become insular, rivalrous and unwilling to import expertise when necessary.

In the project-based organisation, specialist functional departments still exist, but their role is to support the project teams. Since the project teams are staffed from a pool of experts, the functional structure remains intact and is not weakened by secondments to project work.

8 Types of projects

The differences between projects indicate how they should be managed. Brown (2000) sees projects as spreading across a continuum, with complexity increasing on a number of dimensions.

These dimensions include:

- Budget size
- Time span
- Human resources involved
- Complexity of tasks
- Cross-functional involvement
- Co-ordination required

Simple projects, characterised as low budget, short term, simple tasks, within a functional domain, would require more administrative management. Those that are more complex, with higher budgets, often with people from different departments (and maybe organisations) and spanning a longer term would require more sophisticated project management.

ACTIVITY 12.6

Refer to the list you developed in Activity 12.3

Use these, and any other factors that you deem appropriate, to distinguish between the projects in your organisation.

Which types of projects are you most involved with currently? What does this suggest about your role in managing projects?

Obeng (1994) takes a related approach to characterise four distinct project environments, with differences in process uncertainty (ie what to do) and the level of outcome uncertainty (ie what can be achieved) and named the four resulting categories.

1   **Paint by numbers** – Projects are low in process and outcome uncertainty, eg installing point of sale (POS) displays in retailers' outlets. The outcome is the same – the installation of the POS display – and the process (the way in which it is implemented) would be similar. However, differences, such as environmental factors (eg existing store design), time issues (eg minimising staff and customer inconvenience) and cost issues (eg adaptations for a given situation) mean this is not a completely

routine process. Often, organisations have process protocols or manuals detailing core processes. These types of projects are considered 'hard' projects, because of their fixed processes and clarity of outcome.

2   **Making a movie** – Projects are low in process uncertainty and high in outcome uncertainty. Producers and directors know what is involved in making the movie, although the topic, location and people vary. However, predicting the success of the movie is difficult. Projects such as new product or advertising campaign launches often have a similar pattern of high costs and a high risk of failure. These projects need clear, precise definition of outcomes, and stakeholders' expectations must be managed throughout the process. Timescales and budgets must be tightly controlled.

3   **The quest** – Projects are high in process uncertainty and low in outcome uncertainty. These projects have focused outcomes, but it is not clear how or when this will be achieved. Some exploratory development projects, such as AIDS cures for pharmaceutical companies, are in this category. Progress and resources reviews throughout these projects are essential to keep within cost. Further, focus is essential to keep the project on target.

4   **The foggy project** – Projects are vague in what is involved and in the expected results, so they have no set process and uncertainty outcomes. The original dot-com companies, like boo.com and lastminute.com, were foggy projects in their development stages, with little to guide them. Foggy projects need control over costs and level of risk. Marketers need extensive research to minimise the outcome failure, but time and cost management are important for these projects. Project managers need to manage stakeholder relationships as the project develops.

8.1 Hard and soft projects

Project management, as a management discipline, has largely been developed in a context of engineering, where there have been **well-defined, tangible objectives** to be achieved. Examples abound in the civil engineering and aircraft industries. Even where objectives have been events rather than things, such as mounting the Olympic games, it has been fairly clear what the desired outcomes were and what was involved in achieving them. There is, however, a wide category of projects for which **clear-cut scope does not exist** and it is difficult to see quite how to proceed. The project sponsors are aware that something must be done, but they are not quite sure what, precisely, it is, nor how to achieve it. The public sector could provide many illustrations, such as, for example, a perceived need to improve secondary education. Such a mission would be subject to extensive debate: first as to what was to be understood by 'improve'; and, second, how to go about the 'improving'.

8.2 Hard and soft labels

This apparent dichotomy represented by clearly defined, engineering-oriented programmes on the one hand and, vaguer areas of aspiration on the other has led to the use of the terms **hard** and **soft** to label the two types of project. This usage is not confined to the sphere of project management. Professor Mike Pidd of Lancaster University Business School in relation to operations research (OR) says:

'Unfortunate though these terms are, they have crept into common usage in recent years. They are really extreme points on a spectrum …' (Pidd, 2010).

- In hard OR, the question of problem definition is seen as relatively straightforward, and is more a question of finding out what is going on so that some appropriate analysis can be conducted … The key assumption is that this real world can be understood and (sic) a taken-for-granted way.

- By contrast, in soft OR, problem definition is seem as problematic and the process of problem structuring is regarded as crucial to the success of any soft OR. This relates to *John Dewey's* maxim that, 'a problem well put is a problem half solved'. The world is seen as multi-faceted, and the approaches adopted to try to understand it are interpretive or pluralistic. Thus, problem definition is seen as something which must be negotiated between parties who may have different interests and interpretations.'

Professor Pidd's remarks about problem definition are as applicable to project management as to OR. The other insight he offers us here is the idea of hard and soft as extreme points on a spectrum: an awareness that an apparently hard project has some soft aspects will be very useful to the project manager, as will be an awareness of the opposite case.

8.3 Hard and soft projects

Crawford and Pollack (2004) offer further description of what is meant by the terms hard and soft in the context of project management and offer a **seven element analysis** (outlined below) of the practical differences. They say:

Generally, objectivist, scientific approaches are hard, while subjectivist, social approaches are soft.

'Hard' approaches are about seeking and deploying objective knowledge, while soft approaches depend on the construction and subjective interpretation of knowledge.

8.4 Seven dimensions for analysis

Just as the overall classifications of hard and soft should be seen as ends of a spectrum, so Crawford and Pollacks's factors have degrees of presence in a project; they are not qualities that are present or absent. Most of these factors are both visible in the project and in the methods used in its management, though some are more relevant to one or the other.

(a) **Goal/objective clarity**. The degree of definition of the goal or objectives is the first dimension of analysis. Clear and specific desired outcomes are typical of engineering projects, while projects relating to research or organisational change, for example, tend to have less well-defined objectives.

(b) **Goal/objective tangibility**. The clarity and tangibility of project goals and objectives are often linked and the link may be very strong indeed, as with many engineering projects, where the objective is the construction of a physical object. However, this is not always the case: very clear goals can relate to intangible outcomes, such as individual exam success, while some very tangible construction objectives, for example, may be approached *via* ambiguous specifications.

(c) **Success measures**. Generally, it is easier to measure the degree of success of hard projects than of soft ones, partly as a result of their higher degree of goal tangibility and clarity. Quantitative performance measures are associated with hard projects and qualitative with soft. It should not be assumed that quantitative measures are superior to qualitative ones: each has its place. Quantitative measures are generally confined to a few variables considered significant in order to minimise the cost of data capture; this does not give a full picture. Nor are quantitative measures adequate when projects deal with qualitative matters such as attitude, learning and morale.

(d) **Project permeability**. The permeability of a project is the extent to which its objectives and processes are subject to influences outside the control of the project manager. The extent of these influences might be very limited in a short, simple project of a well-understood type. However, larger, less well-defined projects in less well-understood environments are likely to display considerable permeability. A good example of a factor increasing project permeability is the use of sub-contractors: their competence and diligence are far less subject to the control of the project manager than are those of in-house teams.

(e) **Number of solution options**. Hard projects will normally have one or more clearly defined outcomes, possibly handed down by authority. Softer projects will tend to have a range of possible outcomes that require consideration.

(f) **Degree of participation and practitioner role**. This dimension relates specifically to the nature of the appropriate project management practice and is dealt with below under implementation.

(g) **Stakeholder expectations**. Clear and logical stakeholder relationships are typical in hard projects, where the emphasis is on efficiency and predictability. Soft projects, because of their indeterminate nature, require a greater degree of interaction between stakeholders in order to overcome differences of style, language, assumptions and competence. The credibility of project staff in the eyes of stakeholders may become an issue.

8.5 Implementation considerations

The chances of making a project a success are enhanced if project management methods are tailored to the degree of its hardness or softness. Hard and soft approaches are not mutually exclusive and can be combined in ways that reflect the project's position on the various dimensions.

(a) **Goal/objective clarity**. The extent of clarity in the definition of a project's goals and objectives affects the methods that are used to move the project forward. Well-defined goals permit the application of techniques designed to achieve them efficiently. Where there is goal ambiguity, effort must be deployed on consultation, learning and negotiation in order to reach an adequate degree of goal definition. These processes will almost certainly have to be continued throughout the life of the project as new ambiguities arise and have to be dealt with. The management of the project thus entails as much consideration of **what** is to be done as of **how** to do it.

(b) **Project permeability**. Where project permeability is low, hard management methods that concentrate on clear objectives and techniques are appropriate. However, where permeability is high, a softer approach is needed. It may be necessary to deal with, for example, bureaucratic, organisational, cultural and political influences that are capable of affecting both objectives and methods. These influences will probably have to be dealt with sympathetically and diplomatically. They will require a **learning approach** to management and a degree of adjustment to project processes and intended outcomes as understanding of the environment grows.

(c) **Number of solution options**. Hard projects tend to be managed to achieve efficient delivery of clearly defined outcomes. Softer project management methods will tend to explore a range of methods and solutions to problems. This will be appropriate when there is potential benefit in questioning assumptions and exploring a range of options. Crawford and Pollack (2004) say 'the soft paradigm emphasises learning, debate, participation, exploration and questioning'.

(d) **Degree of participation and practitioner role**. A soft approach to project management is participative and collaborative, with expertise in facilitating the efforts of others being a major competence for the project manager. By contrast, the hard project management style tends to be based on individuals' technical expertise in their areas of concern. Project staff will have clearly defined roles and boundaries. This hard approach can achieve faster project delivery, but at a potential cost in lost innovation and learning.

(e) **Stakeholder expectations**. The implementation aspects of this dimension follow on from the previous one. A hard management approach will tend towards command and control, whereas a soft approach 'has culture, meaning and value as central concerns'. Organisations are seen as cultural systems and project success will depend on the perceptions of the stakeholders involved.

ACTIVITY 12.7

Refer to your earlier list of projects from your organisation.

Review how the organisation manages each of these types of projects.

Which of Obeng's categories are most difficult to manage?

The Chartered Institute of Marketing

Pepsi

In 2008, Pepsi unveiled its new logo – its second change in a decade. The process took five months, and it is believed to have cost more than $1 million for the brand experts who came up with the new logo, with its 'series of smiles', with a Pepsi smile, a Diet Pepsi grin and a Pepsi Max laugh.

Modern consumers are not impressed with global megabrands, and Pepsi saw a more engaging brand logo as a step towards a more relevant brand. The brief was to make the logo 'more dynamic', fun and alive, and so better suited to the more individual culture of consumers, and the growing range of soft drinks.

However, changing the new packs is only one part of the new logo launch. Think about how many billboards, vending machines, retail displays and other promotional items need to be replaced throughout the world. And then there are vehicles, packaging, uniforms etc. Co-ordinating the replacement of all old logos would cost hundreds of millions of dollars. For this reason, the full launch did not take place until late 2009.

(Advertising Age, 2008)

ACTIVITY 12.8

Review Obeng's four project categories and the Pepsi case.

Is this project of strategic importance for the company? What are the implications of your view?

Would the range of activities involved in the above project be classified as one project or several projects? Why?

▸ **Assessment tip**

The ability to recognise the context for the project management within the marketing function is a key determinant of assessment criteria that runs throughout this unit. Specifics are imperative and the examiner is looking for a synthesis and cohesion in terms of the situational scenario, subject matter and the organisational problem and solution.

CHAPTER ROUNDUP

- This chapter has given the background to project management.

- We established the three core stages of project management to be initiation, implementation and termination.

- We looked at how projects are usually founded in uncertainty.

- We also established that projects create significant challenges for management but can deliver ultimate successes for the organisation.

- We investigated the project management/marketing paradigm and established the conceptual links and the alignment with a strategic intention.

- This then in turn led us to explore how organisations can incorporate a project management culture into their fabric and how structures could change accordingly.

- Finally, we identified different types of project to include hard and soft definitions and undertakings and the considerations that need to be examined within project management.

FURTHER READING

Burke, R. (2003) *Project Management: Planning and Control*. Chichester, John Wiley & Sons.

REFERENCES

Alexander, J. (2008) *GlaxoSmithKline: Improving Global Project Management Capability*. Chief Learning Office. June 2008, pp58-59.

Anon. (2012) FIFA World Cup Media Kit. VISA, http://corporate.visa.com/newsroom/media-kits/fifa.shtml [Accessed 13 June 2012].

Baker, B. (2008) Filling the gaps. *PM Network*, 22(6), 26–27.

Brown, C.J. (2000) The dimensions of a project management supporting organisational culture. Paper presented to the World Project Management Week Conference, Queensland, Australia.

Crawford, L. and Pollack, J. (2004) 'Hard and soft projects: a framework for analysis'. *International Journal of Project Management*. Volume 22, Issue 8, November pp645-653.

Gray, C. F. and Larson, W. L. (2010) *Project Management: the Managerial Process*. 5th edition. London, McGraw-Hill.

Grundy, T. and Brown, L. (2002) *Strategic Project Management*. London, Thompson Learning.

Johnson, G. Scholes, K. and Whittington, R. (2008) *Exploring Corporate Strategy*. 8th edition. Harlow, Prentice Hall.

Kerzner, H. (2009) *Project Management: A Systems Approach to Planning, Scheduling and Controlling*. 10th edition. New York, John Wiley & Sons.

Lewis, J. P. (2008) *Mastering Project Management*. 2nd edition. Harlow, McGraw-Hill.

Maylor, H. (2010) *Project Management*. 4th edition. Harlow, Pearson.

Meredith, J. R. and Mantell, S. J. (2003) *Project Management: A Managerial Approach*. New York, John Wiley & Sons.

Obeng, E. (1994) *All Change! The Project Leader's Secret Handbook*. New Jersey, Prentice Hall.

Pidd, M. (2010) *Conceptual Modelling for Discrete-Event Simulation*. Abingdon, Taylor & Francis.

Rad, P. F. and Levin, G. (2008) 'What is project portfolio management'. *AACE International Transactions*, 1–4.

Wysocki, R. *et al* (2003) *Effective Project Management*. 3rd edition. New York, John Wiley & Sons.

Zmuda, N. (2008) *Advertising Age*. October, Vol. 79, Issue 40, p6.

QUICK QUIZ

1   What are the two main project management methods in the UK and the US?

2   What is the relationship between project quality, cost, scope and time?

3   What is a breakthrough project?

4   What are the three components of an organisation's configuration?

5   What are the disadvantages of the project-based structure?

ACTIVITY DEBRIEFS

Activity 12.1

Did you realise that each of these activities could form part of a project or, equally, could be part of continuing operations? The point of this exercise is to demonstrate that neither projects nor operations are necessarily defined by the activities involved. You must look beyond the individual activities and discern the wider nature of what is happening.

Activity 12.2

Each World Cup is a separate event, as a different football association in a different country and with different participants hosts it. There are differences in the host countries, the venues and the teams and matches, from competition to competition. However, MasterCard's experience in sponsoring football events can help in understanding processes, timescales and other issues, and to reduce the uncertainty. It will have experience in working with trusted suppliers.

There would be higher output uncertainty for an organisation with no previous experience of this event, but possibly one reason for the switch of sponsor was that FIFA did not believe MasterCard had met FIFA's desired outcomes from the sponsorship. Experience of sponsorship of other major sports events will help VISA, and would have been considered as part of the decision to award VISA the sponsorship contract. Some generic processes could be common between football and golf events, but each event has its unique characteristics. Often, companies seek to reduce input uncertainty by hiring specialists with proven track records.

Activity 12.3

Clearly, the answer to this question will depend on your business. However, you should be looking for examples and issues to help you with your studies.

For example:

If there is an organisation-wide approach to project management, you need to find out about this. Who is responsible for training and communications about this? Is there a circulation list for information on new initiatives? Is it for intra- or interdepartmental projects, or both? Are people running projects happy with this approach? Who monitors the use of this approach and how?

If there is no organisation-wide approach, then you need to find out whether individuals or departments have particular approaches, and what types of projects are undertaken. How is success of these projects measured? How do people learn how to manage projects? Is time allocated for project management, or is it just part of normal job responsibilities?

You do not need to have all the answers just now. But as the assessment for this topic is based on undertaking a project in your work environment, you need to have a general understanding of project management approaches in your organisation.

Activity 12.4

Again, your answers will vary depending on the projects undertaken within your organisation.

If you can find case studies of successful projects, identify what made them successful. Was the process well defined or implemented? Or was it the outcome of the project?

Equally, try to find out about unsuccessful projects. Why were they unsuccessful? Are there any lessons to be learnt here?

Activity 12.5

Again, your answers will vary depending on the projects undertaken within your organisation.
If you can find case examples of successful projects, identify what made them successful. Was the process well defined or implemented? Or was it the outcome of the project? Equally, try to find out about unsuccessful projects. Why were they unsuccessful? Are there any lessons to be learnt here?

Activity 12.6

Once again, your answer will depend on your organisation. But, by now, you should be clear about the difference between routine activities and projects. You should be able to consider the uncertainty levels in your projects and know what forms of uncertainty exist.

Projects differ from routine work in their uniqueness and the resultant uncertainty. Managing this is a key to success.

Some of your projects may be adaptations of earlier projects. These still need project management, but there may be a fairly well-developed process, and your role may be to follow this. Large, new, complex projects may change between projects. You may be involved in managing these or contributing to them. In the latter case, you will be reporting to a project manager.

For your assessed project, look at the above criteria. You need to have a manageable project, which can be completed within the timeframe. Think carefully about what is realistic.

Activity 12.7

Some organisations do not distinguish well between these different types of projects. This can result in poor use of management and administrative time.

Often it is the smaller routine projects that are harder to deal with, if the organisation does not support these appropriately.

Activity 12.8

The Pepsi case shows a strategic project – probably one of the most substantial ones that could be undertaken.

There is one 'master' project, but in each country, brand, type of activity (eg merchandising, trade marketing and advertising).

These must ultimately all link together. Once the master project is agreed, then all the smaller components would automatically have priority. However, the WAY in which these are delivered in each market, for each brand, would have to be approved (ie have a business case for a specific subproject). Your project may be one of these smaller projects that are part of a bigger project.

QUICK QUIZ ANSWERS

1   PRINCE2 and PMBOK

2   Project scope is the totality of what is to be done during the life of the project and what is to be achieved at the end of it. Lewis describes it as the area of a triangle whose sides are quality, time, cost. Time, cost, scope and quality are therefore interrelated variables. If any one or more of these variables changes there is an impact on one or more of the other variables. If you have an agreed project timescale, budget, scope of work and quality outcome, then a change to any of these variables must affect one or more of the others.

3   One that will have a material effect on either the business's external competitive edge, its internal capabilities or its financial performance

4   Structures, processes and relationships

5   It can be expensive in staff and loss of economies of scale; and project teams can become insular, prone to rivalry and unwilling to import expertise when necessary.

CHAPTER 13

Project process

Introduction

Having considered the nature of a project in the previous chapter, we are now in a position to look at project management in more detail and we will focus on managing marketing projects in particular. We will look at a simple model of how projects can be expected to progress and then examine in detail the important ideas affecting how a project is initiated. Determining project scope is a very important aspect of this process and is unlikely to be an easy task.

Project stakeholders are likely to be a major concern for project managers and skill in dealing with them is an essential quality for such managers. Finally we will look at the problem of providing adequate and appropriate resources for the project.

Topic list

The project life cycle ① | Project management plan ⑨

Defining the project ②

Developing an understanding of project scope ③

Project implementation ④

Project termination and project evaluation ⑤

Stakeholder interests ⑥

Project resources – skills and people ⑦

Project management methodologies ⑧

4.3	Develop the main stages of a marketing project plan, identifying the activities, estimating time and cost, sequencing of activities, and assess the competency and skills required of the people needed to deliver the project:
	■ Project initiation
	■ Scope and objectives
	■ Beginning/end dates
	■ Key/core deliverables
	■ Methodology adaptation
	■ Project limitations
	■ Risk management
	■ Outline budgeting
	■ Project implementation
	■ Schedules/schemes of work
	■ Resource reviews
	■ Personnel requirements
	■ Project termination
	■ Project evaluation
4.4	Critically assess the importance of and techniques for establishing the marketing project's scope, definition and goals relative to the organisational marketing plan
	■ The project scoping document
	■ Goals, objectives and critical success factors
	■ In/out of scope
	■ Risk highlights
	■ Assumptions
	■ Roles and responsibilities
	■ Stakeholder management

1 The project life cycle

> ▶ **Key terms**
>
> An **initial project plan** is an outline plan, detailing the outcome and key participants and stages. This is developed in the initiation stage of the project.
>
> The **integrative project plan** is the detailed project plan, developed and used throughout the implementation stage. This includes details of schedules, budgets and resourcing.
>
> **Project stakeholders** are the individuals and organisations that are involved in, or may be affected by, project activities and outcomes.
>
> The **project team** comprises the people who report directly or indirectly to the project manager.

Projects may be thought of as having a **life cycle**. This concept is useful for understanding the processes involved in project management and control, since the resources required and the focus of management attention vary as projects move from one stage to the next.

1.1 A typical four-stage project life cycle

Typically, four stages exist within a project life cycle. It may help you to remember the four stages if you think of them as the **four Ds** (definition, design, delivery, development).

1.1.1 Project definition

Project definition is the first stage. Its essential element is the definition of the purpose and objectives of the project. This stage may include abstract processes of conceptualisation, more rigorous analysis of requirements and methods, feasibility studies and, perhaps most important, a **definition of scope**. As discussed in the previous chapter, the scope of a project is, effectively, what is included and what is not, both in terms of what it is intended to achieve and the extent of its impact on other parts of the organisation, both during its execution and subsequently. An important initial consideration will always be **projected cost**, even if this cannot be estimated very accurately at this stage.

The project definition stage may also include the procedures required for **project selection**. We will discuss this further below, but for now we simply point out that an organisation may be aware of a larger number of worthwhile projects than it has resources to undertake. Some rational process for deciding just which projects will proceed is therefore required.

1.1.2 Project design

The project design phase will include detailed planning for **activity**, **cost**, **quality**, **time** and **risk**. Final project authorisation may be delayed until this stage to ensure that the decision is taken in the light of more detailed information about planned costs and benefits.

1.1.3 Project delivery

The project delivery phase includes all the work required to deliver the planned project outcomes. Planning will continue, but the emphasis is on getting the work done. Sub-phases can be identified:

(a)   The people and other resources needed initially are assembled at **start-up**.

(b)   Planned project activities are carried out during **execution**.

(c)   **Completion** consists of success or, sometimes, abandonment.

(d)   The delivery phase comes to an end with **handover**. This is likely to include **project closure** procedures that ensure that all documentation, quality and accounting activities are complete and that the customer has accepted the delivery as satisfactory.

1.1.4 Project development

Handover brings the delivery phase to an end but the project continues through a further stage of management largely aimed at **improving the organisation's overall ability to manage projects**.

(a)   There should be an **immediate review** to provide rapid staff feedback and to identify short-term needs such as staff training or remedial action for procedure failures.

(b)   **Longer-term review** will examine the project outcomes after the passage of time to establish its overall degree of success. **Lifetime costs** are an important measure of success. There should also be longer-term review of all aspects of the project and its management, perhaps on a functional basis.

It is tempting to ignore the need for project review, especially since, done properly, it imposes significant costs in terms of management time and effort. It is, however, essential if the organisation is to improve the effectiveness of its project management in the future.

2 Defining the project

Limits to resource availability mean that not all potential projects will be undertaken; rational methods are used to select them.

Project initiation tasks include the appointment of project manager and sponsor; stakeholder analysis and the definition of project scope. The business case explains why the project is needed, while the project charter gives authorisation for it to be undertaken.

2.1 Project selection

As already mentioned, it is likely that an organisation will be aware of a greater number of potentially advantageous projects than it has resources to undertake. It is, therefore, necessary to **select projects carefully** in order to make the best use of those limited resources. Project assessment and selection is analogous to strategic choice, not least because many projects are of strategic significance. The techniques used for making strategic choices are, therefore, also applicable. The criteria of **suitability**, **acceptability** and **feasibility** are applicable to many project choice problems, perhaps reinforced by the use of more detailed assessment techniques such as those below.

(a) **Risk/return analysis** using **discounted cash flow** techniques, expected values and estimates of attractiveness and difficulty of implementation.

(b) **Weighted scoring** of project characteristics.

(c) Assessment of **organisational priority**.

(d) **Feasibility studies** addressing technical, environmental, social and financial feasibility; such studies are costly and time-consuming and are likely to be restricted to front-running project proposals.

(e) **SWOT analysis**, assessing the strengths and weaknesses of individual projects against the opportunities and threats facing the organisation.

2.2 Project initiation

When a project has been approved in general terms, it should be the subject of a number of management processes and tasks in order to initiate it and move into the execution phase. The exact nature of these processes may well vary from project to project and according to the particular project management methodology adopted. Schwalbe lists **pre-initiating tasks** and **initiating tasks**. The pre-initiating tasks follow on directly from the formal project selection process.

The Chartered
Institute of Marketing

2.2.1 Pre-initiating tasks

Pre-initiating tasks are the responsibility of the senior managers who decide that the project should be undertaken.

(a) Determination of **project scope** and quality, time and cost targets.

(b) Identification of the **project sponsor** (a senior manager who is accountable for the resources used by the project manager).

(c) Selection of the **project manager**.

Note: The roles and responsibilities of the project manager are discussed later in this chapter.

(d) **Senior management meeting** with project manager to review the process and expectations for managing the project.

(e) Decision whether the project actually needs to be divided into two or more smaller projects.

2.2.2 Initiating tasks

Initiating tasks are carried out by the **project manager**.

(a) Identification of **project stakeholders** and their characteristics.
(b) Preparation of a **business case** for the project.
(c) Drafting of a **project charter** (PRINCE2: project initiation document).
(d) Drafting an initial statement of **project scope.**
(e) Holding a **project initiation meeting** (PMBOK: 'kick-off' meeting).

2.3 More on project definition

It will be common with 'hard' projects, managed in a top-down fashion, to proceed directly from project selection to project initiation. However, many projects, especially 'soft' ones, will require an extensive project definition stage. This will help to increase the clarity with which overall objectives are understood, increase motivation and reduce **mission creep**, which is the tendency for expectations to increase as time passes.

2.3.1 Developing vision and shared understanding

It is important to spend time at the earliest stage of project planning on reaching a shared understanding of what the project is about. This applies to all projects but is particularly vital to the kind of 'soft' project that will be common in marketing. Lewis (2008) recommends a process of brainstorming, discussion and group activity in order to create a sense of ownership and an agreed vision and understanding of what the project is to achieve. Lewis also recommends the use of mindmaps as an aid to this process and suggests that the outcome should effectively be a list of desired features to be provided at the culmination of the project. These features or attributes should be prioritised into three groups:

- Musts
- Wants
- Nice to haves

When this stage is complete, it is appropriate to move on to more detailed consideration of consideration of **project scope and strategy**.

3 Developing an understanding of project scope

As we have already indicated, the word '**scope**' is used in project management to mean both the outcomes that are required and the work that is to be done to achieve them. It is obviously of great importance that everyone involved in a project should have a common understanding of these matters. If this common understanding is not reached, sooner or later there will be acrimonious disputes. A **careful specification of project scope** is, therefore, of great importance and the project management methodology in use may require that this be a separate document, known as a **project scoping document.** Equally, it may be that the business case and the project charter between them provide a clear statement of agreed scope. Under the **PRINCE2** method, the **business case** performs the role of a statement of project scope.

Gray and Larson (2010) say that the document defining scope should be developed under the direction of the project manager and customer (or project owner). It will be an essential foundation for project planning and measuring the extent of project success, and needs to be developed in conjunction with key project stakeholders.

The following diagram shows the process of scope definition.

Figure 13.1   Scoping process

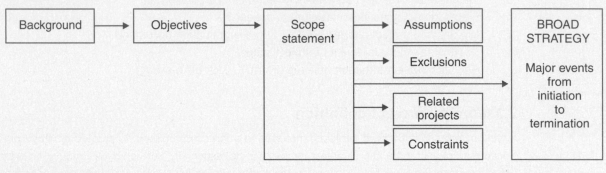

Scope statements identify all of the elements of work in the project. A scope statement must be linked directly to meeting the defined project requirements. For example, a marketing project may be to investigate and recommend a low cost communication strategy for improving awareness of a new brand of high fibre bread and thereby increasing sales by 15%.

The project scoping document would specify factors to be considered:

- Ways to achieve the sales target
- Likely audience/stakeholders
- Costings
- Timeframes
- Resource considerations
- Effect on sales of other products

It is likely that in larger projects it will become necessary to **adjust the project scope**. This might occur, for example, if resources are unavoidably reduced or it becomes clear that a feasibility study was too optimistic or too pessimistic. When a change to project scope becomes apparent, it is important that it is **clearly stated** and that the revision is **approved by the interested stakeholders**.

Grundy and Brown (2002) summarise the process of **project definition** as the preparation of answers to a series of questions.

- What **opportunities and threats** does the project present?
- What are its **objectives**?
- What are its potential **benefits**, **costs** and **risks**?
- What is its overall **implementation difficulty**?
- Who are the **key stakeholders**?

A number of techniques that aid analytical thinking may be used when addressing these questions.

3.1 Defining the key issues – fishbone analysis

Fishbone analysis (root-cause, cause and effect or *Ishikawa* diagram analysis) is useful for establishing and analysing key issues. It can be used both on existing problems, opportunities and behavioural issues, and on those that may be anticipated, perhaps as a result of the construction of a scenario.

The essence of fishbone analysis is to break down a perceived issue into its smallest underlying causes and components, so that each may be tackled in a proper fashion. It is called fishbone analysis because the overall issue and its components are traditionally analysed and presented on a diagram such as the one below.

Figure 13.2   Fishbone analysis

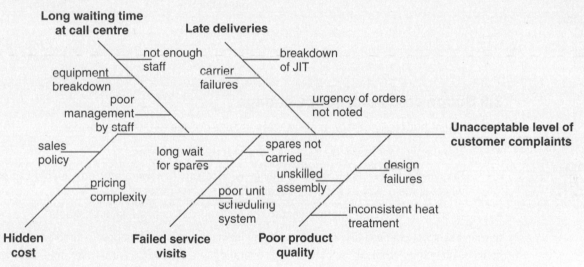

The major issue or problem is shown at the right-hand side of the page and the perceived causes and influences are shown, in no particular order, on the 'bones' radiating from the central spine. Each 'bone' can be further analysed if appropriate. It is common to use familiar models such as the Ms list of resources (men, money, machines and so on) to give structure to the investigation, though not necessarily to the diagram. The fish bone diagram itself is not, of course, essential to the process of analysis, but it forms a good medium for brainstorming a problem and for presenting the eventual results.

3.2 Determining performance drivers

Many projects are aimed at or include improving some aspect of the performance of a department, activity or function: this is true at the strategic level and is likely to be true of projects at lower levels, such as marketing projects. **Performance driver analysis** is useful in such cases; essentially it is another brainstorming and presentation technique.

The essence of the technique is to identify two groups of performance-related influences: those that **enable good performance** and those that **hinder or prevent it**. The factors in these two groups are drawn as arrows against a baseline, the length of each arrow representing the perceived strength of the influence it represents.

Figure 13.3   Performance drivers

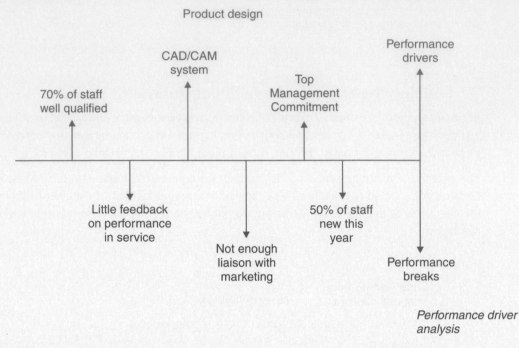

Performance driver analysis

3.3 Scope creep and scope change

As the earlier materials identify, projects often change over time. Changes may be:

- Mandatory – for example, resulting from changes in legislation.

- Required – for example, where a change is necessary to solve a problem, such as an error in copy; or where something was not defined correctly in the first instance.

- Optional – where an improvement to the original work is possible or desirable.

In many sectors, changes to a project plan may indicate that there has been a problem with the initial project goals or planning. However, as marketing is operating in a dynamic environment, often changes will be required by factors that are outside the control of the project team. For example:

- The target market segment is changing preferences, for example owing to the economic environment.
- A competitor has launched a new product.
- An external partner has withdrawn from the project.

Chapter 12 referred to research that showed that IT personnel were uncomfortable with changes caused by the changing business dynamics. These changes make managing scope in marketing projects difficult.

IT consultant Gopal Kapur (2004) says that project managers should act like guide dogs at times, and show 'intelligent disobedience'.

He comments that as the business environment and business knowledge change, then it is tempting for project sponsors to ask for changes in the project scope. However, he comments that some of these changes can be 'half-baked', and that accepting these can lead to extensive scope creep.

He advises project managers to learn to say no to their sponsors, using the analogy of a guide dog and its owner going to cross the road. If the owner wishes to cross the road, it is the guide dog's responsibility to sense the danger, and overrule its owner when appropriate.

Many people working on projects find managing unreasonable expectations from sponsors to be the most difficult. However, practicing 'intelligent disobedience' can result in a more focused project.

Scope creep is the term when work is added to the project after the scope has been established and agreed. Scope creep involves the changes to the project's ongoing requirements or activities increasing, without approved changes to cost and schedule allowances. Changes can and will occur, but these need to be managed through a scope management process.

Scope creep often changes many aspects, such as the timescales, costs and often outcomes. Scope creep often starts with small changes, in the total project or in one aspect of the project. These could include changes to fulfilment processes, or extent of catering menus etc or venues. Often, these will have 'knock on' effects, such as cancellation charges, additional costs, delays in completion etc. Indeed, it is commonly believed that small incremental changes can lead to project failure. Although small, these can impact on the costs, schedule and the risk of the project.

Saunders *et al* (2005) undertook research on the screening and evaluation criteria for new product development (NPD) research. They found that criteria for acceptance or rejection of product concepts vary through the NPD process. At the initial screening stage, there is a focus on the financial criteria. In the detailed screening and predevelopment stages, evaluation focuses on marketing issues, including the product, brand, promotional and market requirements. Post-launch, the decision-makers are more interested in how the new product fits with the business commercially and with its production processes. Only financial criteria are highly valued at all stages of the project.

3.4 Avoiding scope creep

Scope creep can be limited by setting systems in place. Common approaches for avoiding scope creep include:

(a)   **Education of the project team or sponsor**. Explaining the impact of change on the project success often focuses people on avoiding the 'best' solution (eg adding every feature to a new product, rather than those specified in the project plan or that meet the target segment's requirements).

(b)   **Establishing processes for changes, such as a change request process**. Often, individuals make decisions that may impact on others in the project. Using formal processes for approving changes can stop regular and minor changes – or indeed more substantial ones. Change request processes can be initiated, with supporting documentation, which are to be submitted in writing to the project manager, and (depending on the scale of the change) reviewed by the project manager, the project team and/or the project sponsors. Clearly, agreed (and openly communicated) criteria to judge whether changes are appropriate (ie fitting to the project outcomes) and viable (in terms of value for money, ROI etc) can reduce changes.

Projects should also have a project contingency fund to be used in case of essential changes.

ACTIVITY 13.2

In your organisation, are projects considered as they emerge, or in a formal project evaluation process?

What are the advantages and disadvantages of your organisation's approach?

If you have a formal evaluation process, what criteria are used to evaluate these projects?

What method of selection is used?

THE REAL WORLD

IBM

IBM is one of the world's top brands. Much of IBM's work involves planning and implementing complex bids and solutions. These are essentially project management tasks. IBM has implemented project management training for many staff involved in these roles.

Subsequently, IBM sought to measure the benefits of project management training, and its research showed that projects with qualified project managers were less likely to fail. Alongside this, these results also showed increased customer satisfaction. These trained project managers also received more positive project approvals. In a pattern similar to Heskett's service profit chain, these project managers were also less likely to leave IBM (suggesting higher job satisfaction). Staff retention is important – other companies seek PM-qualified staff.

(Shaw, 2011)

ACTIVITY 13.3

Think about the people who should be involved in your assessed project. Do not just think about who is 'usually' involved in these projects – think about the types of roles that need to be part of the project team.

You need to start thinking about the roles and involvement of each of these in the assessed project. You will need to consider this more formally later in your work.

THE REAL WORLD

London Olympic bid

Bidding to host the Olympics required outline project planning to gain the approval of the Olympics committee. London 2012 prepared a written document as part of its submission to the Olympics Bid Committee.

Amongst the issues, the London 2012 organisation have to consider are media operations, transport, security, venues etc, and the work to bring these to the required standard. These issues were considered individually and in detail in its bid document – an initial project plan – and plans for key areas at: http://www.london2012.com/plans/ index.php.

The Chartered
Institute of Marketing

4 Project implementation

The majority of the work in projects takes place within the project process. However, this section is shorter than that for initiation. This is because many of these issues are considered in the following chapters.

The first part of implementation is developing an outline plan into an integrative project plan (Meredith and Mantell, 2003), including:

1   Overview of the objectives and scope.

2   Detailed objectives – profit, technical and competitive aspects of the project.

3   The general approach of the managerial and technical aspects of the project – how this links or deviates from existing approaches and projects. This would include the choice of the appropriate project management methodologies.

4   Contractual requirements – the reporting processes of all parties, the review processes, agreements with third parties and schedules. Information on changes to the plan, including rescheduling, the substitution of suppliers or cancellation of the contract should also be determined.

5   Schedules for the work – the components parts and key milestones in the progress of the project. The project scope should be broken down ('decomposed') into parts. This depends on the chosen work breakdown structure (WBS). At its simplest, a WBS is a structured and itemised 'to do' list. Each task should be detailed, with time estimates. Timings should be agreed by the project manager.

6   Resource issues – the detailed budget should be included, as should the project budget monitoring process.

7   Personnel requirements – the skills required, and processes and criteria for selection of employees, training programmes.

8   Methods and standards of evaluation – mechanisms for collecting and storing data on the progress of the project should be determined.

9   Potential problems or assumptions – including terrorist threats, weather problems or governmental bureaucratic factors that might be outside the project manager's control.

10 Contingency planning – most plans have some form of contingency planning. The approach and allowances for this is part of the main project plan.

5 Project termination and project evaluation

The third stage of the project management life cycle is project termination. A decision to terminate a project occurs when one or more of the following occur:

(a)   A project is superseded, possibly by competitors' actions or a new technical development.

(b)   A project is 'killed' by management before completion, often once its internal sponsor leaves or another initiative has greater priority or fit.

(c)   Projects are deprived of funds and starve to death.

(d)   Projects are integrated into the routine activities of an organisation.

The decision to terminate a project is not the end of the project management process, which ends after the project evaluation. Evaluation determines how well the project met its objectives, including time, cost and

quality, and how well the needs of its stakeholders were met. Project evaluation helps develop learning to guide future projects.

Small projects may have informal reviews, but larger projects need formal reviews. Although evaluation takes place throughout the project, an integrated evaluation at the end of the project reflects on reasons for success and failure that may be missed in operational management. Project audits are rigorous reviews, using a structured approach, and often undertaken by an independent party.

6 Stakeholder interests

It is important to understand who has an interest in a project, because part of the responsibility of the project manager is **communication** and the **management of expectations**. An initial assessment of stakeholders should be made early in the project's life, taking care not to ignore those who might not approve of the project, either as a whole, or because of some aspect such as its cost, its use of scarce talent or its side-effects. The nature and extent of each stakeholder's interest in, and support for (or opposition to) the project should be established as thoroughly as possible and recorded in a stakeholder register. This will make it possible to draw on support where available and, probably more important, anticipate and deal with stakeholder-related problems. The project manager should be aware of the following matters for each stakeholder or stakeholder group:

(a)   Goals
(b)   Past attitude and behaviour
(c)   Expected future behaviour
(d)   Reaction to possible future developments

6.1 Managing stakeholders

It is important to be thorough in assessing stakeholders: a failure to identify and consider a stakeholder group is likely to lead to problems. Here is a list of individuals and groups that might be expected to have a stake in a project.

(a)   **The project manager** – reputation and even employment are at stake.

(b)   **The project team** – they have to work on the project but may have other roles and higher personal priorities.

(c)   **The project sponsor/ budget holder** – this senior figure will demand high standards but may be reluctant to fund all the desirable resources.

(d)   **The customers** – may be external or internal and may break down into several groups, such as an internal user group and an external group who should receive improved service as a result of the enhanced capability the user group should acquire on successful completion of the project.

(e)   **Managers and staff in supporting functions** such as finance and HR can have extensive influence on the project and its chances of success.

(f)   **Line managers of seconded staff** – their own work and prospects may be disrupted.

(g)   **Other project managers**, **teams and sponsors** – rivalry for resources may cause conflict.

(h)   **Regulators and auditors** of all kinds, both internal and external, are likely to take an interest in a project.

Project stakeholders may be divided into two main groups.

(a) **Process stakeholders** have an interest in how the project process is conducted. This group includes those involved in it, those who want a say in it, and those who need to evaluate and learn from it.

(b) **Outcome stakeholders** have an interest in the outcomes, results or deliverables of the project. This group includes not only the customer groups described above, but also, typically, some regulators and compliance staff.

The project manager must manage a broad range of complex relationships if the project is to succeed. This amounts to achieving co-operation through influence rather than authority. Gray and Larson (2008) speak of creating a social network to manage the relationships with those the project depends on. The project manager should know whose co-operation, agreement or approval is required for the project to succeed and whose opposition could prevent success. It is particularly important to enlist the support of top management. This not only brings an adequate budget, it signals the project's importance to the organisation and enhances the motivation of the project team.

7 Project resources – skills and people

7.1 The project manager

All projects require a person who is ultimately responsible for delivering the required outcome. This person (whether officially given the title or not) is the **project manager**. The duties of a project manager are summarised below.

Table 13.1   Project manager roles and responsibilities

Duty	Comment
Outline planning	<ul><li>Project planning (eg targets, sequencing).</li><li>Developing project targets such as overall costs or timescale needed (eg project should take 20 weeks).</li><li>Dividing the project into activities and placing these activities into the right sequence.</li></ul> Developing a framework for procedures and structures, manage the project (eg decide, in principle, to have weekly team meetings, performance reviews etc).
Detailed planning	Work breakdown structure, resource requirements, network analysis for scheduling.
Teambuilding	Build cohesion and team spirit.
Communication	The project manager must keep supervisors informed about progress as well as problems, and ensure that members of the project team are properly briefed.
Co-ordinating project activities	Between the project team and users, and other external parties (eg suppliers of hardware and software).
Monitoring and control	The project manager should estimate the causes for each departure from the standard, and take corrective measures.
Problem-resolution	Even with the best planning, unforeseen problems may arise.
Quality control	There is often a short-sighted trade-off between getting the project out on time and the project's quality.
Risk management	A key consideration is project failure and hence project risks and potential risk areas must be identified and monitored.

Project management as a discipline developed because of a need to co-ordinate resources to obtain desired results within a set timeframe. Common project management tasks include establishing goals and objectives, developing a work-plan, scheduling, budgeting, co-ordinating a team and communicating.

The project management process helps project managers maintain control of projects and meet their responsibilities.

7.2 The responsibilities of a project manager

A project manager may be regarded as having responsibilities both to management and to the project team.

Responsibilities to management:

(a)　　Ensure resources are used efficiently – strike a balance between cost, time and results.

(b)　　Keep management informed with timely and accurate communications about progress and problems.

(c)　　Manage the project competently and take action to keep it on schedule for successful completion.

(d)　　Behave ethically, and adhere to the organisation's policies.

(e)　　Maintain a customer orientation (whether the project is geared towards an internal or external customer) – customer satisfaction is a key indicator of project success.

Responsibilities to the project team:

(a)　　Ensure the project team has the resources required to perform tasks assigned.

(b)　　Provide new team members with a proper briefing and help them integrate into the team.

(c)　　Provide any support required when members leave the team either during the project or on completion.

(d)　　Listen properly to team members so that potential problems are identified and can be dealt with as soon as possible.

7.3 The skills required of a project manager

To meet these responsibilities a project manager requires a broad range of skills. The skills needed are similar to those necessary when managing a wider range of responsibilities. A project manager requires excellent technical and personal capabilities. Some of the skills required are detailed in the following table.

Table 13.2   Project manager skill set

Type of skill	How the project manager should display the type of skill
Leadership and team building	▪ Be **enthusiastic** about what the project will achieve.
	▪ Be **positive** (but realistic) about all aspects of the project.
	▪ Understand where the project fits into the '**big picture**'.
	▪ **Delegate** tasks appropriately – and not take on too much personally.
	▪ Build team spirit through encouraging **co-operation** and sharing of information.
	▪ Do not be restrained by organisational structures; a high tolerance for ambiguity (lack of clear-cut authority) will help the project manager.
	▪ Be prepared to motivate team members and give due praise and encouragement.
Project administration	▪ Ensure all project **documentation** is clear and distributed to all who require it.
	▪ Use project **management tools** to analyse and monitor project progress.
Communication	▪ **Listen** to project team members. Exploit good ideas whatever the source.
	▪ Use **persuasion** to win over reluctant team members or stakeholders to support the project.
	▪ Ensure management is kept **informed** and is never surprised.
	▪ Encourage team members to share their knowledge and support each other.
Technical	▪ By providing (or at least access to) the **technical expertise** and experience needed to manage the project.
Personal	▪ Be **flexible**. Circumstances may develop that require a change in plan.
	▪ Show **resilience**. Even successful projects will encounter difficulties that require repeated efforts to overcome.
	▪ Be **creative**. If one method of completing a task proves impractical a new approach may be required.
	▪ **Patience** is required even in the face of tight deadlines. The 'quick-fix' may eventually cost further time than a more thorough but initially more time-consuming solution.
	▪ **Keep in touch** with team members as their performance is key to the success of the project.

You should note carefully the difference between the skills required and the responsibilities of the project manager.

7.4 Building a project team

Project success depends to a large extent on the team members selected. The ideal project team achieves project completion on time, within budget and to the required specifications – with the minimum amount of direct supervision from the project manager.

The team will comprise individuals with **differing skills and personalities**. The project manager should choose a balanced team that takes advantage of each team member's skills and compensates elsewhere for their weaknesses.

The project team will normally be drawn from existing staff, but highly recommended **outsiders with special skills** may be recruited. When building a team the project manager should ask the following questions.

(a)   **What skills** are required to complete each task of the project? This list will be based on the project goals established previously. (This process is explained in the next chapter.)

(b)   **Who** has the talent and skills to complete the required tasks, whether inside or outside the organisation?

(c) Are the people identified **available**, **affordable**, and able to join the project team?

(d) What level of **supervision** will be required?

This information should be **summarised in worksheet format**, as shown in the following example.

Figure 13.4 Worksheet example

Project Skill Requirements		
Project Name: _____	Date worksheet completed: _____	
Project Manager: _____		
Task	*Skill needed*	*Responsibility*

The completed worksheet provides a document showing the skills required of the project team. Deciding who has the skills required for each task and if possible seconding those identified to the project team, should be done **as early as possible**. Team members should then be able to **participate** in the planning of schedules and budgets. This should encourage the acceptance of agreed deadlines, and a greater commitment to achieve project success.

The individuals selected to join the team should be told **why they have been selected**, referring both to their technical skills and personal qualities. This should provide members with guidance as to the role they are expected to play.

Although the composition of the project team is critical, project managers often find it is not possible to assemble the ideal team, and have to do the best they can with the personnel available. If the project manager feels the best available team does not possess the skills and talent required, the project should be **abandoned or delayed**.

Once the team has been selected each member should be given a (probably verbal) project briefing, outlining the overall aims of the project, and detailing the role they are expected to play.

7.5 Developing the project team

Group cohesiveness is an important factor for project success. It is hoped that team members will **develop and learn from each other**, and solve problems by drawing on different resources and expertise.

The performance of the project team will be enhanced by the following.

(a) Effective communication
(b) All members being aware of the team's purpose and the role of each team member
(c) Collaboration and creativity among team members
(d) Trusting, supportive atmosphere in the group
(e) A commitment to meeting the agreed schedule
(f) Innovative/creative behaviour
(g) Team members highly interdependent, interface effectively
(h) Capacity for conflict resolution
(i) Results orientation
(j) High energy levels and enthusiasm
(k) An acceptance of change

Collaboration and interaction will help ensure the skills of all team members are utilised, and should result in 'synergistic' solutions. Formal (eg meetings) and informal channels (eg e-mail links, a bulletin board) of **communication** should be set up to ensure this interaction takes place.

8 Project management methodologies

Project management approaches vary substantially, across a continuum, with the following extremes:

Organisations have no formal methodology, which means that the project manager has all the information and plans. Team members may be less involved or committed because they lack information. Management may be given only limited information on progress, as reporting takes time.

An organisation-wide methodology is applied for all projects and departments. Usually, this is a sophisticated methodology, which prepares plans, metrics, communications tasks etc. Often, these methodologies require training for all participants. However, an overly complex methodology may be cumbersome for some projects, such as simple, 'soft' or creative projects, and may demotivate people.

Between these extremes, there are many off-the-shelf software packages for managing projects, including Microsoft Project. Typically, these require some training, but are not the highly specialist project management methodologies. These packages identify the core processes and reporting that is required in project management, and can be bought or licensed for application. Pre-established packages are cheaper than the specialist packages. They may increase project management efficiency by automating planning and reporting processes. In turn, this improves effectiveness, such as reducing risks.

These packages are flexible enough to take account of a project's unique aspects and can be customised for marketing projects, but there are also 'off-the-shelf' software packages specifically for marketing projects.

A second option is to buy an existing methodology and customise it (or have it customised) for a specific situation. This is generally for more sophisticated projects and project-focused organisations. There is a fine line here between the adaptation of an existing methodology and the development of in-house methodologies, customised for an organisation's skills, values and best practices. The latter are becoming less common with ever-increasing numbers of quality project management software. Sophisticated customised packages are typically time consuming and expensive, and staff must be trained to use these.

The Microsoft Office Project package details its key benefits, gives you the chance to see a demonstration and also to download this for a 60-day free trial. If you do not know any other package, you might like to plan your assessment for this module on this package. (But remember the 60-day limit, if your company does not have a license for this!)

http://www.microsoft.com/project/en-us/project-management.aspx

This software offers a quick tour of the highlights of the software, and also offers a trial. There is detailed information on product features, including various reports. Also check out the case studies for insight.

http://www.wrike.com/

This is an online project management service, and offers the product features, free demonstration and also case studies and testimonials. Interestingly, this software works directly with e-mail systems to ensure better team collaboration. It also specifically targets marketing professionals and products.

http://www.projectminder.com/

The site makes available software for project management that is focused on vertical markets, including consultancies and agencies. This is very strongly focused on managing time and cost. This site has interesting white papers for those in these sectors. It also offers a small business version.

8.1 Core project management methodologies

Using existing methodology is increasingly common, especially in larger organisations that have extensive project management experience. Often, job advertisements for projects managers detail the methodology to be used, and ask for experience in using this technology.

This discussion presents features of two common process methodologies:

- PRINCE/PRINCE2
- Scalable methodology

Process methodologies are those that follow a formal planning stage, whereby processes are determined for undertaking the project.

8.2 PRINCE/PRINCE2

PRINCE (PRojects INControlled Environments) methodologies are commonly used in public sector project management, although they were originally designed for developing and implementing information systems. It is the default methodology for public sector organisations in the United Kingdom, and is widely used by large organisations across Europe. A related approach is Managing Successful Programmes (MSP). Both approaches are structured, but adaptable to different projects and programmes.

PRINCE methodologies have:

- A clear management structure

- Formal allocation of project roles and responsibilities

- Plans for resourcing and technical issues

- Control procedures

- A focus on products – deliverables to the customer and project deliverables for the management of the project

PRINCE methodologies have three separate progress assurance roles:

- **The business** – The Business Assurance Co-ordinator (BAC) ensures that the project meets the organisation's mission.

- **The specialist** – The Technical Co-ordinator is responsible for ensuring that the project does not have technical problems.

- **The user** – The User Assurance Co-ordinator represents the user throughout the process.

These different roles ensure that the various stakeholders agree that the project is satisfactory (in terms of the cost, quality and delivery) from all perspectives.

In terms of progress planning and monitoring, PRINCE2 shows:

- The project life cycle stages
- Progress against plan and key user-defined decision points
- Alerts for any variance from plan

In addition, PRINCE2 enables:

- Management and stakeholder involvement at critical times in the project
- Effective communication within the project team and other stakeholders

However, PRINCE2 has its critics, who claim it will:

- Make projects longer
- Increase project costs
- Tie up resources
- Delay payback on the project
- Increase risks of failure

The Chartered Institute of Marketing

Read more information on PRINCE2 at http://www.prince2.com/.

8.3 Scalable methodology

Scalable methodology recognises the differences in project size, risk and complexity, and allows a customised best practice management approach for each project. This approach builds on the Project Management Institute's PMBOK (Project Management Body of Knowledge), identifying differences between minor and major projects on nine dimensions and their impact on project management.

8.4 Agile methodologies

A change in recent years has come about owing to criticisms of the process-driven methodologies (such as PRINCE2 and scalable methodology) because they lacked the capacity to adapt as the project developed. New agile methodologies were developed, which allow the project to adapt to changes in the changing environment and business challenges. Although they are seen as contrasting with the process methodologies, they are actually considered to be 'half-way' between a process methodology and no methodology.

Agile methodologies are defined as being:

Adaptive rather than predictive – Agile approaches welcome changes, rather than have fixed plans.

Focused on people rather than process – Process methods focus the process set, and anyone could implement the plans. Agile approaches recognise that people have skills that can add to the project as it progresses.

- Adaptive Project Framework (ADF): ADF is a customer-focused methodology, which is based on being:
    - Client focused and client-driven
    - Frequent and early results reporting
    - Focused on questioning and introspection
    - Change is good, when it is moving to a better solution

ADF allows project scope to vary within defined time and cost levels. The project scope is reviewed in several iterations, by involving the client in identifying the issues that are of most value to the business. This means that the project changes course to deliver the maximum business value.

This approach was developed for IT projects, after many of them failed to deliver using the traditional and more rigid methodologies. However, its focus and flexibility make it appropriate for marketing projects.

8.5 Choosing a methodology

The choice of a project methodology is commonly set given the preferences of the commissioning organisation. However, if you have an open choice of methodology, you should consider the following issues to make an informed choice:

- Availability of software
- Number of team members
- Team member communications
- Complexity of the task
- Training required to effectively utilise the methodology
- Cost of the methodology to acquire or use

9 Project management plan

The following is a good template to use when creating a marketing project plan.

The **project management plan** should include:

(a)   Project objectives and how they will be achieved and verified.

(b)   How any **changes** to these procedures are to be **controlled**.

(c)   The **management and technical procedures**, and **standards**, to be used.

(d)   The **budget** and **time-scale**.

(e)   **Safety**, health and environmental policies.

(f)   Inherent **risks** and how they will be managed.

An example of a simple **project management plan** is shown below. This plan was produced by the American Project Management Institute (PMI) – to manage a project to produce formal project management principles.

The project management plan **evolves** over time. A high-level plan for the whole project and a detailed plan for the current and following stage is usually produced soon after project start-up. At each subsequent stage a detailed plan is produced for the following stage and, if required, the overall project plan is revised.

Table 13.3   Project planning template

Project management plan	
Project name	The full name of this project is 'Project Management Principles'.
Project manager	The project manager is Joe Bloggs. The project manager is authorised to (1) initiate the project, (2) form the project team and (3) prepare and execute plans and manage the project as necessary for successful project completion.
Purpose/ Business need	This project addresses a need for high-level guidelines for the project management profession through the identification and presentation of project management principles. The project sponsor and accepting agent is the Project Management Institute (PMI) Standards Program Team (SPT). The principal and beneficial customer is the membership of PMI. Principles are needed to provide high-level context and guidance for the profession of project management. These Principles will provide benefit from the perspectives of practice, evaluation, and development.
Project management	The project team will use project methodology consistent with PMI Standards. The project is to be managed with definitive scope and acceptance criteria fully established as the project progresses and the product is developed.
Assumptions, constraints and risks	The project faces some increased risk that without a clearly prescribed definition of a Principle, standards for product quality will be more difficult to establish and apply. To mitigate this risk, ongoing communication between the project team and the project sponsor on this matter will be required.
Resources	The PMI SPT is to provide the project team with the following. **Financial**. SPT will provide financial resources as available. The initial amount for the current year is $5,000. The project manager must not exceed the allocated amount, and notify the SPT when 75% of the allocation has been spent. **Explanation of Standards Program**. SPT will provide guidance at the outset of the project, updates as changes occur, and clarifications as needed. **Personnel/Volunteers**. SPT will recruit volunteer team members from within the membership of PMI through various media and liaisons. The project team is to consist of no less than ten members, including the project manager. General qualifications to be sought by SPT in recruiting will be: **Mandatory** ▪ Acceptance of project plan ▪ Demonstrated capability for strategic, generalised or intuitive thinking ▪ Capability to write clearly on technical subject matter for general audiences

	■ Capability to work co-operatively with well-developed interpersonal skills
	■ Be conversant in English and be able to use telephone and internet e-mail telecommunications
	As possible
	■ Time availability (Team members may contribute at different levels. An average of approximately five to ten hours per month is desired.)
	■ Diversity (Team members collectively may represent diverse nationalities, types of organisations or corporate structure, business sectors, academic disciplines, and personal experience.)
	■ Travel (As determined mutually by the project sponsor and manager, some travel for face-to-face meetings may be requested.)
Approach	The project will progress through the following phases.
	Phase 1: Team formation – Recruit and orient volunteer team members. Establish procedures and ground rules for group process and decision-making.
	Phase 2: Subject matter clarification – Identify and clarify initial scope and definitions of project subject matter.
	Phase 3a: Exploration – Begin brainstorming (through gathering, sharing, and discussion) of data and views in unrestricted, non-judgemental process.
	Phase 3b: Selection – Conclude brainstorming (through evaluation and acceptance or rejection) of collected data and views. As the conclusion to this phase, the SPT will review as an interim deliverable the selection made by the project team.
	Phase 4: Development – Conduct further research and discussion to develop accepted subject matter.
	Phase 5: Articulation – Write a series of drafts to state the accepted and developed subject matter as appropriate for the project business need and product description.
	Phase 6: Adoption – Submit product to SPT for the official PMI standards approval and adoption process. Revise product as needed.
	Phase 7: Closeout – Perform closure for team and administrative matters. Deliver project files to SPT.
Communication and reporting	The project manager and team will communicate with and report to the PMI Standards Program Team as follows.
	Monthly status reports – Written monthly status and progress reports are to include:
	■ Work accomplished since the last report
	■ Work planned to be performed during the next reporting period
	■ Deliverables submitted since the last report
	■ Deliverables planned to be submitted during the next reporting period
	■ Work tasks in progress and currently outside of expectations for scope, quality, schedule or cost
	■ Risks identified and actions taken or proposed to mitigate
	■ Lessons learned
	■ Summary statement for posting on PMI website
	Monthly resource reports – Written monthly resource reports are to include:
	Financial resources
	■ Total funds allocated
	■ Total funds expended to date
	■ Estimated expenditures for the next reporting period
	■ Estimated expenditures for entire project to completion
	Human resources
	■ List of all volunteer team members categorised by current involvement (ie active, new (pre-active), inactive, resigned)
	■ Current number of new and active volunteer team members
	■ Estimated number of volunteer team members needed for project completion

Project management plan	
	Milestone and critical status reports – Additional status reports are to be submitted as mutually agreed upon by SPT and the project manager and are to include at least the following items. ▪ Milestone status reports are to include the same items as the monthly status reports, summarised to cover an entire project phase period since the last milestone report, or entire project to date. ▪ Critical status reports are to focus on work tasks outside of expectations and other information as requested by SPT or stipulated by the project manager.
Acceptance	The project manager will submit the final product and any interim deliverables to the Standards Program Team (SPT) for formal acceptance. The SPT may (1) accept the product as delivered by the project team, or (2) return the product to the team with a statement of specific requirements to make the product fully acceptable. The acceptance decision of the SPT is to be provided to the project manager in writing.
Change management	Requests for change to this plan may be initiated by either the project sponsor or the project manager. All change requests will be reviewed and approved or rejected by a formal proceeding of the Standards Program Team (SPT) with input and interaction with the project manager. Decisions of the SPT will be documented and provided to the project manager in writing. All changes will be incorporated into this document, reflected by a new version number and date.

Table 13.4   Project sign-off card

Plan acceptance	Signature and Date
By PMI Standards Program Team	_____ 12 July 20XX Fred Jones – PMI Technical Research & Standards Manager
By Project Manager	_____ 20 July 20XX Joe Bloggs – PMI Member

The format and contents of a project management plan will **vary** depending on the organisation involved and the complexity of the project.

THE REAL WORLD

Volvo

Volvo Cars' integrated global campaigns for their range of models are excellent examples of project management in marketing.

These multimedia campaign projects by Volvo were primarily created to centralise the brand essence and message, predominantly in the United States, China, United Kingdom, Ireland, Spain, Belgium, Netherlands, France, Luxembourg and Switzerland. The theme 'There's more to life than a Volvo. That's why you drive one' is designed to differentiate the product through passion and refinement.

The campaign in the United Kingdom blends radio, television, cinema, digital and mobile advertising, which all link to online sites with other content and engaging full-length film. Online banner advertising also drives traffic to the site.

Detailed schedules were prepared to manage and communicate consumer promotions and to share these with dealers, so they could plan local activities to support and build on the national multimedia campaigns.

Volvo uses these campaigns to create a 'buzz' through its unusual approach. Timescales need to be consistent across the participating markets to ensure that the effectiveness and success of the campaigns can be closely monitored, measured and evaluated. All elements of the project process much operate in tandem in order to minimise the risk of failure and maximise the opportunity for success.

(Volvo, 2012)

Mars

Mars offers Galaxy and Dove brands in various international markets. The former brand name was used in the UK and Middle East; the latter used in China. While the brands looked alike, each market had ownership of its strategy.

Mars decided to change Galaxy's strapline to 'Why have cotton when you can have silk?'. It was decided to project manage this on an international basis and develop a global strategy for the brand.

A global project team was established, with people from Mars and members of their research, communications and design agencies. Starting by understanding the global market, establishing the business objectives, agreeing the methodology, examining the risks, formulating the budgets and briefing the agencies, the outcomes were to redesign and implement the global brand strategy.

Mars decided to keep the existing brand names, but with a common global positioning. The packaging and the shape of the chocolate bar was changed to give a more sensual look and feel after the company realized that its customers considered the product to be indulgent, and that the entire product experience begins with anticipation, before the chocolate is even consumed.

The results from this project showed the success of the new strategy. Brand value has increased by 42% since 2004, at just under $ 2billion in 2011. Some individual markets grew substantially – sales in the US more than doubled over this period. This project is now being reformulated in 2012 to enhance the global digital media presence.

(*Marketing* magazine, 2012)

▶ **Assessment tip**

Whatever template you use for the marketing project plan in your assignment, you must outline and populate all stages thoroughly. The most obvious advice is to use and adhere to all stages of the template that will always be published within your CIM assignment brief.

- These generic stages and the content of plans at each stage should be helping you firm up your thinking about your assessed project.

- We introduced the fact that most projects have a life cycle that moves through the four stages of definition, design, delivery and development.

- Having identified and selected the project, it is then time to initiate it.

- We learned that initiation sets the whole procedure into action and an implementation process needs to be set up.

- The whole project process travels through 13 stages from initiation to termination.

- We next turned our attention to stakeholders and stressed the importance of identifying all those who will be impacted by the project.

- We looked at the role of the project manager, the skills required and the ultimate responsibilities.

- We looked at the importance of the project team, how it needed to be formed and how it could be developed.

- We also examined the different methodologies available to include the formalised, Prince, the customised, Scalable and the adaptive, Agile.

- Finally we showed how all of this must fit within the confines of a dedicated project management plan.

FURTHER READING

Coleman, F. (2009) Project deadlines put pressure on security. http://www.tmcnet.com [Accessed 27 April 2009].

REFERENCES

Gray, C. F. and Larson, W. L. (2010) *Project Management: the Managerial Process*. 5th edition. London, McGraw-Hill.

Grundy, T. and Brown, L. (2002) *Strategic Project Management*. London, Thompson Learning.

Kapur, G. (2004) *Project Management for Information, Technology, Business and Certification*. Harlow, Prentice Hall.

Lewis, J. P. (2008) *Mastering Project Management*. 2nd edition. Harlow, McGraw-Hill.

Meredith, J. R. and Mantell, S. J. (2003) *Project Management: A Managerial Approach*. New York, John Wiley & Sons.

Saunders, J., *et al* (2005) How screening criteria change during brand development. *Journal of Product and Brand Management*, 14(4), pp239–249.

Shaw, E. (2011) Compare IBM's project management methodology with PMBOK. http://www.projectsmart.co.uk/forums/viewtopic.php?f=2&t=780 [Accessed 30 May 2012].

Shearman, S. (2012) Galaxy to revive 'silk' strapline. Marketing, http://www.marketingmagazine.co.uk/news/1112282/ [Accessed 30 May 2012].

Volvo (2012) https://www.media.volvocars.com/global/enhanced/en-gb//Search/Results.aspx [Accessed 23 June 2012.

QUICK QUIZ

1   What are four phases of a typical project life cycle?

2   What is the purpose of the project development phase?

3   What is the aim of fishbone or Ishikawa analysis?

4   What document does the PRINCE2 methodology assume drives the project?

5   What are the project manager's responsibilities to the project team?

ACTIVITY DEBRIEFS

Activity 13.1

Project definition

Purpose of holiday: rest, recreation, broadening of mental horizons or merely spend some time in the sun?

Scope: how many involved? How to travel? Where to stay? Package deal? Activity holiday?

Estimated overall budget? Allow for extra living expenses but note reduced normal expenses – heat, light, travel.

Project design

(Let us assume we have selected a summer activity package holiday)

Project: White water rafting, Colorado, 6-13 June 2009, for four people. Outline budget: £6,780 + pocket money.

Travel Agent: Crazee Travel, Shepherds Bush; project liaison staff: Juanita.

Flight itinerary: outbound – depart Heathrow 6 June 14.30hrs Whiteknuckle Airways flight 13, arrive Denver 23.30hrs (local time); inbound – depart Denver 12 June 11.50hrs, Bugle-air flight 69, arrive Heathrow 13 June 07.45hrs.

Local arrangements: stay night 6 June at Denver Holiday Inn – hotel shuttle bus from airport. Collected 7 June 10.00hrs for transfer to Rancho Jornada del Muerto. 7 – 11 June – at ranch, bunkhouse accommodation, full board. Liaison: Randy Q Scott III.

Finance: £500 pocket money per person is advised as there will be several opportunities to visit local townships. Deposit £850 each to be paid to travel agent by 1 May 2009. Copy invoices available.

Risk management: full travel health insurance is advised for travel to the USA – available online from Flybenite.com for £55 per person.

Project delivery

Delivery involves assembling the party at Heathrow, with luggage and all travel documentation, locating the Holiday Inn shuttle bus at Denver, dealing with misunderstandings and failures of communication at hotel check-in, assisting Rancho staff with transfer bus breakdown, giving EAR and CPR to tourists after river raft overturns, preserving patience and equanimity when return flight delayed for 17 hours with no explanation,

accommodation or even a cup of tea and dispersing party for own arrangements return home from Manchester, where eventual return flight actually lands.

Project development

Immediate review: never travel with Crazee Travel again.

Longer-term review: actually it was all quite exciting, apart from being held at gun point on arrival in the US, which was a bit OTT.

Activity 13.2

Hopefully, you will be able to find some evidence of evaluation of projects. Try to find out about the criteria that are used and when (eg is there a schedule for this evaluation – such as around the time that budgets are submitted) these are reviewed.

You may find a mix of both planned projects (which could be related to investment decisions, or promotional objectives, for example), and those that are necessitated by changing market opportunities, and those that are considered independently. The latter may need funding from some contingency fund.

You will have to justify the project that is the focus of your CIM assessment, even if there is no internal assessment process. So take time to think about this topic and apply to your project.

Activity 13.3

It is commonly assumed that marketing staff can become capable project managers, but that is not always the case. Some marketing managers are poor at working with others, keeping to budgets and schedules etc. Good project managers work at this. Developing project management skills can – as the IBM case shows – make a better manager, in many disciplines. You may find that additional training and/or mentoring could help you develop skills and competences in these areas.

QUICK QUIZ ANSWERS

1   Definition, design, delivery, development

2   To provide rapid staff feedback and to identify short-term needs such as staff training or remedial action for procedure failures

3   To break a perceived issue down into its smallest underlying causes and components

4   The business case

5   Provide resources, brief new members, support departing team members and listen carefully

The Chartered Institute of Marketing

CHAPTER 14

Project tools and techniques

Introduction

Project tools and techniques are intended to give a structure and series of guidelines to work within. They are aimed at producing a logical and disciplined progression from the initial idea to the handover of the project (and sometimes a little beyond that when supplementary work is needed).

Managing a project can be very demanding. Effective project management requires thorough planning, monitoring and control.

We start this chapter by studying some of the **management tools and techniques** available to help the project management process. These tools and techniques are likely to be relevant to your project, so it is essential that you understand and are able to apply the techniques covered.

As with many tasks, project management activities are now usually carried out using computers. **Project management software** packages are covered in Section 2 of this chapter.

Topic list

Management tools and techniques	1
Determining the work breakdown structure	2
Estimating timing and task duration	3
Determining requirements – a resource checklist	4
Sequencing work	5
The project budget	6
Risk management	7
Project management software	8

4.5	Utilise a range of tools and techniques to support project planning, scheduling, resourcing and controlling of activities within the project to enable effective and efficient implementation:
	▪ Work breakdown structure
	▪ Cost analysis
	▪ Estimate forecasting
	▪ Gantt charts
	▪ Critical path analysis
	▪ Histograms
	▪ Phase management
	▪ Feedback control systems

1 Management tools and techniques

▶ **Key terms**

Work Breakdown Structure This is 'a deliverable-oriented grouping of project elements that organises and defines the total work scope of the project. Each descending level represents an increasingly detailed definition of the project work'.

Deliverables Tangible outputs from work undertaken, delivered to sponsors or managers that can be signed off.

Scheduling is the process of identifying and detailing the timings of project activities involved in completing the work.

Milestones mark the end point of an activity.

Network analysis requires breaking down the project into tasks, arranging them into a logical sequence and estimating the duration of each.

The techniques we discuss in this section are concerned with the fundamentals of planning projects and controlling their progress. As with most activities, it is difficult to separate the process of planning a project from that of controlling it: planning is likely to continue throughout the life of the project. A **baseline plan** will show the following:

(a) Start and end dates for the project and its major phases or activities

(b) The resources needed and when they are required

(c) Estimates of cost for the project and the major phases or activities

Several books report on marketing mistakes, many of which come from poorly planned marketing projects. Good planning is essential for project success, as is clear in the 6 Ps of project management: Prior Planning Prevents Poor Project Performance (this may be also be familiar in a rather more earthy form).

Often, the problems start with vague or poor project definition. Typically, projects have requests such as:

(a) Prepare a marketing communications plan for a new product launch *or*
(b) Develop an improved new product development process

At one level, these seem fine. However, exploring these further highlights issues that must be addressed before planning can be undertaken.

▪ What sort of marketing communications plan?
▪ What targets – trade or consumer markets?
▪ What timescale?
▪ Are there any specific media to be used or avoided?
▪ What is meant by improved?
▪ How would this project be measured?

Initial scoping helps identify some aspects of the project, but this next stage of planning adds to the detail for the project plan and clarifies more precisely what is involved. There is an old saying that 'the devil is in the

detail' and it is certainly true that you will have the devil of a time trying to successfully manage a marketing project if you fail to pay attention to detail.

The general process of project planning is the structure of this chapter.

1   Determining the work breakdown structure
2   Estimating timing and task duration
3   Determining resource requirements
4   Allocating responsibilities
5   Sequencing work
6   Developing the project schedule or network
7   Preparing the integrated planning document

The key project management tools will be identified within these headings. You should work through this chapter and consider how to incorporate the frameworks and tools in your assessed work

2 Determining the work breakdown structure

The key element of good project plans is the work breakdown structure. PMI defines the WBS as: 'A deliverable-oriented grouping of project elements that organises and defines the total work scope of the project. Each descending level represents an increasingly detailed definition of the project work'.

In his book *Project Management: Planning and Control Techniques*, Rory Burke (2003) argued a structure that is based on the four project phases of Concept, Design, Implementation and Handover. He contends that each of these individual phases can also be broken down into the full four at a subproject level. Let us take the concept phase as an example. It would include within it the original idea, but that idea would need to be checked and researched to put an overview together. That rough design overview needs to be built into enough of a case to allow the project to gain approval, and that is the implementation that is aimed for. Once that has been gained, then there is a handover to those responsible for the next stage in the process.

The WBS is a structured hierarchy of the work that needs to be accomplished on a project. This organises work in an organisational chart-type structure, with different levels showing how goals, objectives, topics etc. can be broken down into increasingly detailed activities (see Figure 14.1).

Figure 14.1   WBS — implementing a customer relationship management system

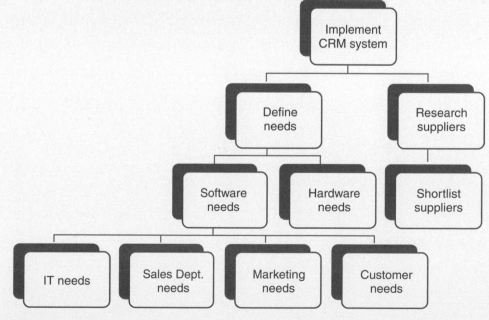

(Adapted from Mayer, 2005)

1   Define the needs – what do we need to allocate to the system and what do we need in return?

- What do we want from the software package?

- What are the IT requirements eg compatibility?

- What does the sales team expect to get?

- How will we able to fit it in to our overall marketing processes?

- We must remember that the customer is the C in CRM

- What are the hardware requirements – do we need to upgrade?

2   Research the suppliers that potentially have suitable software/hardware to satisfy our needs

- Shortlist those suppliers we will invite to bid after more detailed research eg costs, testimonials, product limitations.

(Note that this is only the start of the structure for illustrative purposes and it may go down through many more levels until it is broken down into discrete work packages. You may also note that the text that follows the diagram reflects the hierarchical structure of the diagram.)

The WBS will go down through a series of levels until the project tasks produce manageable outputs. These are called **work packages**. Work packages are normally viewed as being **deliverables** or products at the lowest level of the WBS. Deliverables are the tangible outputs from work, which are normally then signed off as complete. This may be a milestone – the end of a period of work.

Identifying the work packages forms the foundation for developing schedules, budgets and resource requirements, and also forms the foundation for assigning responsibilities.

Work packages can be split into activities or tasks that are used to create a workflow. These contrast with activities and tasks, which are about what is involved in doing work.

Figure 14.2 looks at the process that would be involved in the purchasing of the CRM software outlined in Figure 14.1. It considers a traditional purchasing of traditional physical goods with the alternative of buying software. Again, remember that it is included as an illustration, and you may very well see variations in your organisation.

Figure 14.2   Buying physical or electronic products

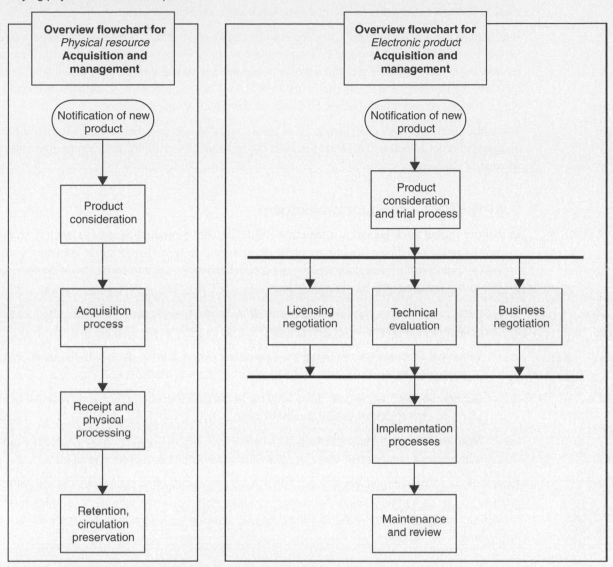

Some people refer to the 80-hour rule to make the decision about the bottom level. The bottom level of a WBS should identify 80 hours or fewer of work. This WBS is the foundation for the other elements of the project plan. The project manager's mantra states that 'if it is not in the WBS, then it is not in the plan'. Clearly, there must be attention to this for the project to be successful, but you may well miss some issues if you are new to project management.

Seek advice from others to check that this is not a major issue.

Some key things to review concerning a WBS are:

- Does the WBS go outside the scope of the project?
- Does the WBS cover the entire scope of the project?
- Does the WBS ultimately result in deliverables?

2.1 Dependencies and interactions

A very important aspect of project planning is the determination of **dependencies** and **interactions**. At any level of WBS analysis, some tasks will be dependent on others; that is to say, **a dependent task cannot commence** until the task upon which it depends is completed. Careful analysis of dependencies is a major step towards a workable project plan, since it provides an **order in which things must be tackled**. Sometimes, of course, the

dependencies are limited and it is possible to proceed with tasks in almost any order, but this is unusual. The more complex a project, the greater the need for analysis of dependencies.

Interactions are slightly different; they occur when tasks are linked but not dependent. This can arise for a variety of reasons: a good example is a requirement to share the use of a scarce resource. If there were two of us working on our vegetable plot but we only possessed one spade, we could not use it simultaneously both to cultivate the plot itself and to dig the trench in which we wish to place the kerbstones. We could choose to do either of these activities first, but we could not do them both at the same time.

The output from the WBS process is a list of tasks, probably arranged hierarchically to reflect the disaggregation of activities. This then becomes the input into the planning and control processes described in the rest of this section.

2.2 PRINCE2 – product breakdown

Rather than using **work breakdown structure**, PRINCE2 uses a **product-based** approach to planning. This has the advantage of directing management attention to *what* is to be achieved rather than *how* to do it, thus providing an automatic focus on achieving the product goals. Also, it can be helpful in complex projects, where the processes involved may be initially unclear.

Under this approach, work breakdown is preceded by **product breakdown**. PRINCE2 starts this analysis by dividing the **project products** into three groups.

(a) **Technical products** are the things the project has been set up to provide to the users. For an IT system, for example, these would include the hardware, software, manuals and training.

(b) **Quality products** define both the quality controls that are applied to the project and the quality standards the technical products must achieve.

(c) **Management products** are the artefacts used to manage the project. They include the project management organisation structure, planning documentation, reports and so on.

Each of these groups of products is then broken down into manageable components as part of the planning process, using the traditional work breakdown structure approach if the complexity of the project requires it. Project and stage plans may make use of the normal planning tools such as CPA, Gantt charts and resource histograms.

---

3 Estimating timing and task duration

Project duration defines the length of time (in hours, days, weeks or months) to complete an activity. Typically, in marketing projects, the deadline will be set, such as to launch in time for a Christmas holiday or before the Olympics. Working back from the set deadlines is stressful for a project manager, and often for all other members of the project team too.

Task and activity duration also needs to be determined for planning purposes. Estimating the task duration for work packages is one of the most difficult things for a novice project manager. There are several ways to try and determine this:

■ Consider similar activities for which you have information about the task duration. However, this may not be possible for all tasks.

■ Historical data may identify how long tasks or activities have taken in the past. However, some project tasks may be new tasks.

■ Expert advice – or knowledge – from senior managers can give indications of the likely – or desired – outcomes.

Problems with establishing time periods include:

- Lack of experience in planning time duration for tasks, and in doing activities.

- Clearly, novices will typically take longer than experienced workers to do the same tasks, and may be unaware of the problems that take time. Clearly, lack of experience here can lead to unrealistic timescales.

- Complexity of the marketing problems – often these involve creative tasks, for which focusing on time may detract from quality.

- Unexpected events or delays due to illness etc. Also, mistakes or other problems can add to the time needed. Contingencies may have to be built into the systems.

- Novices tend to underestimate the amount of work involved in any tasks. Expert project managers tend to use the longest predicted duration in scheduling, as this allows for possible delays.

There is a dual issue here. It is very difficult to judge the time taken for new projects or new activities or tasks. Some tasks involved in marketing activities – such as creative work – are especially difficult to do 'to a timescale'. This in turn will impact on the feasibility of the project completion date.

ACTIVITY 14.1

Many students underestimate the amount of time taken to undertake a project or dissertation. They look at the word count, compare this to an essay and then say 'I can write a 2,000 word essay in three hours, so a dissertation of 10,000 words will take 15 hours'.

Is this the case? What assumptions underpin this? How valid are they?

4 Determining requirements – a resource checklist

Project resourcing clearly varies depending on the type and size of projects. The central issue in identifying this is using the WBS and estimated timings to determine the resource requirements to complete the project on time and budget:

(a) **The people** to be involved in the project, the level of their commitment, and the required level of skills.

(b) **The facilities** for the project planning, and depending on the project, its implementation.

(c) **The equipment** required, such as computers, cameras, or other audio-visual equipment.

(d) **The money** – a budget needed to complete the task. There will often be an iterative process to determine budgets, taking account of the costs, timescales etc.

(e) **The materials** – what tangibles, consumables or other items will be required in the process.

The resources need to be determined at this stage, and this becomes a reference point for monitoring resource use once the project starts. While the WBS tends to work top-down, many argue that resources should be determined from the bottom-up. Contingencies may need to be built in for some resources.

5 Sequencing work

The tasks so far have complexities, but the real difficulties in project planning come through scheduling. Scheduling is essentially about the links between and among activities/tasks and or people and organisations. Some work tasks will be completed in parallel, while others will be dependent on the completion of other activities.

Scheduling examines the sequence of tasks, both independent and interrelated, that will be undertaken. This is then organised into a series of subschedules and charts, which can be prepared from the master plan, detailing what will happen when, by whom, and detailing the interfaces and the milestones for the tasks.

For example, a brochure cannot be printed until the content has been prepared. The content cannot be prepared until a copywriter has been appointed and the R&D team has provided the product information. However, a printer can be sourced while the copy is being written.

Once you know what needs to be done, you need to examine the work involved to determine:

Predecessor tasks: those required for another task to be completed.

Successor tasks: those that cannot start until another task has been completed.

The schedule can be prepared once this workflow is established. The schedule becomes a key tool in managing progress.

Detailed scheduling turns the project plan into action plans, on the basis of the WBS. Each WBS task is normally named and numbered, and the duration of tasks, any lead or lag times, and resources and budget involved must be estimated in order for a detailed schedule to be undertaken. Clearly, this reinforces the need for good time and resource estimates. Each WBS task should become the responsibility of a named individual.

However, schedules will often feature ideal start dates and late finish dates. Ideal start dates are the latest dates for an activity to start, if delays are to be avoided. Late finish dates are the latest dates for an activity to finish without causing delays in the project.

Later in the project, revised schedules are prepared as issues emerge. Rescheduling does not always result in delays in completion, as contingencies – for time or budget – may be built into the project plan. However, if the delays exceed this, and there is no flexibility with the delivery date or resources, terminating the project should be considered. Many tools are used to present schedules.

THE REAL WORLD

BMA Software is a company that specialises in bespoke software for wholesalers of durable goods. The organisation needed to employ a robust project methodology in order to decrease severe problems throughout its implementations. It took the decision to invest in a dedicated program from Microsoft, Dynamics Sure Step, and adapt it to fit the individual needs within its customer base. The methodology enables BMA to manage a seamless sales process which instils greater confidence in its customers. The program allows BMA to streamline implementation, define roles and responsibilities and manage multiple concurrent projects, while at the same time maximising the efficient use of existing organisational resources.

(TechRepublic, 2009)

The Chartered Institute of Marketing

Marketing writer Philip Kotler said:

'In a downturn, it can be common for a CEO to put the stoppers on marketing projects that are costing the company, as they want to save money. Along with R&D, marketing is often one of the first things to suffer.'

(Business and Leadership, 2009)

For a valid project of your choice (ie one which you believe will achieve results), identify how you would defend your chosen project from being terminated.

5.1 Gantt charts

Gantt charts are a **visual** planning tool useful for projects but are limited in their use as they do not recognise the interrelations between tasks.

A **Gantt chart**, named after the engineer Henry Gantt who pioneered the procedure in the early 1900s, is a horizontal bar chart used to plan the **time scale** for a project and to estimate the **resources** required.

The Gantt chart displays the time relationships between tasks in a project. Two lines are usually used to show the time allocated for each task, and the actual time taken.

A simple Gantt chart, illustrating some of the activities involved in a network server installation project, follows.

Figure 14.3   Gantt chart

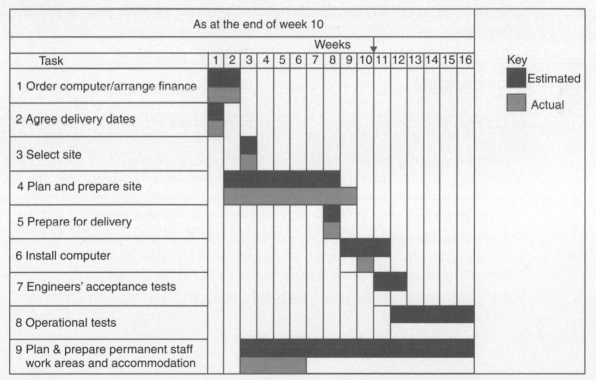

The chart shows that at the end of the tenth week Activity 9 is running behind schedule. More resources may have to be allocated to this activity if the staff accommodation is to be ready in time for the changeover to the new system.

Activity 4 has not been completed on time, and this has resulted in some disruption to the computer installation (Activity 6), which may mean further delays in the commencement of Activities 7 and 8.

5.2 Network analysis tools

Network analysis tools show dependencies in work activities. Two common network analysis tools are Critical Path Methodology (CPM) often called Critical Path Analysis and Program Evaluation and Review Technique (PERT). These techniques are commonly combined, as PERT/CPM. Their focus is on managing the total length of the project, rather than the time for each aspect of the project (like Gantt charts).

A path is a series of connected activities. Projects have several potential paths. The term critical path describes the sequence of activities that takes the longest total time required to complete the project. A delay in any activity in the critical path means that the project will face a delay.

PERT is used to determine how much time a project needs before it is completed, on the basis of activities being completed within a best, worst and most likely time estimate resulting in an average time for completion.

Project management software simplifies the preparation of these schedules – and revised schedules as the project continues. These can also be designed to show schedules for the whole project, or by task, person or date, so that these facilitate the project communications.

Later in the project, revised schedules are prepared as issues emerge. Rescheduling does not always result in delays in completion, as contingencies – for time or budget – may be built into the project plan. However, if the delays exceed this, and there is no flexibility with the delivery date or resources, terminating the project should be considered.

Although this may appear to you to be far removed from marketing, these methods should not detrimentally affect the creative elements involved in building a campaign, but it should ensure that basic managerial functions such as setting target dates, monitoring progress and identifying potential problems are carried out rigorously.

6 The project budget

Building a project budget should be an orderly process that attempts to establish a realistic estimate of the cost of the project. There are two main methods for establishing the project budget: **top-down** and **bottom-up**.

Top-down budgeting describes the situation where the budget is imposed 'from above'. Project managers are allocated a budget for the project based on an estimate made by senior management. The figure may prove realistic, especially if similar projects have recently been undertaken. However, the technique is often used simply because it is quick, or because only a certain level of funding is available.

In **bottom-up budgeting** the project manager consults the project team, and others, to calculate a budget based on the tasks that make up the project. Detailed analysis of the deliverables and work to be done to achieve them will be necessary in order to produce an accurate and detailed budget.

It is useful to collate information on a **budgeting worksheet**.

The Chartered
Institute of Marketing

Figure 14.4   Budget estimate

Budgeting worksheet				
Project Name: _____		**Date worksheet completed**		
Project Manager: _____		_____		
Task (code)	Responsible staff member or external supplier	Estimated material cost	Estimated labour costs	Total cost of task

Estimates (and therefore budgets) cannot be expected to be 100% accurate. Business **conditions may change**, the project plan may be amended or estimates may simply prove to be incorrect.

Any **estimate** must be accompanied by some **indication of expected accuracy**.

Estimates can be **improved** by:

(a)   **Learning** from past mistakes.

(b)   Ensuring sufficient design **information**.

(c)   Ensuring as **detailed a specification as possible** from the customer.

(d)   Properly **analysing the job** into its constituent units.

The overall level of cost estimates will be influenced by:

(a)   **Project goals**. If a high level of quality is expected costs will be higher.

(b)   **External vendors**. Some costs may need to be estimated by outside vendors. To be realistic, these people must understand exactly what will be expected of them.

(c)   **Staff availability**. If staff are unavailable, potentially expensive contractors may be required.

(d)   **Time schedules**. The quicker a task is required to be done the higher the cost is likely to be – particularly with external suppliers.

The budget may express all resources in monetary amounts, or may show money and other resources – such as staff hours.

Budgets should be presented for approval and **sign-off** to the stakeholder who has responsibility for the funds being used.

Before presenting a budget for approval it may have to be revised a number of times. The 'first draft' may be overly reliant on rough estimates, as insufficient time was available to obtain more accurate figures.

On presentation, the project manager may be asked to find ways to cut the budget. If he or she agrees that cuts can be made, the consequences of the cuts should be pointed out – eg a reduction in quality.

It may be decided that a project costs more than it is worth. If so, scrapping the project is a perfectly valid option. In such cases the budgeting process has highlighted the situation before too much time and effort has been spent on an unprofitable venture.

Risk Management Strategy of Virgin Group

Virgin is a massive sprawling conglomerate of over 200 companies and you can imagine that all aspects of the risk management process must be watertight. Here is a short look at some of the issues the group faces

1   **Strategic planning**: The group is in private ownership and business decisions are made in-house. No short-term focus on stock market performance pervades and therefore plans are made on a sound business project platform.

2   **Strategic business entities**: The group is structured under a corporate brand and the individual companies operate independently. Therefore each individual company is charged with managing and mitigating its own risk while protecting the collective.

3   **Risk splitting**: Whenever an individual company hits a certain volume of business it is divided into two or more units. This minimises failure and reduces overall risk to the group. This strategy is in effect one of anti-risk contagion.

4   **Source of funds**: Partnerships with other organisations owning superior competencies are leveraged with the Virgin corporate brand so as to pool resources and spread the risk.

(Sonia Jaspal's RiskBoard, 2010)

7 Risk management

Project managers must address the levels of risk. You should refer to the chapters in this book specifically addressing this. However, the foundations of project risk management are summarised here.

7.1 The project risk management process

1   **Risk identification** – have you identified the risks for the project, and the implications of these on the business?

2   **Risk analysis** – have you identified risks, and the chances of these affecting the time, cost, performance and outcomes of the project, and what the consequences of these risks are?

3   **Risk planning** – have you prepared contingency plans to avoid, address or minimise risks to the project achieving its time, cost and performance outcomes?

4   **Risk monitoring** – have you got a system in place to monitor these potential risks and to pick up on any other risks that might impact on the project process or outcomes?

 The Chartered Institute of Marketing

A B2B manufacturer set in place a project to develop and launch a website for its partners (ie intermediaries), which would offer a range of information, administration and support activities. The intention was to move the partners away from more labour intensive forms of dealer support, which would enable the partners to give better service to their customers. The project budget was set at the cost of running a call centre for handling partner enquires and support over a two year period. The cost-saving was to be split between the manufacturer and its trade partners. Therefore moving to this new website, once developed, would improve channel margins. The basic form of 'Microsoft Project' was engaged and this was supported by other in-house physical planning and scheduling techniques.

The website development went through several project stages, such as specification, routing, content development and testing. The initial testing involved mirroring a sample of queries managed through the dealer support call centre. Beta testing of the site amongst selected partners was put in place, with pop up questionnaires, observations and discussions to review their site usage, attitudes, etc.

Modifications as a result of the pilot project were made to the process, and the full-scale launch was signed off into the mainstream company activity within the original time schedule.

8 Project management software

Project management techniques are ideal candidates for computerisation. Inexpensive project management software packages have been available for a number of years. *Microsoft Project* and *Micro Planner X-Pert* are two popular packages.

Software might be used for a number of purposes:

(a) **Planning and scheduling**

Calendars, **network diagrams** (showing the critical path) and Gantt charts (showing resource use) can be produced automatically once the relevant data is entered. Packages also allow a sort of 'what if?' analysis for initial planning, trying out different levels of resources, changing deadlines and so on to find the best combination.

(b) **Estimating and controlling costs**

As a project progresses, actual data will become known and can be entered into the package and collected for future reference. Since many projects involve basically similar tasks (interviewing users and so on), actual data from one project can be used to provide more accurate estimates for the next. The software also facilitates and encourages the use of more sophisticated estimation techniques than managers might be prepared to use if working manually.

(c) **Monitoring**

Actual data can also be entered and used to facilitate monitoring of progress and automatically updating the plan for the critical path and the use of resources as circumstances dictate.

(d) **Reporting**

Software packages allow standard and tailored progress reports to be produced, printed out and circulated to participants and senior managers at any time, usually at the touch of a button. This helps with co-ordination of activities and project review.

Most project management packages feature a process of identifying the main steps in a project, and breaking these down further into specific tasks. A typical project management package requires four **inputs**:

(a) The length of **time** and the resources required for each activity of the project.

(b) The **logical relationships** between each activity.

(c) The **resources** available.

(d) **When** the resources are available.

The package is able to analyse and present this information in a number of ways. The views available within Microsoft Project are shown in the following illustration – on the drop down menu.

Figure 14.5   Microsoft project screenshot

The advantages of using project management software are summarised in the following table.

Table 14.1   Software benefits

Advantage	Comment
Enables quick replanning	Estimates can be **changed many times** and a new schedule produced almost instantly. Changes to the plan can be reflected immediately.
Document quality	Outputs are accurate, well presented and easy to understand.
Encourages constant progress tracking	Actual times can be captured, enabling the project manager to compare **actual** progress against **planned** progress and investigate problem areas promptly.
What if? analysis	Software enables the effect of various scenarios to be calculated quickly and easily. Many project managers conduct this type of analysis using **copies** of the plan in separate computer files – leaving the actual plan untouched.
Complexity	Software can handle projects of size and complexity that would be very difficult to handle using manual methods.

The Chartered
Institute of Marketing

The software also has several **disadvantages**, some of which also apply to manual methods.

(a) **Focus**. Some project managers become so interested in software that they spend too much time producing documents and not enough time managing the project. Entering actual data and producing reports should be delegated to an administrator.

(b) **Work practices**. The assumptions behind work breakdown structure are not always applicable: people tend to work in a more flexible way rather than completing discrete tasks one by one.

(c) **Estimates**. Estimation is as much an art as a science and estimates can be wildly wrong. They are subject to the **experience** level of the estimator; influenced by the **need to impress clients**; and based on **assumptions** that can easily change.

(d) **Human factors**. Skill levels, staff turnover and level of motivation can have profound effects on performance achieved. Also, human variation makes rescheduling difficult since employing more people on an activity that is running late may actually slow it down at first, while the newcomers are briefed and even retrained.

ACTIVITY 14.3

How many different types or packages of project management software can you name or identify?

> **Assessment tip**

It is important that all of your schedules, budgets and actions are illustrated within the main body of your project report as opposed to being appended.

The terminology here can be a bit confusing if you are new to project management. However, the following summarises the most important elements from this section:

- Start the WBS from the top-down, not bottom-up.
- Identify all resources required for the project, and ensure that the budget addresses these.
- Assign responsibilities for each work package or activity.
- Identify concurrent activities.
- Examine and understand predecessor and successor tasks.
- Prepare and circulate schedules.

FURTHER READING

Hughes, B. and Cotterall, M. (2009) *Software Project Management*. 5th edition. London, McGraw Hill.

REFERENCES

Anon. (2009) Industry-Focused IT Firm Increases Capacity with Better Project Planning, TechRepublic, http://www.techrepublic.com/whitepapers/industry-focused-it-firm-increases-capacity-with-better-project-planning/1248083?cname=project-management&tag=content;selector-1 [Accessed 30 May 2012].

Burke, R. (2003) *Project Management: Planning and Control Techniques*. 4th edition. Chichester, John Wiley & Sons.

Jaspal, S. (2010) Risk Management Strategy of Virgin Group. SJR, http://soniajaspal.wordpress.com/2010/11/10/risk-management-strategy-of-virgin-group/ [Accessed 30 May 2012].

Kotler, P. (2009) The age turbulence. Business and Leadership, http:www.businessandleadership.com/marketing/news/article/12249/marketing/the-age-of-turbulence [Accessed 26 January 2009].

QUICK QUIZ

1   What is the purpose of work breakdown structure?

2   What is the probable effect on the project budget of introducing a requirement for higher quality than originally anticipated?

3   What are some of the main purposes of using project management software?

4   What is the critical path?

5   How much float is available for critical activities?

Activity 14.1

This is absolutely **not** the case. A longer task is a more complex task. Complexity increases the time involved. Further, this task usually has developmental or reflective issues. These require time to review.

Take this advice, and build in contingencies into your assignment project plan!

Activity 14.2

You will get some clues if you read the article. Kotler says:

'This (putting the stoppers on the projects) is not the answer. It is better to keep investing, or work smarter.'

This is the central issue – projects should be continued or culled on their individual merits. Therefore, the project must be considered in terms of the fit with strategy and the returns on the project. A good project will have these specified at the outset. These should be reviewed throughout the process as these may be required to defend your project in events of cutbacks.

Activity 14.3

There are hundreds of packages available in addition to the traditional packages referred to in this chapter and throughout the section. Any straightforward browser search will identify numerous packages and their specific features.

QUICK QUIZ ANSWERS

1   To analyse the work required to complete the project into manageable components

2   Budgeted cost will almost inevitably rise

3   Planning and scheduling; estimating and controlling costs; monitoring and reporting

4   The series of tasks that determines the minimum possible duration of the project

5   By definition, there is no float on the critical path

CHAPTER 15

Project control, termination, review and evaluation

Introduction

With this chapter we conclude our coverage of project management. There are two main elements here. The first is the project control process. No project will run itself and all project managers must expend effort on constant review of progress and the taking of control action where necessary. A number of techniques have been developed to aid in the process of project control.

The other main topic is the extensive work that is required when the project seems to be at an end. There is first the problem of closing it down in an effective and tidy fashion so that no loose ends are left to unravel. Second, there must be a process of review so that the lessons learned during the project are not immediately forgotten. This review process can take a considerable time to complete.

Project termination is when work on the project is complete. Ideally, this should be when the project has reached its successful conclusion. Alternatively, it can be stopped when a project has problems or will fail to achieve the outcomes.

Termination clearly is at the end of a project life cycle (whether the expected end or a premature end), so activities at termination rarely impact on the success of the project. However, it can impact on the success of future projects and on attitudes to the terminated project and the project team.

Managing termination is therefore the final stage in effective project management. Project termination begins with the project termination decision (how to decide and whether to terminate). This is followed by the termination implementation process. Finally, once a project has been terminated, a project review will then take place, which will use evaluation tools to address the dimensions of success and failure. These topics are the focus of this chapter.

Topic list

Project monitoring ①

Reporting progress ②

The project termination decision ③

The project report ④

The project scorecard ⑤

4.6	Utilise a variety of methods, measurements and control techniques to enable effective monitoring and measuring of progress throughout the project to ensure that it is completed to specification, on time and within budget:
	■ The project scorecard
	■ Objective review
	■ Budget review
	■ Update reporting
	■ Productivity
	■ Corrective action plans
4.7	Critically assess the main techniques for evaluating effectiveness, success or failure of a marketing project on its completion:
	■ Variance analysis
	■ Outcome matrices
	■ Profit/loss analysis
	■ Liquidity analysis
	■ Investment performance analysis
	■ Productivity analysis
	■ Value analysis
	■ Marketing mix analysis
	■ Lessons learned

▶ Key terms

A **progress report** shows the current status of the project, usually in relation to the planned status.

Project monitoring 'Monitoring is the collecting, recording and reporting information concerning any and all aspects of project performance that the project manager or others in the organisation wish to know', Meredith and Mantell (2003).

Project control 'Control is the last element in the implementation cycle of planning— monitoring— controlling. …. In essence, control is the act of reducing the difference between plan and reality', Meredith and Mantell (2003).

At all stages of a project, activities need to be monitored. Targets should have been established as part of the project plan, but progress against these must be measured. Control mechanisms must exist that will allow corrective actions to occur if there is a substantial deviation from that which was projected.

Some project managers acknowledge that a perfect plan cannot exist. Plans are implemented in a fast-moving environment, with a range of interrelated activities and participants. Given that change is inevitable, then the project manager's role is to monitor progress to direct and enable to ensure that the project continues to make progress. If it is not making the progress intended, it is the project manager's responsibility to manage the project control by making adjustments to the plan.

This chapter focuses on monitoring and control. These terms are commonly 'unified', but are actually separate issues. Accordingly, these two separate terms become the structure for this chapter.

Objective measures of progress on performance are essential to realise project objectives and outcomes. These should be in the project document.

1 Project monitoring

Marketers are familiar with the concept of a planning and control cycle. Planning and control is different within the project environment from the analysis, planning, implementation and control cycle in marketing. Project managers focus on planning, monitoring and controlling. Planning was addressed earlier, and so now the focus moves to the monitoring phase.

According to Meredith and Mantell (2003): 'Monitoring is the collecting, recording and reporting information concerning any and all aspects of project performance that the project manager or others in the organisation wish to know.'

Tracking and monitoring progress helps to ensure an effective and efficient project, by reviewing project implementation against the approved plan and budget. Monitoring focuses on tracking data about activities and progress. It needs to be built on a good plan and substantial data. The design of a realistic chain of results, outcomes, outputs and activities is particularly important.

Monitoring cannot make a project successful – it is a 'neutral' part of the project process. However, timely monitoring (followed by effective control) can help identify – and avoid if necessary – the three Cs that challenge projects:

- Crises
- Catastrophes
- Change

Monitoring is usually the responsibility of the project co-ordinator and may be carried out informally (through weekly briefs) or through routine review of the project documents. The minimum forms of review for a project should be on the 'triple constraints' or:

- Time (schedule)
- Cost (budget)
- Performance

Within this, the key parameters are:

- Current project status
- Progress to date

1.1 The project monitoring system

The key stages in designing a monitoring system are:

- Identify the information requirements
- Identifying the key factors to be monitored
- Identifying the boundaries

Project monitoring normally relies on the parent organisation having a robust internal information system for monitoring and control.

The project monitoring system needs to be specified at the project initiation. Typically, this will look at the data collection process, the standards and the performance criteria. Unfortunately, these may change over time, because of changes affecting scope, legal changes or other budgetary or business priorities.

The monitoring system should also consider project milestones of performance criteria (such as the number of changes to plan or variations in resources usages).

The project action plan, WBS system and the further more detailed subplans are the reference for this. These describe the project activities, tasks, schedules, resource levels and costs for all elements. However, these factors may not identify all elements needed for project monitoring. Indeed, focusing on monitoring activity, rather than the output, is a common error. A project may have a considerable amount of activity, but the output may still be hidden. Focusing on the activity may mask the problems in creating output.

2 Reporting progress

The above material has identified various ways of monitoring progress, but these analyses are not only for the project manager. Commonly, monitoring is communicated to others through reports and meetings. Reports can be prepared by the project team, or prepared by independent auditors, depending on the organisation, type of project and the level of project risk. The reports will also form the record on which the project history will be based. However, the project manager has the ultimate responsibility for defining how reports and meetings are managed.

2.1 Project status reports

Project status reports provide updates on the project status.

Routine reports are normally those that provide updates on the project status.

- **An executive status report**, for the project sponsors or other key stakeholders who are not directly involved in the project activities. These should be prepared on an agreed schedule, often monthly or quarterly, and timed to fit with meetings with executive stakeholders. The focus of this report should be on the 'top-level' issues affecting progress and plans.

- **Project progress status reports** will be prepared on a regular time schedule. Projects with full-time team members or working within a tight schedule will commonly have these prepared weekly. Part-time projects may have a less frequent reporting schedule, as long as they do not have a short time duration.

Project status reports are normally prepared by those in key roles in the project team. These keep the project manager and project team up-to-date with progress or problems, and enable all to be aware of plans to reduce problems or recover from problems.

The frequency and contents of progress reports will vary depending on the length of, and the progress being made on, a project.

The report is a **control tool** intended to show the discrepancies between where the project is, and where the plan says it should be. Major considerations will be time and cost and reports will highlight comparisons of planned and actual progress.

Any additional content will depend on the format adopted. Some organisations include only the 'raw facts' in the report, and use these as a basis for discussion regarding reasons for variances and action to be taken, at a project review meeting.

Other organisations (particularly those involved in long, complex projects) produce more comprehensive progress reports, with more explanation and comment.

Gray and Larson (2010) suggest the following basic format for a control report:

1   Progress since last report
2   Current project status
     Time schedule
     Cost
     Scope
3   Cumulative trends
4   Problems and issues since last report
     Actions and resolution of earlier problems
     New variances and problems identified
5   Corrective action planned

2.2 Budget reports – earned value

The progress report should include cost information: the **earned value** approach is widely used, especially when projects are managed using the US Project Management Institute methodology. The essence of monitoring using earned value is the computation of **variances for cost and schedule** (schedule here means time progress). Three cost figures are required for the computations.

(a) **Actual cost of work completed** (**AC**). This is the amount spent to date on the project.

(b) **Planned value of the work scheduled to date** (**PV**). The amount that was budgeted to be spent to this point on scheduled activities.

(c) **Earned value** (**EV**). This figure is calculated by pricing the work that has actually been done – using the same basis as the scheduled work.

$EV - AC$ = The **cost variance** for the project.

$EV - PV$ = The **schedule variance** for the project.

It should be noted that the schedule variance, while a useful overall indicator, is not the best indicator of time progress: the project network is far more accurate and informative.

ACTIVITY 15.1

At day 30, the earned value of project 23/076 is £3.46 million, the planned value of work scheduled is £4.04 million and the actual cost of work completed is £3.95 million. What are the cost and schedule variances?

2.3 Traffic light reports

Traffic light control can also provide a higher level visual summary of progress.

In the traffic light approach, project members estimate the likelihood of various aspects of a project meeting its planned target date. Each aspect is then colour-coded.

Green   Means 'on target': the work is on target and is expected to meet stakeholder expectations.

Yellow   Signifies the work is behind target, but the slippage is recoverable. Yellow indicates that some problem areas have been identified, but corrective actions can be taken to deal with them.

Red   Signifies the work is behind target and will be difficult to recover. A 'red' traffic light suggests there are major problems: for example, if a major component of the project is behind target it could significantly affect the progress of the project as a whole.

Traffic light control can also be applied to cost and quality aspects of a project as well as time.

Equally, traffic light control could be applied to the three elements of time, cost and quality together. If a project is on course to substantially meet its objectives in all three elements, it will be indicated by a green traffic light. If two out of the three are likely to be substantially met, the traffic light will be yellow, but if less than two objectives are substantially met, the traffic light will be red.

2.4 Control charts

Several different types of chart may be used to display project progress. The **Gantt chart**, described in the previous chapter, is inherently suited to use as a control chart, displaying planned and actual usage of resources, as is, to some extent, the **resource histogram**. A 'project schedule control chart' displays overall progress against plan. An example is shown below.

Figure 15.1   Sample control chart

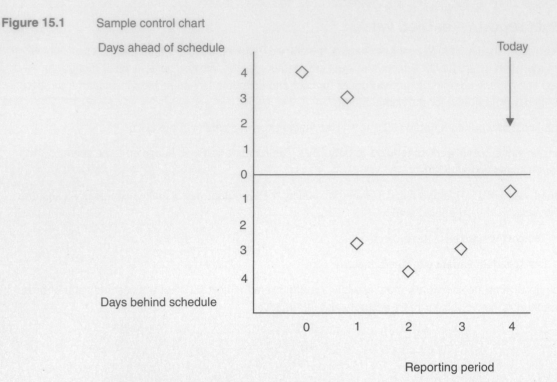

Days ahead of schedule

Today

Days behind schedule

Reporting period

This chart shows that after a good start, by the end of period 3, the project had fallen behind by almost two days. Efforts were obviously made to recover the lost time, because the latest report, at the end of period 8, shows the project only about half a day behind.

Draw a control chart of the type illustrated above showing a project that was:

- Three days behind schedule when it started
- Gradually recovered two days by the end of reporting period 4
- Lost a day during reporting period 6

2.5 Milestones

Milestones should be definite, easily identifiable events that all stakeholders can understand. Monitoring progress towards key milestones can be done on a control chart of the type described above, or on a **milestone slip chart** such as that shown below (Figure 15.2). This chart compares planned and actual progress towards project milestones. Planned progress is shown on the X-axis and actual progress on the Y-axis. Where actual progress is slower than planned progress **slippage** has occurred.

The Chartered
Institute of Marketing

Figure 15.2   Milestone slip chart

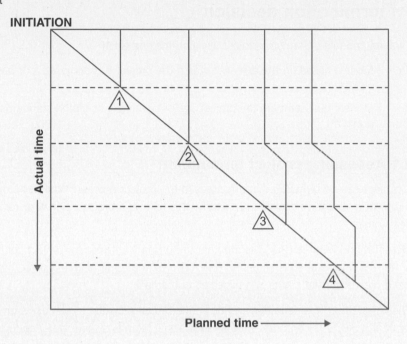

On the chart above milestones are indicated by a triangle on the diagonal planned progress line. The vertical lines that meet milestones 1 and 2 are straight – showing that these milestones were achieved on time.

At milestone 3 some slippage has occurred. The chart shows that no further slippage is expected as the progress line for milestone 4 is the same distance to the right as occurred at milestone 3.

THE REAL WORLD

A milestone example.

Qatargas second new wellhead platform topsides installed

Qatargas recently achieved another major project milestone with the installation of the second of three new wellhead platform topsides in the North Field, 80 kilometres offshore of Qatar.

The QW4 platform topsides was installed safely and without incident on February 9th in a multi-hour operation which involved the use of a special heavy lift crane , NPCC's HLS 2000, that is capable of lifting up to 2,500 tonnes.

The topsides, which weighed approximately 2,200 tonnes, were carefully positioned above the legs of the previously installed jacket structure and successfully lowered over the ten pre-drilled wells onto the jacket.

Mr Faisal M. Al Suwaidi, Chairman and Chief Executive Officer of Qatargas said;

'Qatargas 2 is a project made up of many large projects within a project. This milestone takes the project one step closer to completion. I would like to thank all the parties involved — our staff, and contractors NPCC and Technip — for their dedication to seeing this job completed safely.'

(Qatargas, 2012)

3 The project termination decision

Two key models or forms of project decision-making exist:

- Models based on the extent to which the project has achieved – or failed to achieve – its desired outcomes
- Models that compare the project against generally accepted standards for success and failure for a project

3.1 Assessing project termination

A project can be terminated at any stage in the project process. Whether projects should continue is essentially a resource allocation decision. Generally, this follows a project review, or results from other organisational decisions.

Meredith and Mantell (2003) state 'that the primary criterion for project continuance or termination is whether or not the organisation is willing to invest the estimated time and cost required to complete the project, given the project's current status and expected outcome.'

They argue that this definition can be applied to all projects. In practice, some marketing managers allow tactical projects to continue, without substantial review, if there is no 'bad news' associated with them. A departmental plan will have a range of subprojects, such as those designed to support a new brand launch. Each element will normally continue – unless risk, budget or other factors go right out of control.

While project managers should be committed to their projects, they should also recognise when and how to stop unsuccessful projects. Often, project managers will protect their projects, because of an emotional involvement or concern over their careers. Early project termination can be emotional though, as reflected in the language used.

Projects that finish early are 'culled' or have 'hatchets' taken to them. In reality, continuing some projects may have worse outcomes on the careers of the managers and of the sponsoring organisation. Usually, project termination decisions are made by senior sponsors rather than project managers.

3.2 Criteria for reviewing ongoing project termination

Relatively little attention has been given to criteria for ongoing project termination in formal studies, and especially in marketing. Dean (1968) identified the following criteria for terminating a project early.

Table 15.1   Project termination criteria

Termination evaluation criteria	Possible tools for evaluation
Probability of technical/commercial success	Marketing research, profit/loss analysis, value analysis
Profitability/ROI/market potential	Marketing research, profit/loss analysis, value analysis
Cost growth	Budgeting, variance analysis
Changing competitive factors/market needs	Marketing intelligence, profit/loss analysis
Technical problems that cannot be resolved	Project viability, marketing mix analysis
Competing projects having higher priority within the organisation or department	Investment performance analysis, project priority review

- Low probability of technical/commercial success
- Low profitability/ROI/market potential
- Damaging cost growth
- Change in competitive factors/market needs
- Technical problems that cannot be resolved

- Competing projects having higher priority within the organisation or department
- Schedule delays

Despite the age of Dean's work, these issues remain valid. Note that Dean includes changing market situations, which is not explicitly mentioned in Meredith and Mantell's definition. Studies in 2008–2009 showed that over 50% of US marketing managers were considering culling projects or project expenditure. It is not clear whether this was due to lower budgets, less cash to invest in marketing or changes in potential rewards from projects.

Organisations rarely have formal criteria for evaluating the early termination of projects. Often, it is easier – in terms of the level of investment and the external evidence of the project – to stop marketing projects than those with tangible evidence of work completed, for example construction projects. It is also easier to stop projects that do not have a full-time team as there are no redundancies. Notably, staff motivation and concerns are often not included in project termination decisions.

THE REAL WORLD

Edinburgh

The City of Edinburgh decided to support a new £515 million tram system in 2007 after a period of debate and dispute. However, the work on the project caused major traffic problems with central routes being at 'gridlock' and temporary traffic measures had not worked. Those who opposed the scheme called for the resignation of the CEO of the tram project company (TIE) in September 2008. A month later, he resigned for personal reasons.

In February 2009, chaos again hit Edinburgh's traffic, when work on the famous Princes Street was due to start. TIE said that the dispute arose because contractors were in dispute over 'additional costs', which TIE said would add over £50 million to the project budget. The time delays are of major concern to local retailers, who lobbied over the scheduling of this work in order to ensure that the work was completed before the Christmas holiday shopping period.

It became clear that the project could not be achieved within the £545m budget.

After three years of disruption, £440m (80% of the original budget) has been spent, but only 28% of the infrastructure completed. As the scheduled completion date in February 2011 passed, the trams commissioned from Spanish company CAF started to arrive, forcing TIE to find and pay for storage.

So the City of Edinburgh was left with a difficult choice: abandon ship, and find itself the laughing stock of the world, or retain a semblance of dignity by building the line through to St Andrew Square. Completing the line to St Andrew Square would cost at least another £200m and the Scottish government had already made it clear it was not prepared to plough any more money in.

The decision was taken to continue to completion with a projected total cost of £715m.

(The Scotsman, 2011)

The International Institute for Communication and Development (IICD)

The IICDD, a non-profit organisation, developed a 'project scorecard evaluation tool' to monitor its projects. IICD focuses on facilitating the development of communities in poor communities in countries such as Bolivia, Jamaica, Mali and Uganda through technology – ranging from radio and television to internet solutions – in a range of sectors. This development approach requires a unique project scorecard, with customised measures.

Three broad headings were identified for this scorecard:

Content – Two elements were measured: project and owner success, and the development impact of the project.

Money – the project's financial contribution.

Process – how effective the IICD was in the project.

Project and owner success and the project's financial contribution are monitored by quarterly progress reports from local managers.

The development impact and IICD effectiveness are measured though research and discussion. Questionnaires are targeted at stakeholders, with a series of attitude statements and open-ended questions, including measuring awareness of ICT possibilities, levels of empowerment, perceived income and employment benefits. Local project partners rated IICD's effectiveness on two dimensions : local ownership and IICD's project support.

Focus group meetings are then held to identify how to re-focus projects to enable them to make more impact.

(IICD, 2012)

ACTIVITY 15.3

Review Meredith and Mantell's definition of the project termination decision, and Dean's criteria for evaluating project termination. What is the chance that this project will be terminated as a result? What does this demonstrate about project termination decisions?

As the Edinburgh tram Real World example shows, the decision to end a project is complex. This is particularly the case in marketing projects, where the project is not just measured on the activity, but also on the outcomes that the implementation of the project achieves. Expectations of the outcomes may well exist, but these may not be easily transferred between projects.

For example, commonly, companies will have a facility to share models of successful marketing communications activities (ie share knowledge). This can be through manuals, handbooks, videos or conference presentations. Some campaigns may well have achieved success in the past, but these may not apply in the future:

- New competitor campaigns may be better.
- Customers may already be aware of the communications approach.
- Customer budgets may be cut.
- The new product may not be as relevant as those in the past.

More sophisticated organisations will use decision support systems to decide on project termination. This is similar to the initial project choice review, considering a range of projects on a predetermined range of factors. Managers should specify thresholds to determine which projects should face more specific review.

Some projects die even though there is no formal decision to stop the project, usually because work is no longer being undertaken.

Project progress has slowed down so much that the project is no longer active. Sometimes, this is due to the members of the project team moving on to 'more interesting topics', or even the project manager moving to other work.

The project is no longer achieving the level of resourcing (people and budget) required enabling progress. This could be the result of the project no longer being considered a high priority, because of company budgetary constraints, or even the project champion no longer getting top-level management support.

3.3 Implementation of project termination

By definition, a project will eventually be terminated once it has achieved its outcomes and is no longer required. Examples of this would be the launch of the new product or the implementation of a new communications plan.

Projects – irrespective of whether they are culled prematurely or finish along their expected course – can be terminated:

- Following a planned and structured process
- Suddenly, and without any warning or support

In many cases, the project manager's final responsibility is to complete the project review. The project review is to detail the lessons learnt and the outcomes of the project. However, without full budgeting and scheduling of this activity, it may not happen. Often, organisations forget the value of learning from the project experience, despite increasing commitment to ideas of 'learning from success' or defining themselves as 'learning organisations'.

Project termination decisions consider many aspects that are part of the project process. In minor projects, many of these will be irrelevant. In others, they will be key factors for future project success.

Key termination tasks include:

- **Personnel issues**, which will differ depending on the type of project organisation. In project team organisation, some team members will need help in finding new jobs and in disengaging from the project and project issues. This can also apply to external parties – the loss of a major advertising account can impact on personnel who have been heavily involved in projects for that customer.

- **Operations/Logistics/Manufacturing**, which will change post-project, when this moves to general activity. Support specialists in these functions may return to general management and not focus on issues related to the project.

- **Accounting and financial** matters need to be 'closed'. The project budget and expenditure need to be audited or verified and signed-off. Any balances (positive or negative) need to be addressed.

- **Processes** will need to be clearly specified and operationalised. For example, compliance issues will need to be clearly specified with appropriate training briefs for their implementation in a new financial product. This may require specification for all new procedures.

- **Information systems** are closely related to other processes. However, data protection issues may require more attention to personal details, and examination of personal data into internal systems.

- **Marketing activities**, both internal and external, should be verified as in alignment with the project outcomes.

4 The project report

At the end of the project, two differing views of the project report exist:

1   Project report identifying the success of the project
2   Project history to encourage learning

A Project Success Report focuses on the outcomes of the project, and should identify:

(a)   Whether the project's objectives have been met and identifying the success of the project on the basis of this.

(b)   A comparison of the performance against the planned target time and cost.

(c)   Whether the original project plan needed changes.

(d)   Analysis of any changes to time, cost, outcomes, during the project.

(e)   Any other organisational requirements, eg staff performance, testing etc.

On project completion, the project manager will produce a **completion report**. The main purpose of the completion report is to document (and gain client sign-off for) the end of the project.

The report should include a summary of the project outcome:

(a)   Project objectives and the outcomes achieved.

(b)   The final project budget report showing expected and actual expenditure (If an external client is involved this information may be sensitive – the report may exclude or amend the budget report).

(c)   A brief outline of time taken compared with the original schedule.

Responsibilities and procedures relating to any such issues should be laid down in the report.

4.1 The outcome matrix

A matrix approach may be taken to the presentation of various aspects of the completion report. The simplest kind of matrix will simply list project deliverables in the left-hand column of cells and show an objective assessment of achievement in the right-hand column. The matrix can be made more informative by incorporating further columns to summarise outcomes in terms of, for example, time, cost and stakeholder satisfaction. An example is given below.

Table 15.2   New product development project outcomes

Deliverable	Schedule	Cost	Production engineering	Sales	Finance
Product design	Three weeks late	£10,900 under budget	Complexity considered marginally acceptable	Good market performance anticipated	Breakeven unlikely below 14,600 units per month
Packaging	On time	£2,700 over budget	Satisfactory	Satisfactory	Considered expensive
Service requirements specification	Six weeks late	£4,900 over budget	Satisfactory	Over-complex	Satisfactory

A more complex type of outcome matrix can be used to analyse performance against two interacting criteria. This is the very common two-axis type of matrix that you are probably already familiar with through ideas such as Ansoff's product/market matrix. An example of an outcome matrix would be one that analysed technical aspects of a project deliverable in terms of quality of design and quality of execution.

The Chartered Institute of Marketing

4.2 The post-completion audit

Any project is an **opportunity to learn** how to manage future projects more effectively.

The **post-completion audit** is a formal review of the project that examines the lessons that may be learned and used for the benefit of future projects.

The audit looks at all aspects of the project with regard to two questions:

(a)   Did the end result of the project meet the client's expectations?

     (i)   The actual design and construction of the end product

     (ii)   Was the project achieved on time?

     (iii)   Was the project completed within budget?

(b)   Was the management of the project as successful as it might have been, or were there bottlenecks or problems? This review covers:

     (i)   Problems that might occur on future projects with similar characteristics.

     (ii)   The performance of the team individually and as a group.

The post-completion audit should involve input from the project team. A simple questionnaire could be developed for all team members to complete, and a reasonably informal meeting held to obtain feedback, on what went well (and why), and what didn't (and why).

This information should be formalised in a report. The post-completion audit report should contain the following:

(a)   A **summary** should be provided, emphasising any areas where the structures and tools used to manage the project have been found to be unsatisfactory.

(b)   A **review of the end result** of the project should be provided, and compared with the **results expected**. Reasons for any **significant discrepancies** between the two should be provided, preferably with suggestions of how any future projects could prevent these problems recurring.

(c)   A **cost-benefit review** should be included, comparing the forecast costs and benefits identified at the time of the feasibility study with actual costs and benefits.

(d)   **Recommendations** should be made as to any steps which should be taken to improve the project management procedures used.

Lessons learnt that relate to the way the project was managed should contribute to the smooth running of future projects.

A starting point for any new project should be a review of the documentation of any similar projects undertaken in the past.

4.3 Benefits realisation

It is obviously important that the benefits expected from the completion of a project are actually enjoyed. Benefits realisation is concerned with the planning and management required to realise expected benefits. It also covers any required organisational transition processes.

The UK Office of Government Commerce has identified a **six-stage procedure for benefits realisation**. This is most relevant to projects aimed at process improvement and changing the organisation's way of doing things.

Stage 1   **Establishing benefits measurement**
Measure the start state and record it in the **benefits profile**. The benefits profile defines each anticipated benefit and is used to track progress towards its realisation. Determine how benefit realisation will be measured. Benefits may be complex and spread across departments: designing usable and realistic measures may be difficult.

Stage 2   Refining the benefits profile
The benefits profile should be refined and controlled throughout the life of the project. Project managers should conduct regular benefits profile reviews in collaboration with key stakeholders.

Stage 3   Monitoring benefits
There should be regular monitoring of benefits realisation. It must be accepted that some projects will only be beneficial in enabling other projects to be successful.

Stage 4   Transition management
Projects are likely to bring change and this must be managed in a proper way. Effective communications will be required as will the deployment of good people skills

Stage 5   Support for benefit realisation
Benefits realisation will mainly accrue after the end of the project. Where a project brings changes in methods and processes, there is likely to be a period for settling-down before benefits are fully realised. During this period, costs may rise and problems may occur. Careful management is required to overcome these short-term effects. A philosophy of continuous improvement is required if further benefits are to be achieved.

Stage 6   Measuring the benefits
Benefits achieved should be established by comparison with the pre-improvement state recorded in the benefits profile.

The Project Success Report can be an important way of showing stakeholders that the project has achieved its outcomes, or identifying the reasons for failure. This is critical for the project manager's future career.

The Project History focuses on 'lessons learned' for future projects, rather than on the merits of the project. This report is sometimes called a project history. This history will examine the following to determine what worked and what did not, and when and why problems occurred.

It will address:

Project performance – the outcomes, successes, failures and challenges.

Administrative performance – reports and reporting, communications and meetings, review procedures, scoping and change procedures, financial management.

Project organisation – how this changed throughout the project, and how this helped or hindered the project.

Project teams – how these performed, recommendations for future teams.

Project management – scoping, plans, methodologies, budgets, schedules, risk management etc.

Table 15.3   Project review

Summary of project history			
	What went well	**What went badly**	**Recommendations**
Project performance			
Admin performance			
Project organisation			
Project teams			
Project management			

Often, these reviews will be presented in a meeting or presentation. Simply, this basic finding can be summarised in a presentation, and Table 15.3 will help identify these key issues.

More formal project audits are often undertaken for major projects, and especially those in the public sector.

The Chartered Institute of Marketing

5 The project scorecard

Project scorecards extend the traffic light approach to provide progress summaries on key performance metrics for a project. They are produced on a regular basis, for example weekly, monthly or quarterly, depending on the project. This scorecard approach complements, rather than replaces, other planning and monitoring systems.

Organisations must determine appropriate metrics to include in their project scorecards. These can take one of the two forms. The first focuses on key project management dimensions, including:

- **Cost**, eg between the actual spend against planned spend
- **Quality**, eg the percentage of work completed to standard
- **Time**, eg the extent to which the project is meeting the project schedule
- **Corporate factors**, eg the extent to which corporate goals or standards are being met

The second takes a 'balanced scorecard' approach, and assumes that assessing the following dimensions will deliver the above benefits:

- The financial perspective, eg EVA, ROI

- **The customer perspective**, customer satisfaction, economic value added. (Notice the difference between earned value analysis and economic value added. The commonality of the acronyms can cause confusion.)

- The training and innovation perspective, staff PM expertise, lessons learned

- **The project or other internal business perspective**, eg satisfaction indices, fit with corporate objectives

This information can be presented in different ways. Some organisations produce a simple one-page sheet, which:

- Highlights key developments
- Shows the tracking of the key performance matrices
- Identifies areas that need attention (ie are over budget, late, possible risks on the horizon etc)

The temporary nature of projects means that tracking and monitoring systems must be accessible, easy to use and current. As a temporary initiative, some or all aspects of the project tracking may not fit well within the existing information systems. Further, often only the larger projects have staff with responsibilities, for example information systems or finance. Therefore, the tracking data should be, wherever possible, gathered as part of the normal routine of the project.

Another general rule is that the reporting should be kept brief. Therefore, an updated report should be only a page or two for most projects.

Often, organisations do not require these reports despite their contribution to project management knowledge and future projects. Often, other priorities overtake this, or the project manager has moved to other projects or has a wish to move on. Further, on longer projects, there is much documentation, but often the reasons for changes or problems are not noted.

Project definition and goal (Stage 2)

The main aim of the project was to develop appropriate library services to schools that would improve children's use of their public library.

Benefits of the project

A successful project would improve visitor targets, increase the active borrower count and increase book issues. This would also help to improve the satisfaction rating during the children's' E Plus surveys.

Finance

There was no designated budget for this project. The goals had to be made achievable from within the standard libraries budget.

Staffing

The Children's' Service Development Manager was the project lead for all the libraries in the county initially. Then the area co-ordinators monitored the performance of each library manager who was responsible for the project within each of their libraries.

Head teachers, English teachers, and in some cases school librarians, were involved depending on the responsibility within each school. In the larger libraries the responsibility would then be passed down to the children's librarian and in the smaller libraries the responsibility to organise and deliver the class visits would remain with the library manager.

Support staff were used to process the joining forms so that each child would become a member of the library. This enabled them to borrow a book during their class visit. Staffing numbers needed to be adequate to support the visit while also maintaining a service to the public.

Time Scales

The project started in January and had to be included in all of the library action plans by April . This meant it would then be part of the core service for the remainder of the year. This would also be when all of the libraries would have to meet their targets. These class visits have since been incorporated into library action plans each year as part of the standard service.

Communication

The original idea was communicated to library managers through a joint area managers' meeting to discuss services to children and how they could be improved.

E-mails kept the Service Development Manager (SDM) in touch with library managers. Each manager had a meeting with the SDM to further discuss the need for essential training and staff responsibilities. Operational issues also needed to be discussed such as: staffing numbers required for a class visit; concerns about proof of identification and joining children to the library; carrying out the visits while the library was open to the general public and possibilities and problems if children borrowed books during the visit.

The SDM and the area co-ordinators were informed of progress during the monthly area managers' meetings and by the quarterly library action plan updates. This helped to ensure that targets were being met, the project was on course and to highlight any problems.

Key tasks (Stages 3 and 4)

SDM informs library managers of project and aims.

Project is included in each library action plan with targets set for each library to achieve.

Schools are consulted by the Children's SDM and key contacts passed to library managers.

Library staff were informed during weekly staff meetings.

Meetings are held with library managers to discuss training and operational issues. Feedback from staff was discussed.

Guidance notes on how to deliver class visits were drawn up by the Children's SDM and a team of children's librarians and e-mailed out to library managers and children's librarians.

Library managers/children's librarians contacted schools in their catchment areas to arrange meetings with teachers/school librarians to discuss plans for the class visits, age of children, numbers of children, mutually convenient dates, length of visit, joining procedures. The programme and content to be included in the visit for each age group was also agreed.

Class visits were planned by managers/children's librarians.

Adequate staffing was arranged and roles communicated to staff.

Class visits were rolled out to schools.

Follow-up calls and letters to teachers after the visits were used to assess feedback.

Evaluation (Stage 5)

Evaluation was sought formally within libraries through monthly management meetings and through the library action plans quarterly updates. Performance targets would also be improved through successful visits.

There was no formal evaluation plan recommended to libraries, however, each library would have their own way of gaining this information. Library managers and librarians liaised closely with teachers and other library staff involved before and after each visit to find out what went well and what didn't work so well that could be changed next time. Library staff that had been on duty during the visit were also asked to give feedback as to how they coped with issuing books to large numbers of children, problems with library cards and serving the public during the visits, etc.

Reflection

Key skills needed to develop the project:

Good communication with people of all ages, written and oral
Good ICT skills
Ability to work in a team
Ability to use initiative
Project management skills
Time management skills
Self-motivation and the ability to motivate a team

A set of guidelines were written and sent out electronically to managers to enable them to plan and devise a series of class visits appropriate to the age range of each class visit. Although the guidelines were well thought out it would have been useful to have been supported by a children's librarian for the first class visit or to have been able to observe how they delivered a session. Instead confidence has grown with experience.

Problems encountered:

Staff were extremely unhappy having class visits while the library was open to the public. The previous librarian had taken some class visits but only while the library was closed. This project reflected a belief that a change in culture was necessary to show the children how a library operates and enhance their perspective of a library as part of the community. It was also thought to be good for the public to see children using the library, further evidence that the library service has changed.

Difficulty contacting teachers who are either teaching or in meetings. Librarians needed to find out the best times to contact or ask them to contact the library manager. This was time consuming.

Where more than one class visit was arranged on one day there could be problems if the first class was late. This would then mean that visits would have to be cut short or would overrun thus causing problems for the next class, or problems with library staff not being able to have their breaks.

Some library users complained of the noise generated by the class visits or of having to wait to be served. Meeting all user needs at such times proved challenging.

Some schools did not cancel the visit if they were unable to get the children to the library. This was a particular problem when a series of visits had been planned for one school and books became overdue because parents were told by the school that it didn't matter. The library was unable to contact parents as they did not have a list of the names.

Library books getting mixed up with books at the school. Pupils and teachers failed to differentiate between ownership of these items.

Some schools insisted that they needed to bring two classes at once due to staff/ time but this has been too much for the library to cope with while also serving the public with the resources available.

Teachers not getting joining forms to the library well in advance of the visit to enable library cards to be processed for the children. Library staff levels were not enough to cope with class visits, serve the public and process large numbers of joining forms all at the same time.

The project experience has informed managers/librarians what works and what creates problems. It identified the numbers of staff needed to ensure a successful visit. It also identified the need to communicate the important factors to teachers before the visit so they in turn can inform parents.

The project goal has been achieved and class visits are now included in all library plans each year.

Conclusion and analysis

This is an interesting example of a project that involved policy that evolved as a consequence of external environment factors. The public library needed to improve children's use of their local libraries which had been identified as weak through monitoring of national standards and statistics.

There is a sense of a top-down approach as this was imposed on the libraries. However, the dispersed project leadership ensured that managers were involved in the planning and developing stages so that local issues could be adapted to meet the project goal.

Communication with the schools seemed to present real problems as did the challenge of trying to meet the very different needs of diverse user groups.

Overall, however, it is interesting to read about a project that has become part of standard service delivery.

(The Higher Education Academy, 2012. Contains information for educational purposes under an open copyright policy)

▶ **Assessment tip**

Always read the assessment criteria carefully with respect to whichever option you chose. You may be asked to show how you would evaluate the success or otherwise of your specific project or you may be asked to generally criticise the main techniques for evaluating projects *per se*. Be sure to answer the question you have been asked.

 The Chartered Institute of Marketing

- We have looked at the termination of projects and understand that this can be at full completion or earlier.

- We have looked at the criteria to help decide if an early termination is beneficial.

- We understand that companies may not always follow the path that the logical review indicates.

- We understand what the key termination tasks are and what importance they have.

- We have looked at the use of the project report for the termination stage.

FURTHER READING

Kaplan, R. and Norton, D. (1992) The balanced scorecard: measures that drive performance. *Harvard Business Review,* January–February, pp71-80.

REFERENCES

Anon. (2011) Edinburgh's disgrace II: Tram fiasco threatens to further embarrass capital. http://www.scotsman.com/news/edinburgh-s-disgrace-ii-tram-fiasco-threatens-to-further-embarrass-capital-1-1680151 [Accessed 30 May 2012].

Anon. (2012) Monitoring & Evaluation Methodology. IICD, http://www.iicd.org/about/approach/monitoring_evaluation/methodology [Accessed 30 June 2012].

Anon. (2012) Public Library Schools Visit Project. http://www.ics.heacademy.ac.uk/resources/rlos/chivers/case-study3.doc [Accessed 25 June 2012).

Dean, B. V. (1968) Evaluating, selecting, and controlling R&D projects. *AMA Research Study 89.* American Management Association, Inc.

Gray, C. F. and Larson, W. L. (2010) *Project Management: The Managerial Process*, 5th edition. London, McGraw-Hill.

Meredith, J. R. and Mantell, S. J. (2003) *Project Management: A Managerial Approach*. New York, John Wiley & Sons.

Qatagas (2012) http://www.qatargas.com/Projects.aspx?id=74 [Accessed 24 June 2012].

QUICK QUIZ

1   What is a project milestone?

2   How is earned value calculated?

3   What are the three constraints on project achievement that can be traded-off against each other?

4   What is the main benefit of carrying out a post-completion audit?

5   How are the benefits brought by a project measured?

Activity 15.1

Cost variance = EV – AC = £3.46 – 3.95 million = -£0.49 million

Schedule variance = EV – PV = £3.46 – 4.04 million = -£0.58 million

Activity 15.2

Figure 15.3

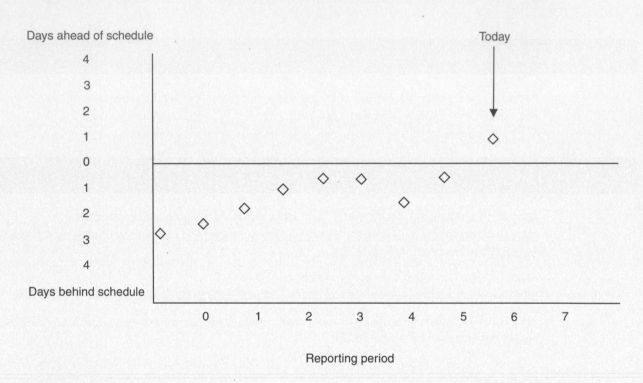

Activity 15.3

Although the project cost appears to be facing approximately 10% increase in cost, and a critical timing delay that will adversely affect some stakeholders (the retailers and the shoppers), it is likely that the project will continue.

This demonstrates why many project budgets increase, and also why deadlines are not met – there are different stakeholder interests, which impact on the project process, but often projects continue in spite of these and cost and timing problems. This is especially common in major public sector costs, especially following considerable initial investment.

However, these factors can cause ill will after the end of the project, and therefore affect the project when it moves into the implementation stage.

The Chartered
Institute of Marketing

1   A significant event in the life of the project, usually completion of a major deliverable.

2   Earned value is the price of the work that has actually been done.

3   Quality, cost and time.

4   The opportunity make the management of future projects more effective.

5   By comparison with the pre-improvement state recorded in the benefits profile.

Project Management in Marketing

Section 4:

Senior Examiner's comments

This section of the syllabus realises the dynamic evolution of the marketing function and the practical fact that organisational management and planning are presenting common denominators. Marketing projects and project management principles are inextricably linked, and a paradigm exists. Content and knowledge will be drawn from all Level 4 units, but ultimately themes and perspectives from the other three units at Level 6 will be investigated and applied.

Students should examine core project management techniques and identify the interface with the principles of marketing management. The appreciation and understanding of this relationship will allow the integration of dual concepts in a practical scenario. For marketing project plan, read marketing plan. There is little difference in format and structure, only nature and scope. It is fully expected that students arrive at this unit in no doubt as to, and fully competent in, the necessary frameworks of the marketing planning process. This is a fundamental imperative and anything less would not permit any candidate to undertake this unit, let alone be successful in it. These frameworks will be adapted to fit any given organisational context or brief.

This section, in turn, becomes the marketing project plan and is built from the study and application of the content from the previous three sections.

Candidates will, therefore, be expected to integrate not only their knowledge from the other units and previous study but also a coherent application of the concepts and frameworks specifically introduced here.

Having arrived at a justified position for the project, the student will now formulate the initiation, the progression, the measurement and the completion of a contextualised marketing project.

The core content of this section is clearly defined and should be used as a template for what becomes the project document. What will emerge is a cumulative and summative understanding and practical application of a concept for managing marketing projects.

There is nothing here that is trying to be overcomplicated for over-complication's sake. The syllabus is clearly defined and indicative content outlined. The examining team will expect nothing less than the consequential and structured approaches referred to by Element 4.3 of the syllabus document.

This element of the assessment carries the most individual weight in relation to the marking criteria, representing up to a quarter of the total mark. This task will always form a part of the candidate's brief, and the full remit within a project plan should always be used. The examiners will be expecting an all-inclusive presentation of the situational context, formalised and quantified objectives, operational delivery and implementation programmes, dedicated timescales, investment/income budgets and monitoring, evaluation and measurement mechanics. Anything less is unlikely to be accepted.

A core understanding of, and an ability to apply, traditional project management techniques in any given context are imperative here.

Senior Examiner's comments on assessment sessions to date

Assessment criteria weighting and mark allocation

The nature of the tasks reflects the weighting across the syllabus sections. The allocation of marks is aligned to the breadth and depth of the assessment criteria. It is, therefore, important that the format and structure of the assignment submission should be directed by the relative weight and mark allocation indicated. In future assessment sessions, it is proposed to further align this to completely mirror the four syllabus area weightings whereby this aspect will become even more of an imperative.

Consequently, critical analysis of findings should be sharp, succinct and to the point. Where key issues are requested, these should be highlighted and presented. Such summary pieces should therefore not extend to more than 10% of the overall assignment or no more than 600 words. Furthermore, this analysis should be directly related to the candidates' findings from their audit work and not be presented as independent material that was not investigated in the first instance, or worse still, has no relevance to the context of the brief. The concentration from the outset must address the contexts and nothing else. The situational specific audit now accounts for five of the total ten marks available for this section of the report.

On the other hand, where it is fairly obvious that a depth and breadth is required around issues such as project planning, justifying business cases and risk, then the appropriate time, effort, research and construction should be apportioned accordingly. These core issues individually or together could potentially represent between 25% to 45% of the overall marks available for any given assignment brief.

Grade differentiation

The grade descriptors indicate what is expected from candidates within the different grade boundaries. In addition, the specific mark schemes indicate the minimum requirements under each assessment criteria. Generally, these can be summarised as follows:

A grade:

- All of the elements under each assessment criteria are comprehensively presented
- Thorough understanding of relevant syllabus areas
- Considerable evidence of wider reading from a range of sources
- Consistently relies upon and refers to situational specific audit and other appended material
- Thorough appreciation and understanding of key issues
- All aspects of the submission relate entirely to the assignment brief
- All aspects of the submission are detailed, complete, applied and evaluated
- All aspects of the submission adhere fully to the command prompts within the assessment criteria
- Consistent and appropriate use of underlying concept and theory
- Professionally researched, structured and presented throughout.

B grade:

- All of the elements under each assessment criteria are competently presented
- Good understanding of relevant syllabus areas
- Some evidence of wider reading from a number of sources
- Relies upon and refers to audit and appended material

- Sound appreciation and understanding of key issues
- Most aspects of the submission relate to the assignment brief
- Most aspects of the submission contain good detail, application and evaluation
- Most aspects of the submission adhere to the command prompts within the assessment criteria
- Appropriate use of underlying concept and theory
- Well researched, structured and presented throughout.

C grade:

- Most of the elements under each assessment criteria are adequately presented
- Reasonable understanding of relevant syllabus areas
- Some but more limited evidence of wider reading
- Some reliance and reference to audit and appended material
- Reasonable appreciation and understanding of key issues
- Aspects of the submission have a tendency to be overly generic and formulaic
- Aspects of the submission contain reasonable detail, application and evaluation
- Aspects of the submission adhere to the command prompts within the assessment criteria
- Reasonable use of underlying concept and theory
- Reasonably researched, structured and presented.

D grade

- Some elements under the assessment criteria are not fully presented
- Limited/lacks understanding of relevant syllabus areas
- Little/no evidence of wider reading
- Little/no reliance or reference to audit or appended material
- Limited/lacks appreciation or understanding of key issues
- Aspects of the submission are irrelevant, inaccurate or inconsistent
- Aspects of the submission contain little/no detail, application or evaluation
- Aspects of the submission ignore command prompts within the assessment criteria
- Limited/no reference to theory and/or incorrect application
- Report lacks structure and focus, is under researched and poorly presented.

One significant point to raise is that a number of candidates fail to refer to core project management texts and even the official CIM course book continues to be ignored. A range of additional reading is highly beneficial and allows a greater appreciation of the published brief, providing the foundations for a sound construction of the report for submission. However, it must be stated that any over reliance on web-based resources and references are unlikely to improve the candidate's work. All the same, it is no coincidence that those candidates who endeavoured to refer to a range of texts tended to achieve a pass grade.

In summary:

The grade descriptors and specific mark schemes are indicative of grade differentiators and minimum requirements under assessment criteria. They are by no means definitive and will evolve with the qualification and within this unit. However, these documents are good benchmarks of what is expected and their content should be studied and absorbed by tutors and candidates alike.

Comments and examples of:

- Strengths and good practice
- Common mistakes when tackling this type of question/task

Strengths and good practice:

- Format and structure to include clear identification of the option chosen, highlighted word counts, title page, contents page, executive summary and Harvard references

- Covering all aspects of assessment criteria and paying particular attention to the fact that these more than likely will be multi-faceted

- Aligning depth and breadth of assessment criteria with indicative weighting and mark allocation

- Demonstrating appreciation and understanding of underlying concept and theory

- Audit and any supporting appended material concentrates solely on context

- Reliance on and reference to audit

- Synthesis and cohesion throughout

- Evidence of equilibrium between concept, application and evaluation.

Common mistakes:

- Over reliance on generic models and formulaic solutions

- Core content not relating to audit or appended material

- Inclusion of irrelevant or inaccurate material

- Unqualified and unquantified cost benefits analysis

- Non-critical analysis

- Lack of recommendation and justification

- Incomplete submissions in relation to aspects of the assessment criteria with dual or multiple facets

- Presenting marketing plans or marketing communications plans in place of outline project plans

- Underlying concepts of risk and control not appreciated

- Non alignment of indicative weighting and mark allocation with word count

- Lack of format or structure, synthesis and cohesion.

Strengths and good practice – Option One:

- Sharp and succinct critical analysis of findings fully based on audit and supporting appended material

- Findings were critically analysed as opposed to listed and described. Using traditional, adapted or original models and illustrations to support the context

- Recommendations for internal marketing management were proposed/justified

- Resourcing capability and capacity was critically assessed relative to existing availability

- Outline project plans were full and concentrated on recommendations and proposals

- terms of organisational impact

- Format and presentation was categorised by an ease of flow and navigation.

Common mistakes – Option One:

- Findings bore no relation to the audit or appended material

- Submissions were text heavy with no diagrammatic or illustrative punctuation

- Only one element of a particular aspect within the assessment criteria was covered when in fact several needed to be examined

- Assessments were not critical

- Recommendations for internal marketing management were not justified

- Resource capacity and capability was not assessed

- Outline project plans were incomplete and not aligned with proposals

- Relevant sources of risk were not identified and no organisational impacts were offered

- Format and presentation was fragmented with no references or evidence of additional reading.

Strengths and good practice – Option Two:

- Findings were critically analysed and manipulated using traditional, adapted or original models and illustrations

- Business cases were drawn from appended material and justified via the same approach. Robust cost benefit analyses were undertaken and presented. The project was further justified in terms of how it would fit with marketing operations

- Outline project plans were complete and concentrated entirely on brand and branding issues

- Sources of risk were critically analysed and assessed

- Risk control programmes were recommended and fully aligned with project implementation

- Effective project evaluation methods were critically assessed.

Common mistakes – Option Two:

- Analysis of findings were descriptive and text laden with little, if any, critical insight

- Business cases were not qualified or quantified

- Cost benefit analyses were shallow and superficial

- Risk control programmes were generic and formulaic

- Evaluation techniques were not critically assessed

- Format and presentation was fragmented with no references or evidence of additional reading.

Recommendations for how performance can be improved in future assessments

- Audits are specific and concentrated, ignoring irrelevant material

- Subject matter within assignment briefs is fully appreciated and understood

- Analysis and assessment must be critical and not descriptive

- Project plans must be detailed from initiation through to evaluation and must outline all stages

- Recommendations must be justified

- Diagrammatic illustration should be included where possible

- All aspects of all elements under assessment must be covered

- Business cases must be robust and justified

- Cost benefit analysis should be qualified and quantified

- Plans and programmes must be consistent and relevant

- All elements of the submission should be framed in context

- Underlying concepts and theories need to be used in support

- Presentation must be professional and fluent with synthesis and cohesion

- All reading and sources must be referenced

- Concept, application and evaluation must be relevant and obvious throughout.

SEMINAL ARTICLES

Marketing Myopia
Theodore Levitt

The article suggests that mismanagement - not market saturation - is the reason for the decline in growth industries. Factors influencing industrial growth include customer-oriented management led by the chief executive. The author argues that there are growth opportunities which can be created and exploited by companies that are organised for this purpose. Topics include E. E. DuPont de Nemours & Company, Corning Glass Works, the four conditions of the self-deceiving cycle, and examples of industries that defined their purpose, policies, and objectives too narrowly.

Levitt, T. (1960) Marketing Myopia. *Harvard Business Review,* Vol 38(4), pp45-56.

Broadening the concept of marketing
Philip Kotler and Sidney J. Levy

Marketing is a pervasive societal activity that goes considerably beyond the selling of toothpaste, soap, and steel. The authors interpret the meaning of marketing for nonbusiness organizations and the nature of marketing functions such as product improvement, pricing, distribution, and communication in such organisations. The question considered is whether traditional marketing principles are transferable to the marketing of organizations, persons, and ideas.

Kotler, P and Levy, S.J. (1969) Broadening the concept of marketing. *Journal of Marketing,* Vol 33(1), pp10-15.

New product adoption and diffusion
Everett M Rogers

This paper summarises what we have learned from research on the diffusion of innovations that contributes to understanding new product adoption, discusses how the background of diffusion research affected its contributions and shortcomings, and indicates future research priorities. Diffusion research has played an important role in helping put social structure back in the communication process. Network analysis and field experiments are promising tools in diffusion studies. The diffusion model has aided our understandings of the consumption of new products.

The Chartered Institute of Marketing

Rogers, E. (1976) New product adoption and diffusion. *Journal of Consumer Research,* Vol 2(4), pp290-301.

Market orientation: the construct, research propositions and managerial implications
Ajay K Kohli and Bernard J Jaworski

The literature reflects remarkably little effort to develop a framework for understanding the implementation of the marketing concept. The authors synthesise extant knowledge on the subject and provide a foundation for future research by clarifying the construct's domain, developing research propositions, and constructing an integrating framework that includes antecedents and consequences of a market orientation. They draw on the occasional writings on the subject over the last 35 years in the marketing literature, work in related disciplines, and 62 field interviews with managers in diverse functions and organizations. Managerial implications of this research are discussed.

Kohli, A.K. and Jaworski, B.J. (1990) Market orientation: the construct, research propositions, and managerial implications. *Journal of Marketing,* Vol 54(2), pp1-18.

Customer-oriented approaches to identifying product-markets
George A Day, Allan D Shocker and Rajendra K Srivastava

The need to identify the boundaries of increasingly complex product-markets has spawned a number of analytical methods based on customer behaviour or judgments. The various methods are compared and contrasted according to whether they are consistent with a conceptual definition of a product-market, and their ability to yield diagnostic insights.

Day, G.A, Shocker, A D, and Srivastave, R,K. (1979) Customer-oriented approaches to identifying product markets. *Journal of Marketing,* Vol 43(4), pp8-19.

A conceptual model of service quality and its implications for future research
A Parasuraman, Valarie A Zeithaml and Leonard L Berry

The attainment of quality in products and services has become a pivotal concern of the 1980s. While quality in tangible goods has been described and measured by marketers, quality in services is largely undefined and unresearched. The authors attempt to rectify this situation by reporting the insights obtained in an extensive exploratory investigation of quality in four service businesses and by developing a model of service quality. Propositions and recommendations to stimulate future research about service quality are offered.

Parasuraman, A., Zeithaml, V,A, and Berrly, L.L. (1985) A conceptual model of service quality and its implications for future research. *Journal of Marketing,* Vol 49 (4), pp41-50.

Consumer perceptions of price, quality, and value: a means-end model and synthesis of evidence
Valarie A Zeithaml

Evidence from past research and insights from an exploratory investigation are combined in a conceptual model that defines and relates price, perceived quality, and perceived value. Propositions about the concepts and their relationships are presented, and then supported with evidence from the literature. Discussion centres on directions for research and implications for managing price, quality, and value.

Zeithaml, V.A. (1988) Consumer perceptions of price, quality, and value: a means-end model and synthesis of evidence. Vol 52(3), pp2-22.

Title	How to...write a business case
Author	Anonymous
Pagination	31
Serial title	People Management
Date of publication	02-Sept-2010
ID	249308
Accession number	A0336530
ISSN	13586297
Record type	Article
Abstract/subtitle	Money. People. Time. Most senior HR professionals want more of those, so they can do the things they need to do: recruitment, internal campaigns, change programmes. so how do you convince those high up (usually the board) to give the resources to you, rather than to the IT director or head of sales?
Thesaurus terms	Writing (general); employee participation; corporate strategy; corporate organisation; resource allocation; budgeting
Purchase information	The Copyright Fee for this article, for commercial purposes, is £12.00 + VAT plus standard CIM photocopying charges.
Member access	Members have a range of online databases available to them giving access to over 3000 journals in full text plus thousands more as abstracts. www.cim.co.uk/elibrary
Record modified	20/04/2011
When catalogued	17/09/2010
Access control	No restriction
Title	ROI and measurement - the business case for social media
Author	Chapman, Tom
Pagination	41
Serial title	B2B Marketing
Date of publication	Jul-2009
ID	241749
Accession number	A0330369

ISSN	14774895
Record type	Article
Abstract/subtitle	With subscription levels for online communities soaring, Tom Chapman, social media strategist at Headstream, provides insight on how you can measure networks against your needs.
Thesaurus terms	Marketing effectiveness; measurement; social networks; social media
Purchase information	The Copyright Fee for this article, for commercial purposes, is £30.00 +VAT plus standard CIM photocopying charges.
Record modified	05/01/2011
When catalogued	18/09/2009
Access control	No restriction

Title	Building a strong business case for investment in a technology project will help all those participating within your organisation and make it more effective.
Author	Oakes, Graham
Pagination	27
Serial title	Marketing
Date of publication	07-Mar-2012
ID	259420
Accession number	A0345192
ISSN	00253650
Record type	Article
Abstract/subtitle	Some dos and don'ts.
Thesaurus terms	Marketing strategy; technology (general); checklists; social media
Purchase information	The Copyright Fee for this article, for commercial purposes, is £12.00 + VAT plus standard CIM photocopying charges.

Member access	Members have a range of online databases available to them giving access to over 3000 journals in full text plus thousands more as abstracts. www.cim.co.uk/elibrary
Record modified	12/04/2012
When catalogued	12/04/2012
Access control	No restriction

Title	Building the business case for internal sponsorship activation
Vol and issue no	1, 3
Author	Rogan, Matt
Pagination	267-273
Serial title	Journal of sponsorship

Date of publication	2008
ID	229196
Accession number	A0322515
ISSN	17541360
Record type	Article
Abstract/subtitle	Employee engagement in the UK is at an all-time low. As businesses understand more about the impact this has on their performance, so the imperative increases to use traditionally externally-focused tools like sponsorship to drive employee as well as customer engagement. Increasingly, sponsors are thinking creatively in terms of how they might engage with employees, using the sponsored property to drive employee engagement, behaviour and, ultimately performance. This is no longer an afterthought as an objective. Data suggests a significant uplift is likely by working with sponsorship in this way. The onus is on marketers to engage earlier and deeper with HR departments to ensure that their rights are maximised as a lever for people as well as a marketing strategy.
Thesaurus terms	Academic theory; sponsorship; employee participation; internal marketing
Purchase information	The Copyright Fee for this article, for commercial purposes, is £25.00 + VAT, plus standard CIM photocopying charges.
Record modified	09/02/2011
When catalogued	16/06/2008
Access control	No restriction
Title	Business case essentials: a guide to structure and content (3rd ed)
Author	Schmidt, Marty J.
Pagination	103
Publisher	Solution Matrix Ltd
Actual cost	£24.00
Date of publication	Jul-2009
ID	257885
Accession number	B0120511
Location	ADB
Record type	Loan
Place of publication	Boston, MA
ISBN	1929500025
	9781929500024
Physical description	Paperback
Abstract/subtitle	'Business Case Essentials' was written in response to requests from consulting clients and seminar participants for a brief but complete outline of what belongs in a business case and why it belongs. It assumes no prior background in finance or business planning. The focus is on questions like

these: How do I prove that one choice is the best business decision? How do I show that all important costs and benefits are included? How do I show that alternative action proposals are compared fairly? How do I establish value for benefits--even non financial benefits? How do I build a business case when I am in a government or non profit organisation? How do I minimise risk and show management how to maximise business results? Since 1998, 'Business Case Essentials' has helped professionals in all lines of business develop practical answers to such questions. The book was first published as a white paper in 1998, and revised in 2006. With nearly one million copies in circulation, it has become one of the world's most frequently cited business case resources. Now published as a 100 page book, 'Business Case Essentials' is the leading complete, concise, authoritative guide to what belongs in a business case and why.

Thesaurus terms	Business plan; business analysis; planning process; risk management
Record modified	07/02/2012
When catalogued	07/02/2012
Access control	No restriction

Title	A business case for corporate social responsibility: a company-level measurement approach for CSR
Vol and Issue no	26, 4
Author	Weber, Manuela
Pagination	247-261
Serial title	European management journal
Date of publication	2008
ID	232633
Accession number	A0324158
ISSN	02632373
Record type	Article
Abstract/subtitle	Although theoretical and empirical research often points to a positive relation between CSR and company competitiveness, approaches to measure the company-specific business impacts of CSR are missing in the current literature. However, such an approach could strengthen the overall CSR involvement and support rational decision-making in this area. This paper thus focuses on the question how to measure the business impact of CSR activities from a company perspective. Using a theoretical approach a multi-step measurement model is developed that allows managers to evaluate their company-specific business case for CSR. A case example illustrates the use of the model in practice.
Thesaurus terms	Academic theory; corporate social responsibility; measurement; company performance; case studies
Purchase information	The Copyright Fee for this article, for commercial purposes, is £20.00 + VAT plus standard CIM photocopying charges.

Record modified	05/01/2011
Electronic access	Articles from this journal may be purchased from www.ingentaconnect.com (Full abstracts available free of charge.)
When catalogued	19/09/2008
Access control	No restriction

Title	The business case for corporate social responsibility: a review of concepts, research and practice
Vol and Issue No	12, 1
Author	Carroll, Archie B.
	Shabana, Kareem M.
Pagination	85-105
Serial title	International journal of management reviews
Date of publication	2010
ID	244951
Accession number	A0333170
ISSN	14608545
Record type	Article

| Abstract/subtitle | In this review, the primary subject is the 'business case' for corporate social responsibility (CSR). The business case refers to the underlying arguments or rationales supporting or documenting why the business community should accept and advance the CSR 'cause'. The business case is concerned with the primary question: What do the business community and organizations get out of CSR? That is, how do they benefit tangibly from engaging in CSR policies, activities and practices? The business case refers to the bottom-line financial and other reasons for businesses pursuing CSR strategies and policies. In developing this business case, the paper first provides some historical background and perspective. In addition, it provides a brief discussion of the evolving understandings of CSR and some of the long-established, traditional arguments that have been made both for and against the idea of business assuming any responsibility to society beyond profit-seeking and maximizing its own financial well-being. Finally, the paper addresses the business case in more detail. The goal is to describe and summarize what the business case means and to review some of the concepts, research and practice that have come to characterize this developing idea. |

Thesaurus terms	Academic theory; corporate social responsibility; company performance; profitability
Purchase information	The Copyright Fee for this article, for commercial purposes, is £22.00 + VAT, plus standard CIM photocopying charges.
Record modified	05/01/2011
When catalogued	18/02/2010

The Chartered Institute of Marketing

Access control	No restriction
Title	How SAP made the business case for sustainability
Vol and issue no	52, 1
Author	Hopkins, Michael S.
Pagination	69-72
Serial title	MIT Sloan management review
Date of publication	2010
ID	251396
Accession number	A0338400
ISSN	15329194
Record type	Article
Abstract/subtitle	How are leading companies evaluating the costs and benefits of sustainability investments? As SAP's first-ever chief sustainability officer, Peter Graf was prepared to lay out the business case for sustainability to stakeholders and customers of every kind. But he had to make the case to SAP's own board of directors first.
Thesaurus terms	Academic theory; environmental issues; corporate social responsibility; case studies; personalities
Purchase information	The Copyright Fee for this article, for commercial purposes, is £3.71 + VAT plus standard CIM photocopying charges.
Member access	Available in full text up to the end of 2004 on the Ebsco's Business Source Corporate database, www.cim.co.uk/elibrary
Record modified	05/05/2011
When catalogued	14/01/2011
Access control	No restriction
Title	The 20 minute course in... project management
Author	Hilpern, Kate
Pagination	39-42
Serial title	The marketer
Date of publication	Feb-2009
ID	239165
Accession number	A0328103
ISSN	17435528
Record type	Article
Abstract/subtitle	Fastlane: this months continuing professional development focus is project management. The author has been filing away tips.
Thesaurus terms	Continuing professional development (cpd); project management; team development

Purchase information	The Copyright Fee for this article, for commercial purposes, is £12.00 + VAT plus standard CIM photocopying charges.
Member access	Members are reminded that they have access to a range of articles from The Marketer at www.themarketer.co.uk. Log in using the same user name and password as the CIM website.
Record modified	26/01/2012
When catalogued	21/05/2009
Access control	No restriction
Title	Competence-based risk perception in the project business
Vol and issue no	24, 3/4
Author	Veres, Zoltan
Pagination	237-244
Serial title	Journal of business and industrial marketing
Date of publication	2009
ID	242445
Accession number	A0331005
ISSN	08858624
Record type	Article

Abstract/subtitle

The perceived risk of services is not characterized by being inevitably higher than that of tangible products but rather by the fact that performance risk is bilateral and process-like. The aim of this paper is to explore the nature of this competence-based risk perception during different project transactions. The research approach is a qualitative, exploring one. The elements of the theoretical framework have been explored with the help of parallel supplier and buyer in-depth interviews. In terms of industry coverage the focus of the study was in the traditional engineering areas including some other players of b2b project markets in the participant group. Buyers' perceived performance risk can be linked to the presumed weaknesses of the supplier in professional background, personnel, size or technology, and to certain external factors. Risk perception coming from mainly competence asymmetry can be reduced by interactive communication but it must be adjusted to the buyer's comprehension level. Intensive two-way communication may be to justify the appropriateness of the buyer's decision. Understanding the risk perception of buyers can improve the management of purchasing activity and the purchasing process as well as the proactive behaviour of the supplier. Exploring the risk behaviour of the supplier can help to harmonize the selling/procuring activities of the supplier/buyer. The originality of the paper lies in the process-like, bilateral modelling of risk perception in the service transaction. Based upon this approach a comparative interviewing has been carried out.

Thesaurus terms

Academic theory; risk management; project management; business-to-

business marketing

Purchase information	The Copyright Fee for this article, for commercial purposes, is £15.00 + VAT plus standard CIM photocopying charges.
Member access	Hard copy held from 1993-2006. Members have access to this Emerald journal from 1994 onwards via www.cim.co.uk/elibrary
Record modified	29/03/2012
Electronic access	Articles from this journal may be purchased from http://www.emeraldinsight.com (abstracts available free of charge).
When catalogued	16/10/2009
Access control	No restriction

Index

The Chartered
Institute of Marketing

The Chartered
Institute of Marketing